AF599045

Preservation *in* Action

Publication of this book is funded by the
Beatrice Fox Auerbach Foundation Fund
at the Hartford Foundation for Public Giving

Preservation *in* Action

TEN STORIES OF STEWARDSHIP: RESTORATION, REHABILITATION, RENOVATION, ADAPTATION, AND REUSE

Anne Crofoot Kuckro

PHOTOGRAPHY BY PETER R. BROWN

Wethersfield, Connecticut

Webb Deane Stevens Museum

Published in association with Wesleyan University Press

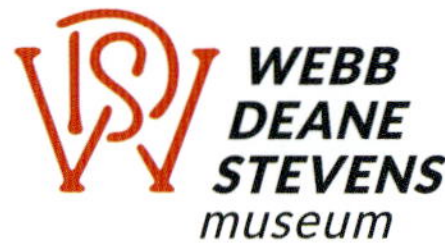

Published by
Webb Deane Stevens Museum
211 Main Street, Wethersfield, CT 06109

Published in association with
Wesleyan University Press
215 Long Lane
Middletown, CT 06459
www.weslpress.org

Copyright © 2024 by Lee G. Kuckro.
Photographs copyright © 2024 Peter R. Brown.

All rights reserved. No part of this book may be reproduced by any means, in any media, electronic or mechanical, including motion picture film, video, photocopy, recording or any other information storage retrieval system, without prior permission in writing from Wesleyan University Press.

Publication of this book is funded by the
Beatrice Fox Auerbach Foundation Fund
at the Hartford Foundation for Public Giving

First edition, 2024
ISBN: 978-0-8195-0146-2
Printed and bound in China

CONTENTS

For ANNE

A NOTE FROM THE PUBLISHER

Without Anne and Lee Kuckro, the preservation community in Old Wethersfield would not look as it does today. Through a half-century of board and committee leadership and tireless work behind the scenes, they are the common thread connecting the several entities responsible for stewarding the town's history. Anne's last role was as President of the National Society of The Colonial Dames of America in The State of Connecticut, which owns and operates the Webb Deane Stevens Museum. But it was the Wethersfield Historical Society, whose board she and Lee both chaired, that became most intimately involved in preparing this manuscript for posthumous publication. With gratitude for the robust community in which we work, the Webb Deane Stevens Museum is pleased to honor Anne's legacy by bringing this work forward for publication to the credit of many and for the benefit of all.

Brenton Grom
Executive Director, Webb Deane Stevens Museum

Alice R. M. Hyland
President, National Society of The Colonial Dames of America in The State of Connecticut

This publication has been made possible by an Historic Preservation Enhancement Grant administered by The State Historic Preservation Office of The Connecticut Department of Economic and Community Development with federal funds from the Historic Preservation SP Municipal AA form rev. 12-01-21 21 Fund of the National Park Service, U.S. Department of the Interior. Any opinions, findings, and conclusions or recommendations expressed in this material are those of the author(s) and do not necessarily reflect the views of the Department of the Interior.

The Town of Wethersfield, CT, as a Certified Local Government, provided support to this publication by applying for the Historic Preservation Enhancement Grant. In addition, this publication received funding through the *Wethersfield Tourism & Cultural Commission* and the *Wethersfield Economic Development & Improvement Commission*. Any opinions, findings, and conclusions or recommendations expressed in this material are those of the author(s) and do not necessarily reflect the views of the Town of Wethersfield.

Additional funding for this publication was provided by the Wethersfield Beautification Trust.

FOREWORD

Ten stories of stewardship: restoration, rehabilitation, renovation, adaptation, and reuse.

The ten stories of stewardship collected in this book are a small part of the culture of historic preservation in Wethersfield. What we call historic preservation was traditionally practiced by thrifty, practical, and pragmatic Yankees for whom adaptation and reuse were normal, usual, and unremarkable. This natural repurposing can be seen with the village's public buildings.

The Old Academy, for example, built as a school in 1801-1804, also served as a site for town meetings after the separation of church and state in 1818, temporarily housed three religious congregations, became the town hall and library and then the Wethersfield Historical Society's Museum. It now serves as the Society's headquarters and houses offices, a library, and archives.

The Keeney Memorial Cultural Center was originally built as the town's high school and grammar school (what we today call a junior high) and thereafter served as the Governor Thomas Welles School (elementary grades). It also functioned as a venue for town meetings, the town court, the draft and rationing boards during World War II, and the Board of Education offices before its present incarnation.

The Baptist Church became the American Legion Hall and is now a dance studio, the Methodist Church is Temple Beth Torah, and the Grange Hall is a food establishment and private home.

And Wethersfield homeowners have maintained, repaired, remodeled, enlarged, and brought their homes up to date since the town 's founding, adapting to changes in family needs with additions that reflect the fashions of the times yet are by and large respectful of the original structures.

The formal efforts to preserve individual houses in Wethersfield date from Wallace Nutting's 1916 purchase of the Joseph Webb House because of its historic association (yes, George Washington slept there). But it was the purchase of the Webb House from Nutting only three years later by The National Society of The Colonial Dames of America in The State of Connecticut (NSCD-CT) that marks the beginning of a sustained institutional commitment to historic preservation in town. The NSCDA-CT's subsequent acquisition of the Isaac Stevens House in 1957 and the Silas Deane House in 1959 has created the Webb Deane Stevens Museum, a professionally accredited museum on an eight acre campus which includes a Colonial Revival garden, a historic barn and a new educational and visitors center, whose construction occasioned an archeological dig that discovered evidence of the very beginning of the Connecticut Colony, the palisaded homesite of Clement Chaplin and evidence of the interaction between the colonists and the native Wangunks.

Both the Joseph Webb House and the Silas Deane House are National Historic Landmarks, and the Isaac Stevens House is on the National Register of Historic Places. The Museum's historic houses, the important stories they tell, and its exhibits and activities, are Old Wethersfield's principal tourist attraction, and with its event spaces and tourist and visitor facilities the Webb Deane Stevens Museum anchors the Historic District.

In 1949 The Antiquarian and Landmarks Society (now Connecticut Landmarks) acquired the Belden Tavern (Buttolph-Williams House) and in 1971 the Wethersfield Historical Society received the Thomas Chester (Hurlbut-Dunham) House by bequest.

More significantly, the town fathers and mothers also took steps to protect the townscape, the town itself. When the state proposed routing a state road through the old village center in the 1930s, long before it had adopted zoning, the town hired New York city planner Herbert Swan to design the Silas Deane Highway to divert the north-south state highway traffic away from Old Wethersfield.

The creation of the Wethersfield Historic District in 1962, the largest and oldest in Connecticut, institutionalized the town's stewardship of the old village, reinforced the efforts of home and business owners, fostered preservation, and encouraged and attracted new homeowners interested in the challenges and rewards of restoration and the charm of living in a protected New England town center.

But despite the Historic District Commission protecting the architectural fabric of Old Wethersfield and individual property owners improving their properties, making the district more attractive and increasing property values, Old Wethersfield was still something of a backwater.

The combined impact of two floods in the 1930s, the Depression, World War II rationing of building materials, and the relocation of town offices to the Silas Deane Highway in the 1960s sapped the old village of economic vitality, leaving vacant and underused buildings.

The revitalization of Old Wethersfield started in 1984 when the Wethersfield Historical Society Board made the courageous decision to submit its proposal to the town to redevelop two vacant surplus town buildings in the heart of the Historic District, creating new businesses with foot-traffic potential: the Henry Deming house as a restaurant and the Governor Thomas Welles School as a museum and cultural center.

The agreement by the Town to entrust the Wethersfield Historical Society with the responsibility for the restoration, rehabilitation, and oversight of the Deming House and the rehabilitation and operation of the old high school has been rewarded with economic vigor, rising property values, and a thriving village stimulating new investments and reinvestments safeguarded by the oversight of the Historic District Commission.

The stories in this book range from the oldest house in town with a seventeenth-century addition added in the twentieth to a nineteenth-century commercial building whose greenhouse was repurposed for additional café seating in 2022. Some are stories of stewardship sustained over generations of successive owners, of institutions and congregations proudly restoring the buildings for which they are responsible. Some stories are of heroic efforts—buildings brought back from the brink of destruction; some are of patient incremental improvements over decades of restoration.

All tell the tale of Historic Old Wethersfield, Preservation in Action.

Lee G. Kuckro
Wethersfield, May 2023

THE EVOLUTION OF AN AMERICAN BEAUTY

Thomas Chester (Hurlbut-Dunham) House

— 212 Main Street —

In 1794, Thomas Chester (1764–1831) engaged a builder to construct a brick house at 212 Main Street and contracted James Francis to do the joinery. His brother, Colonel John Chester (1749–1809), who had been serving in the Connecticut legislature since 1774, was appointed chairman of the building committee in 1792 to oversee the construction of the new State House in Hartford. That summer, Colonel Chester and a Hartford builder traveled to Boston to consult with architect Charles Bulfinch about the design. The Chester House was built while the State House was taking shape, perhaps best explaining its sophisticated design.

The Thomas Chester House — centered above the portico is a Palladian window. The original lights were replaced with stained glass and leaded tracery when the house was extensively remodeled around 1865 by Levi Goodwin in the Italianate style, including a new portico over the original entrance, bracketed cornice, rooftop belvedere, and verandah.

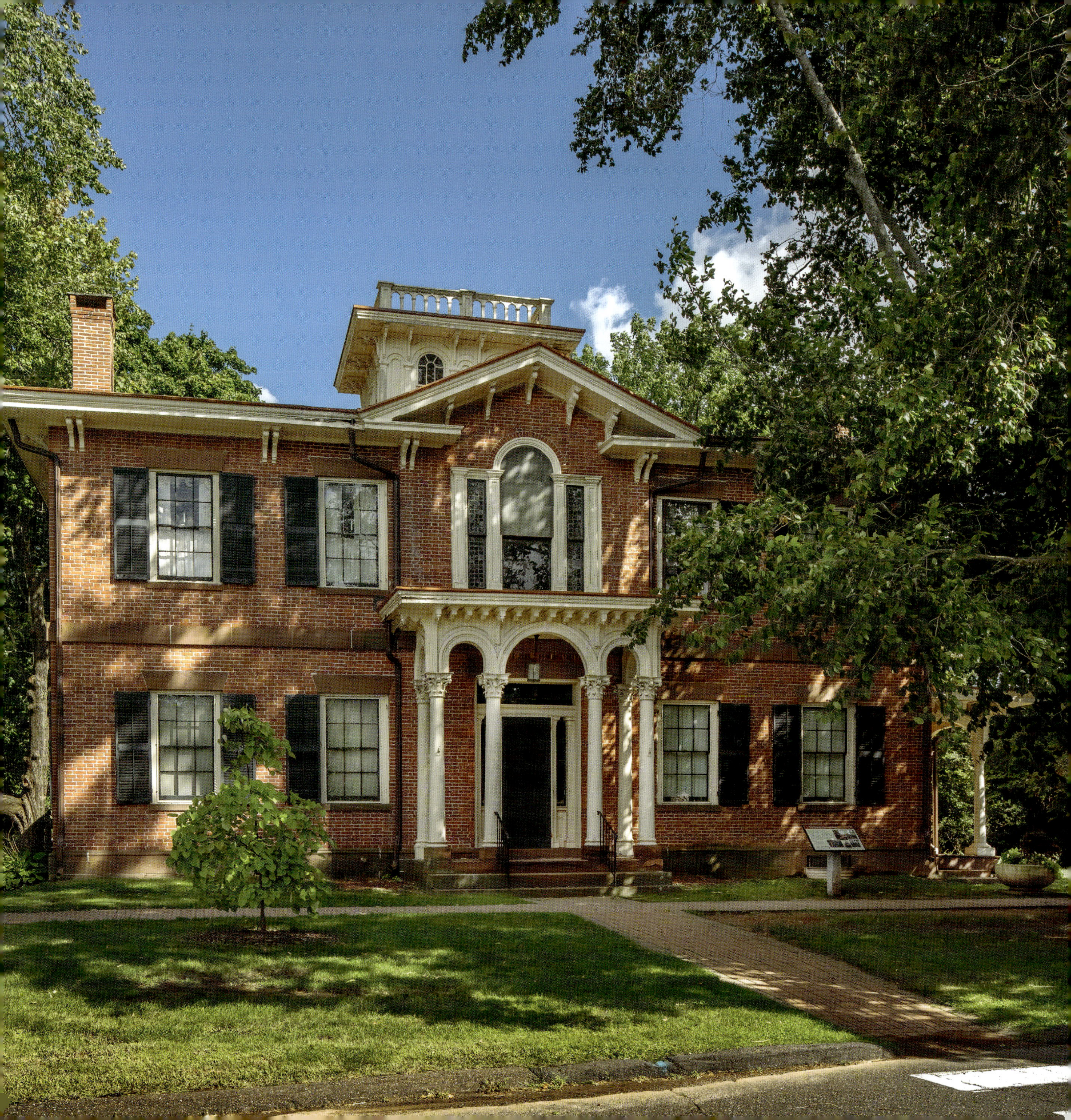

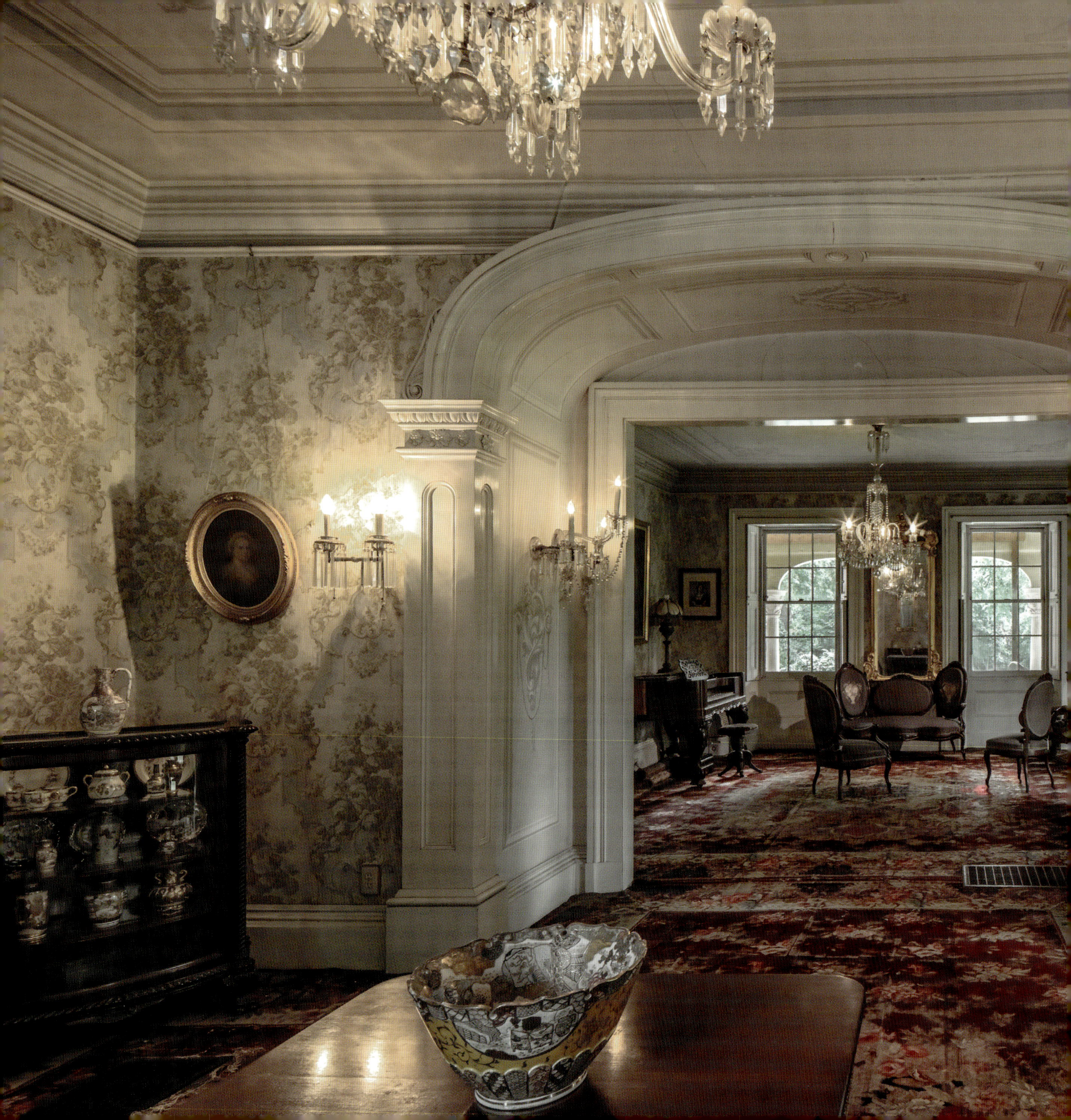

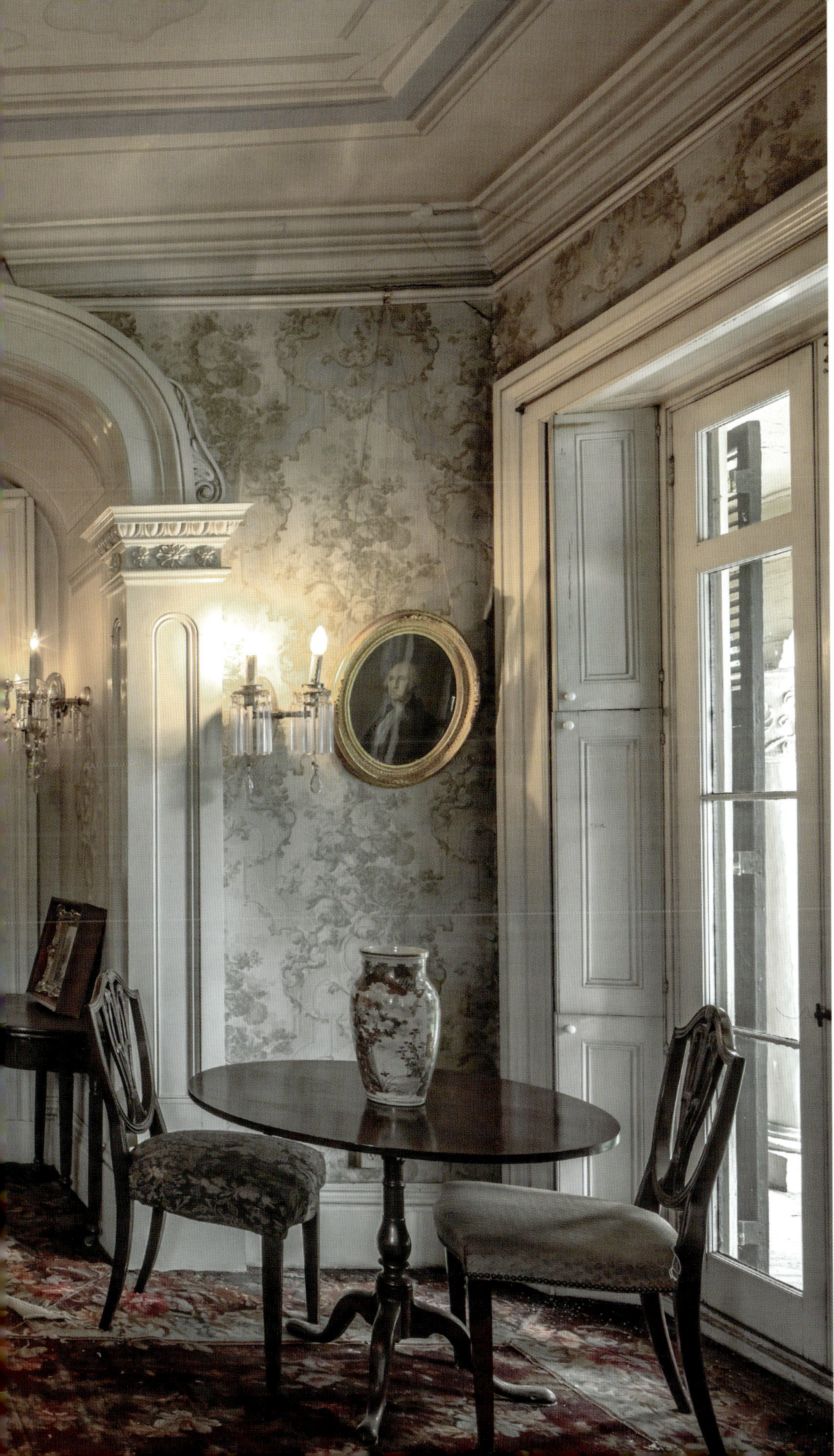

The double parlor on the south side of the house dates from the Goodwin remodeling. Extensive changes included the opening of the wall between the two parlors, installation of the arched opening and closets between the rooms, architrave trim around doors and windows, marble mantels, and lengthened windows and French doors opening onto the new verandah.

The refined details included a carved brownstone drip table separating the brownstone foundation from the brick walls, a brownstone string course between the first and second floors, and brownstone windowsills and lintels. The front entrance included both sidelights and a transom. Although it was altered by a subsequent owner around 1865, the original design included a classical portico. The roof of the original portico fit beneath the brownstone string course. Centered over the portico was a Palladian window, nicely framed by the small intersecting gable that projects from the hipped roof.

A view from the southeast parlor into the center hall.

The house had four separate chimneys built into its north and south walls. The interior consisted of two rooms on either side of a through center hall. The stairs, originally in the center hall, were later located in a separate hall between the two north rooms.

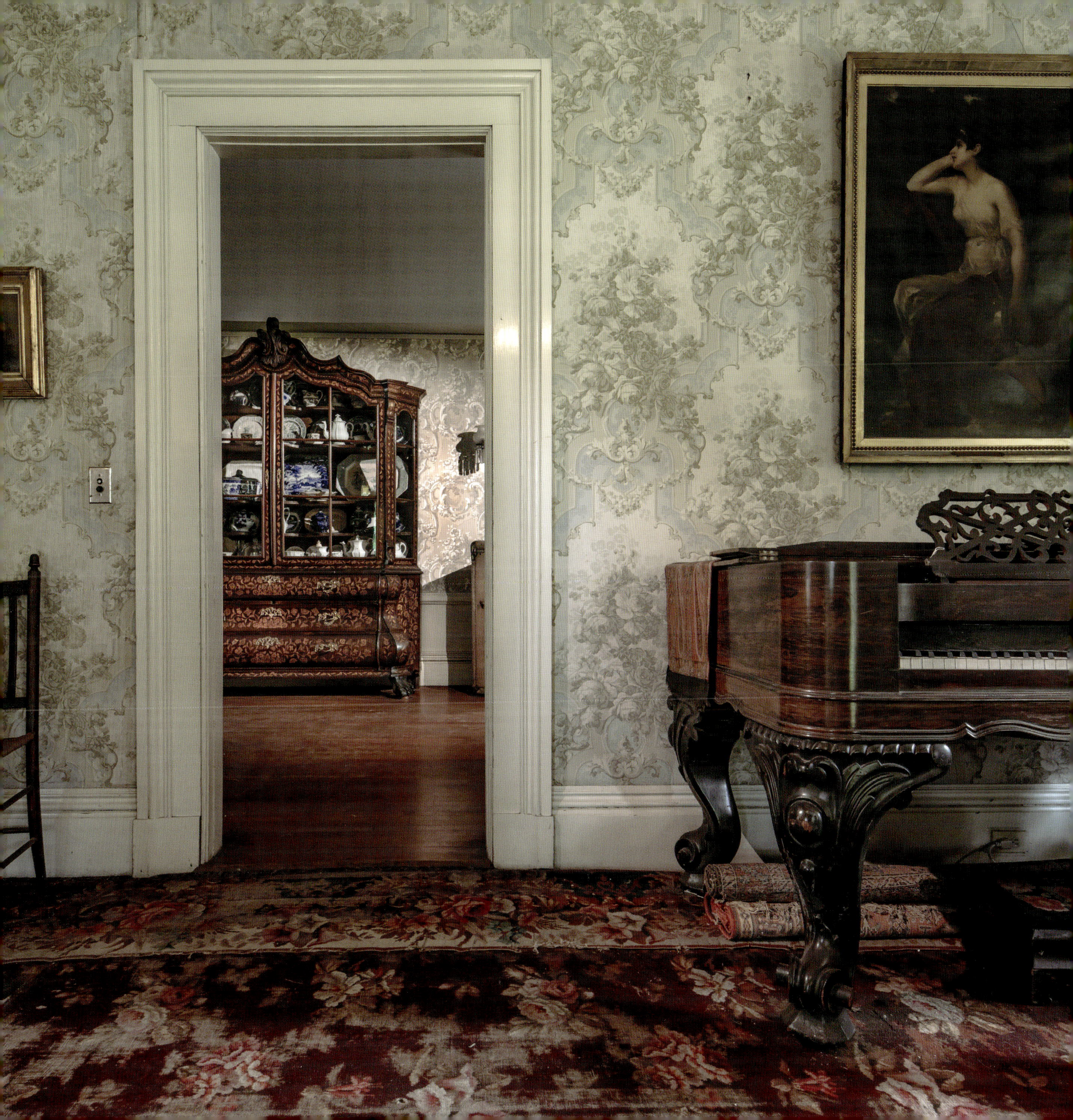

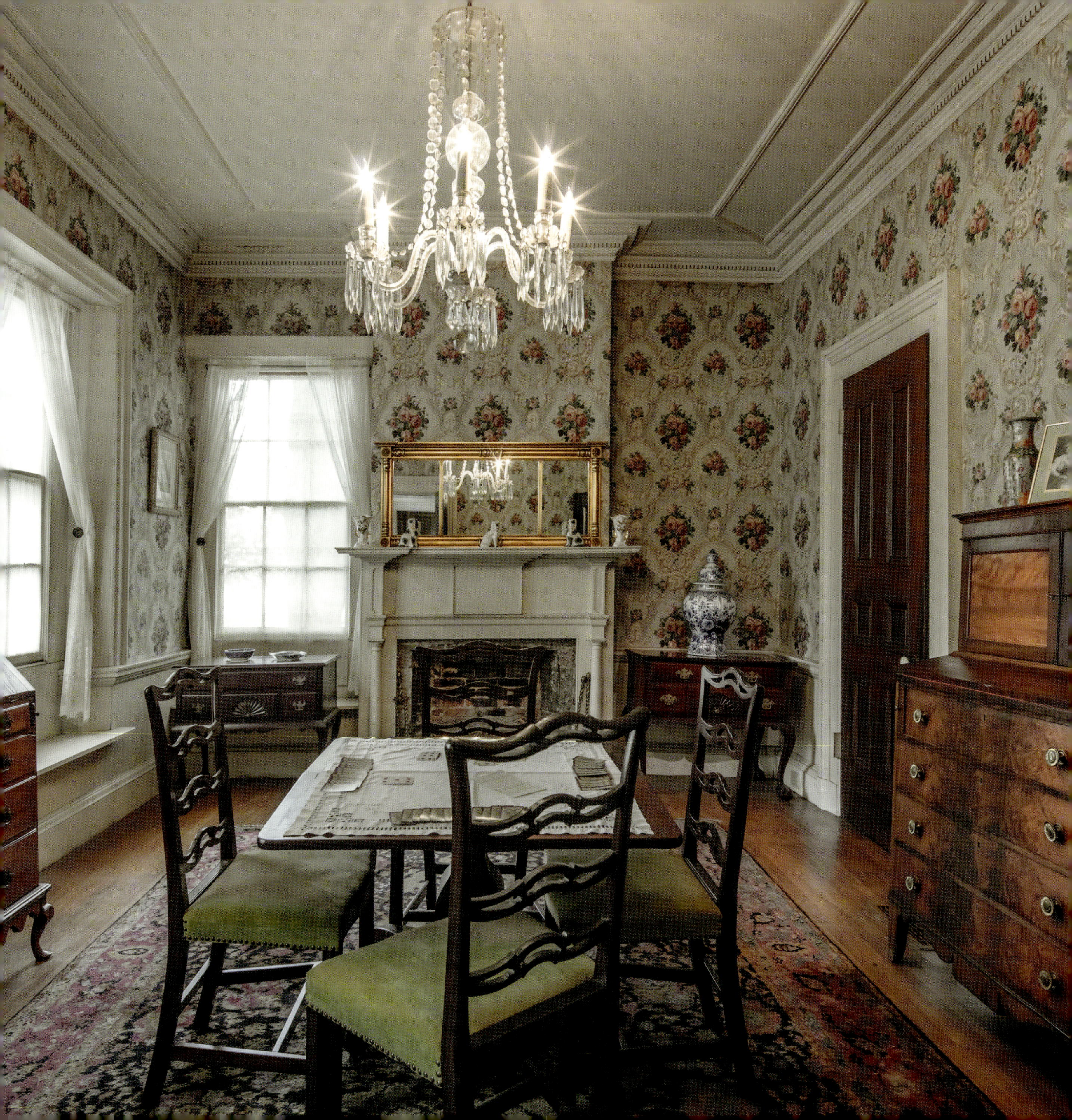

The northwest sitting room — although the late eighteenth-century mantel dates from the house's construction, its size suggests it was originally in one of the south parlors. Its installation likely dates from the Goodwin remodeling of the parlors with marble mantels.

In 1804, John Hurlbut (1770–1808) used the proceeds from his trip to China on the American ship Neptune to purchase Chester's brick home. By the spring of 1805, he had engaged James Francis "to finishing the space way [hall] for 25 dollars," and later "to making a frame for a fanlight."(Francis 1805) The fanlight could only refer to the semicircular part of the Palladian window.

The Palladian window might have been inspired by one at the 1767 Duke of Cumberland Inn in Rocky Hill.

John Hurlbut died in New York of smallpox in 1808. His wife, Anna, died in 1810. Their only surviving daughter, Anne, went to live with her uncle, Ashbel Wright, and then with her older cousin, Martha Wright. Martha's husband was the Reverend Royal Robbins, who became the minister at Berlin.

Anne quitclaimed the Chester House to her uncle and John's brother, James Hurlbut. James and his wife, Wealthy Griswold, had five children, and the family lived in the Chester House until Wealthy inherited the Michael Griswold House at 116 Garden Street.

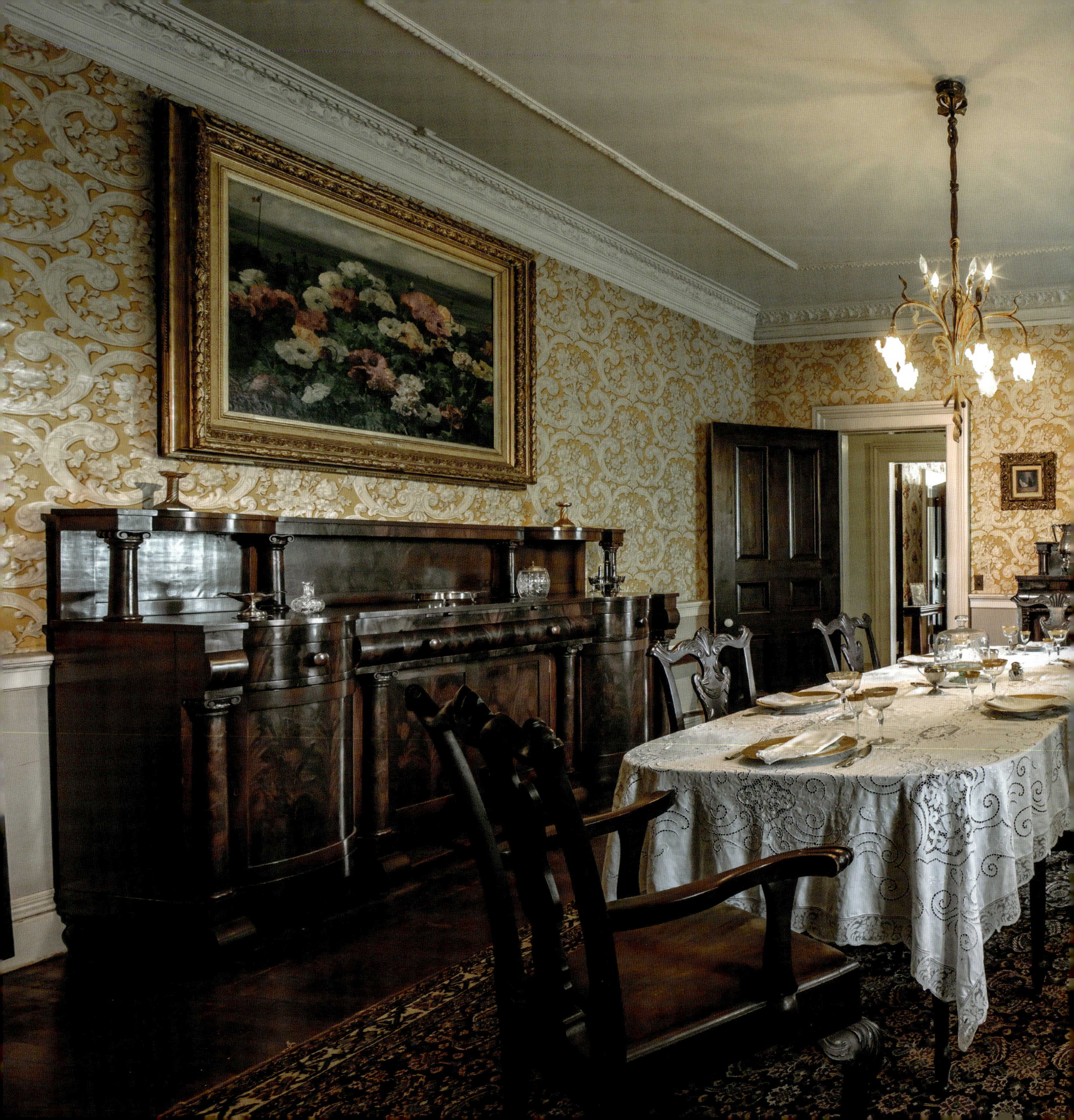

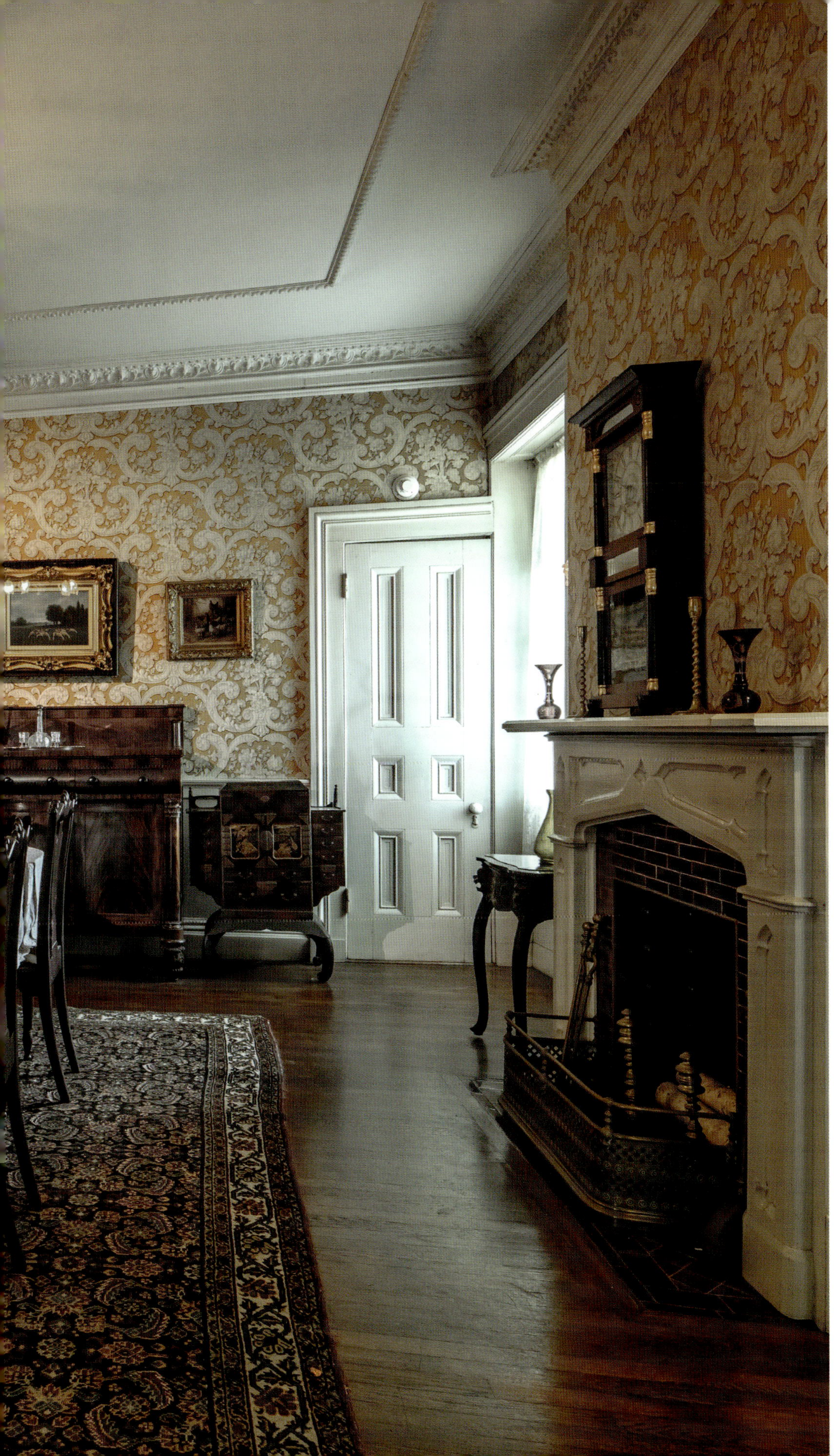

The dining room, the house's original kitchen, dates to Goodwin's addition of the ell and new kitchen between 1865–1873. The Gothic Revival fireplace mantel dates from that time. The ceiling cornice was added in 1891.

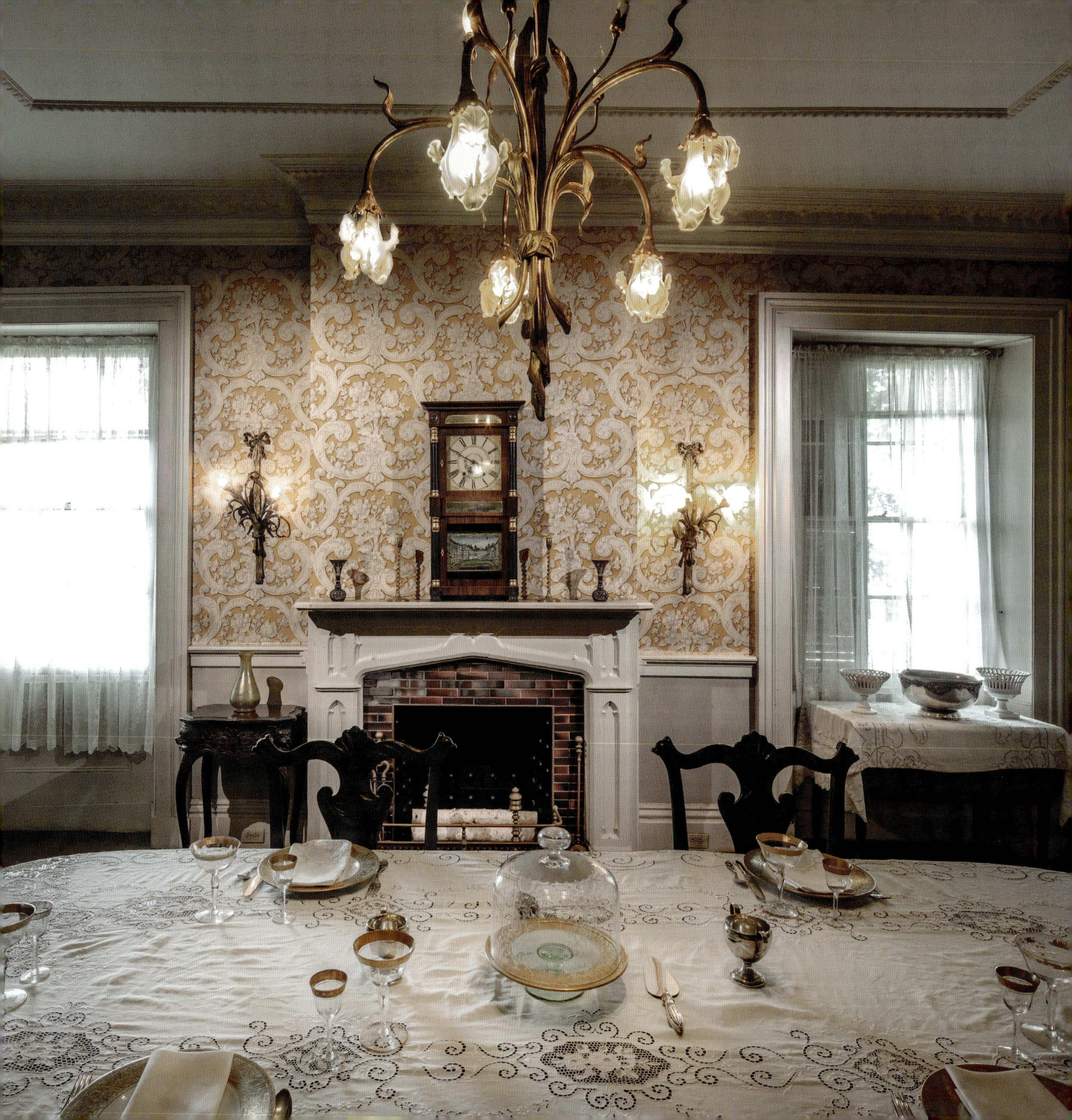

The brass and glass chandelier and sconces are early twentieth century and might have been added for Jane and Howard Dunham's wedding in 1907, in addition to the wallpaper, wainscot, and chair rail.

By 1862, Levi Goodwin had assumed sole ownership of the brick house at 212 Main Street and remodeled it in the Italianate style. Unable to change the underlying structure, horizontal proportions were the norm when Thomas Chester built the house in 1794, Goodwin introduced a degree of verticality with a new entrance portico and a rooftop belvedere. Goodwin's builder must have obtained the various components, including the Corinthian columns; arches, brackets, and cornice of the portico; the arched windows and frames; and brackets and cornice molding of the belvedere from a local lumberyard, because their counterparts can be seen on a number of Hartford buildings such as the brick houses built on Congress Street around 1858–1860.

Goodwin lengthened the first-floor windows on the south side of the house to provide access from the double parlors onto the newly added veranda against the south and east sides of the house. Since the original roof was already a shallow hip, it was relatively easy to have the builder extend the eaves and add heavy brackets and a cornice.

The house's original center staircase, rising on the north side of the back hall to a platform and then along the back wall, was probably removed during Goodwin's remodeling.

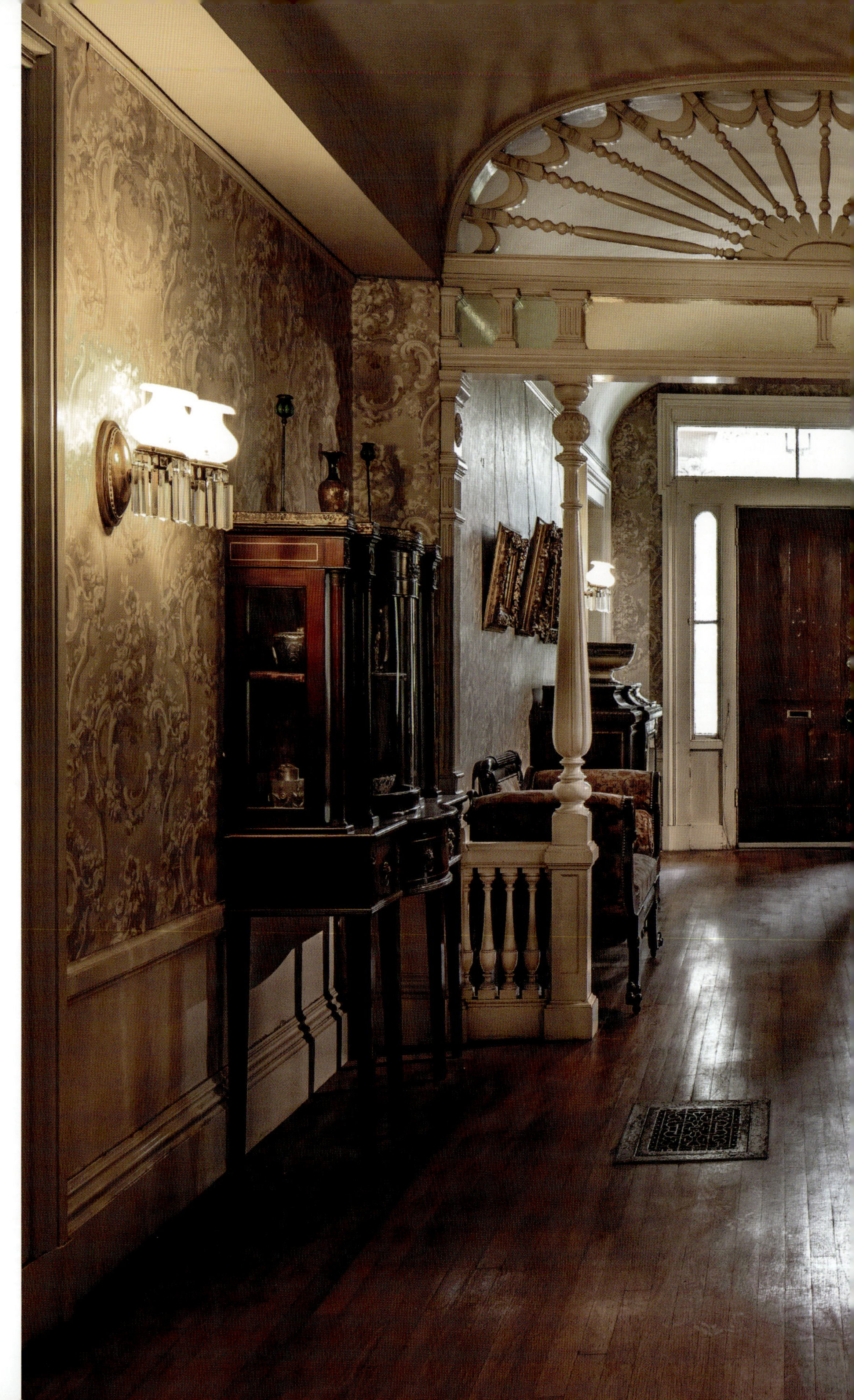

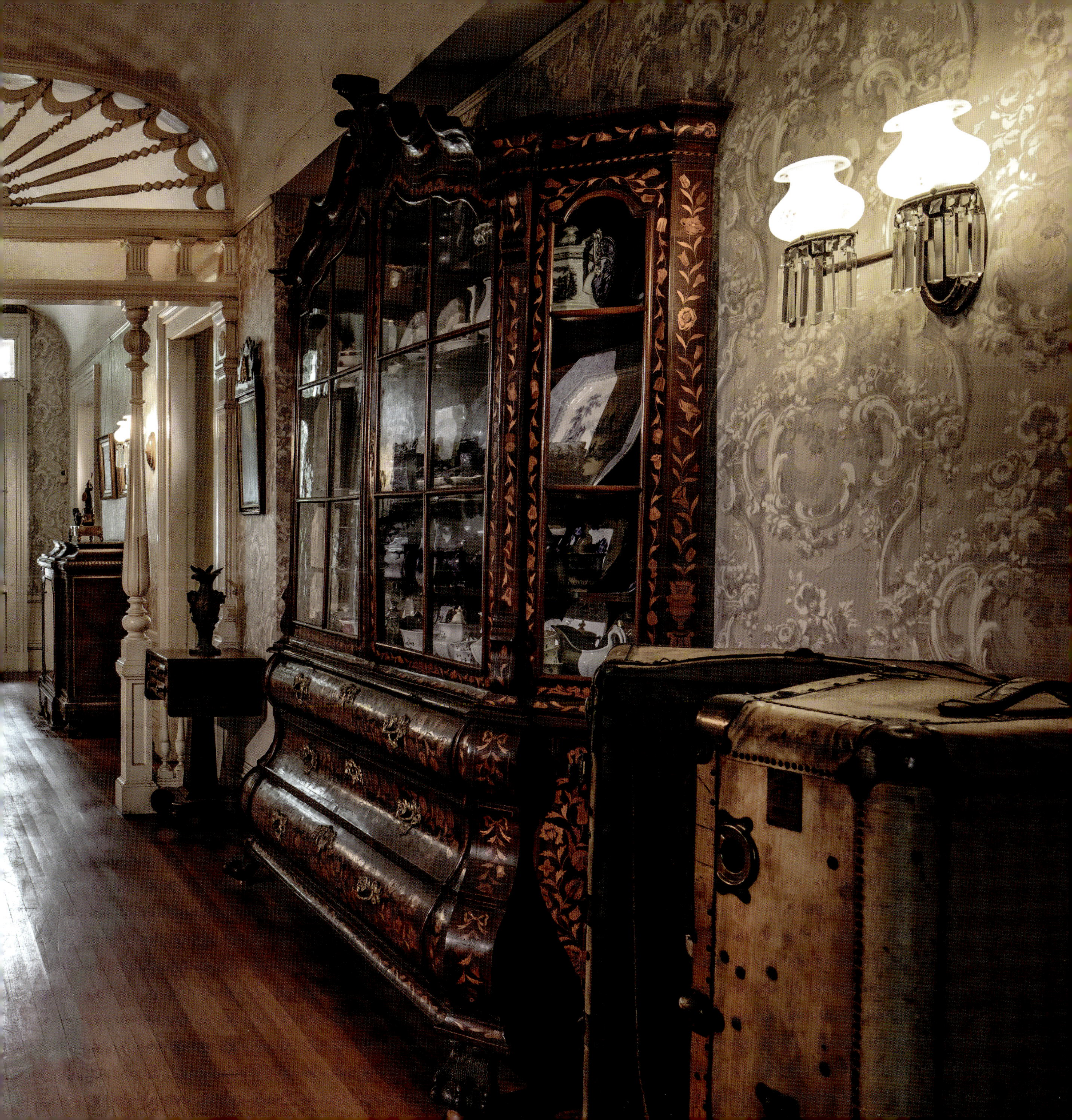

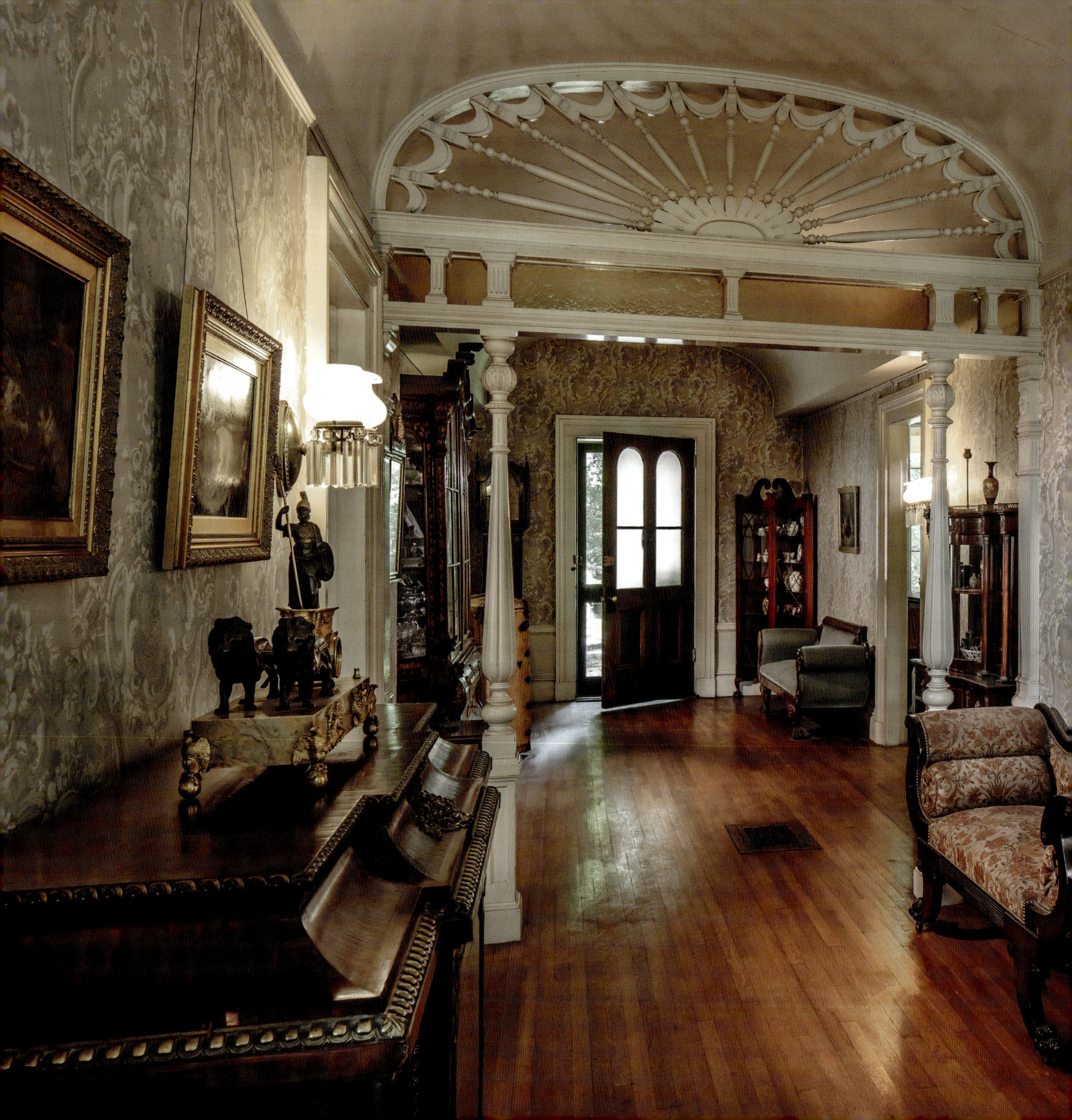

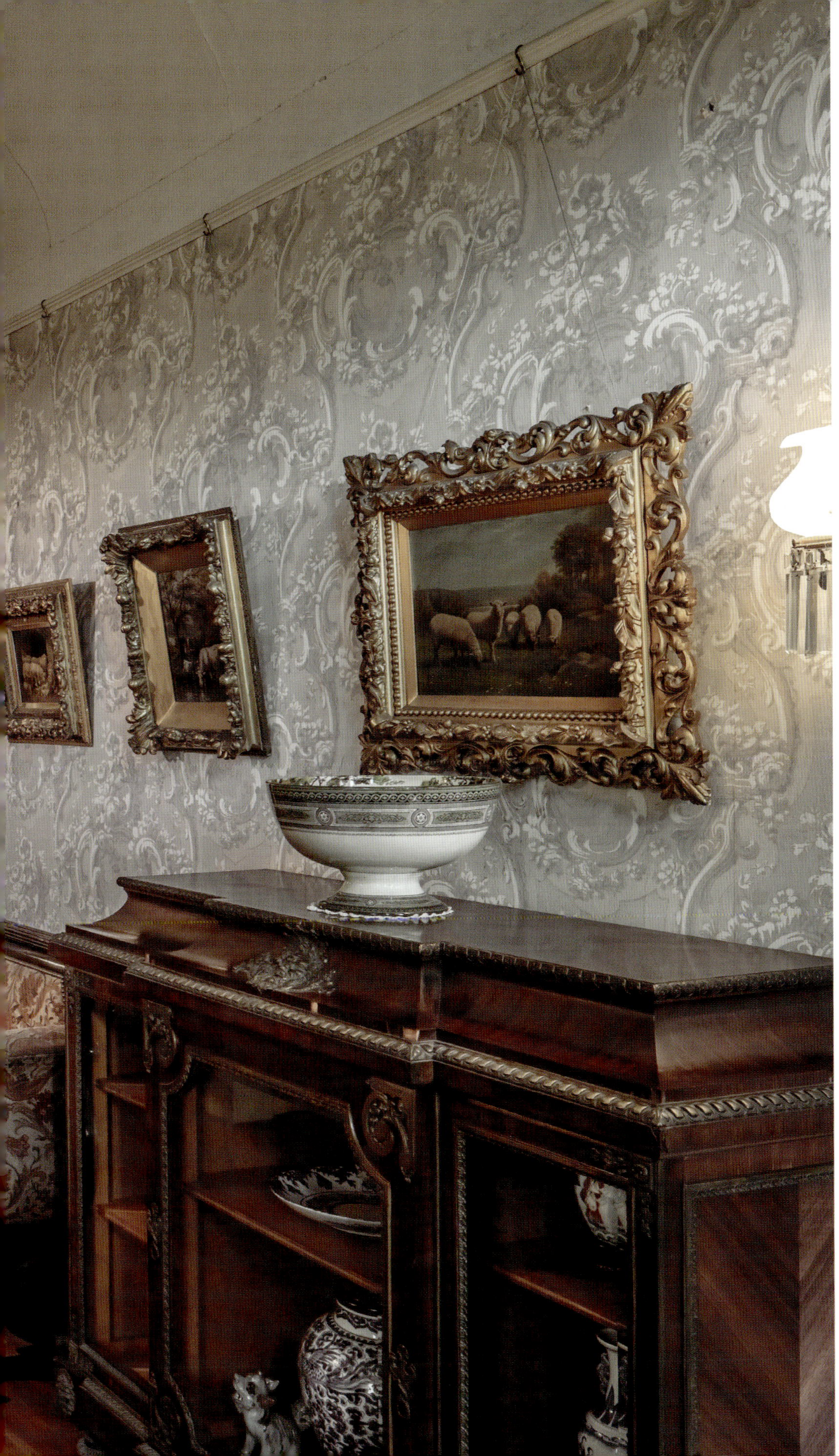

The cove ceiling dates to the Goodwin remodeling. The late nineteenth-century millwork grill, which divides the hall, was probably installed between 1880 and 1900.

The gasoliers, dating from about 1875, were probably installed after Silas Robbins purchased the house that year for his son, Elisha Robbins. They were electrified by the Dunhams.

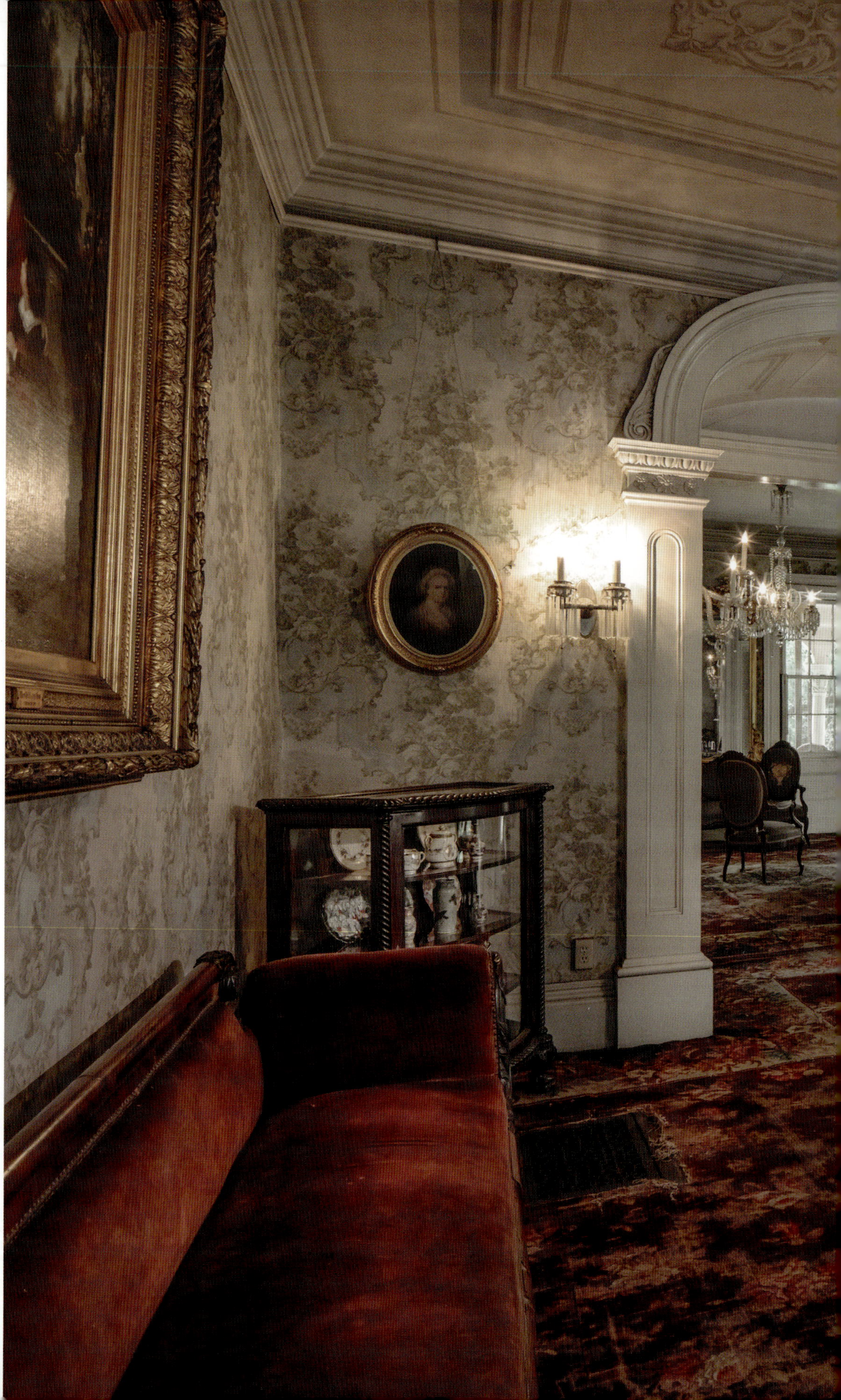

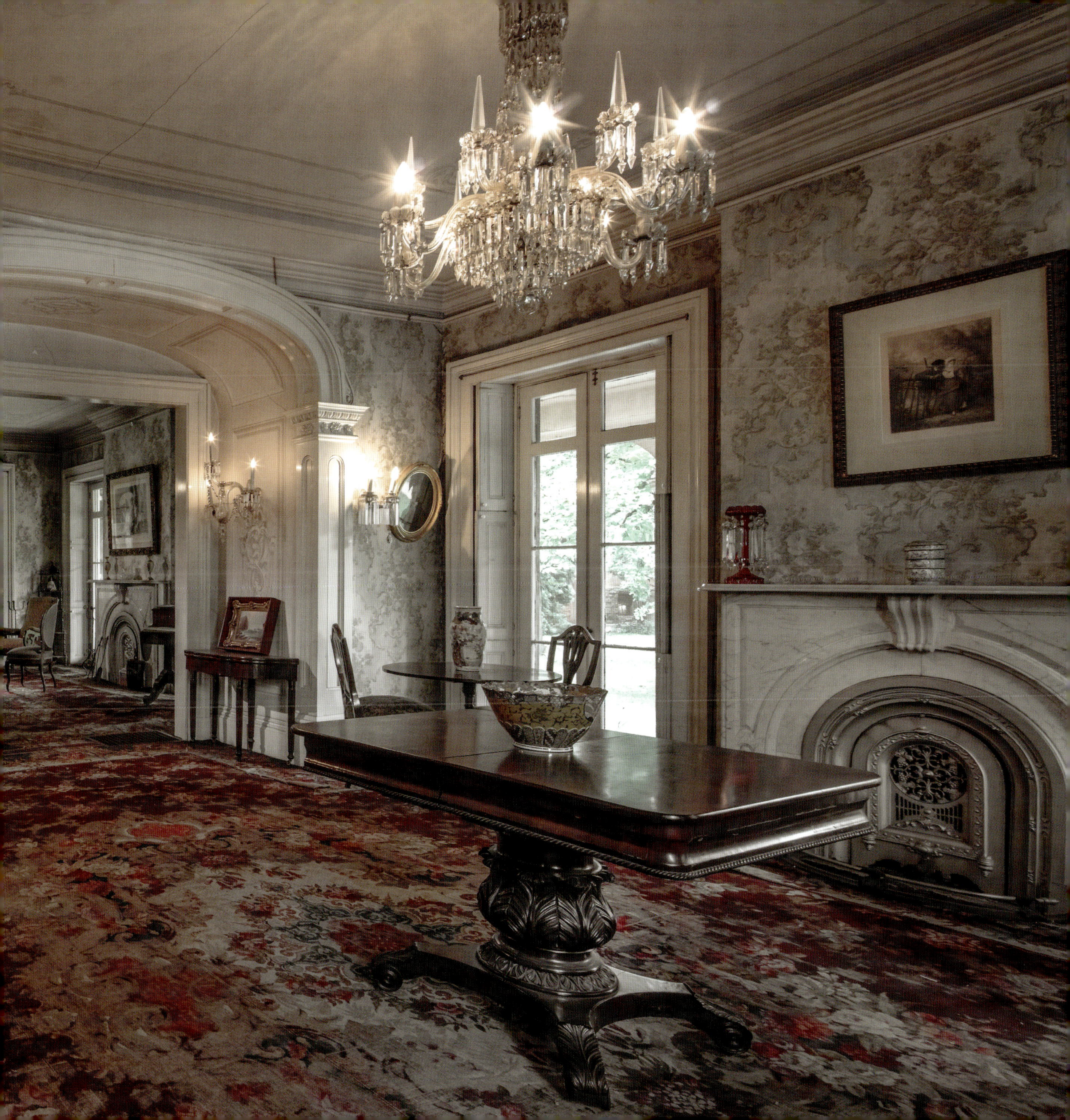

In 1875, Silas W. Robbins (1822–1918) purchased the house for his son and daughter-in-law, Elisha Robbins and Ida Adams. Their daughter, Jane Robbins (1884–1963), inherited the house and lived in it with her husband, Howard Dunham, until the 1930s when they moved to New York City.

Jane Robbins Dunham left the home to the Wethersfield Historical Society, who received it in 1971 after Howard's death. The Society still owns and operates the property and preserves the home as it existed between 1899–1930 when the Dunhams and Jane's mother, Ida Robbins, inhabited it. Howard and Jane Dunham selected a colonial revival color scheme of red brick, cream trim, and green shutters, which they proudly displayed one year on their Christmas card. ♛

The verandah on the south and east sides of the house was part of Goodwin's Italianate remodeling.

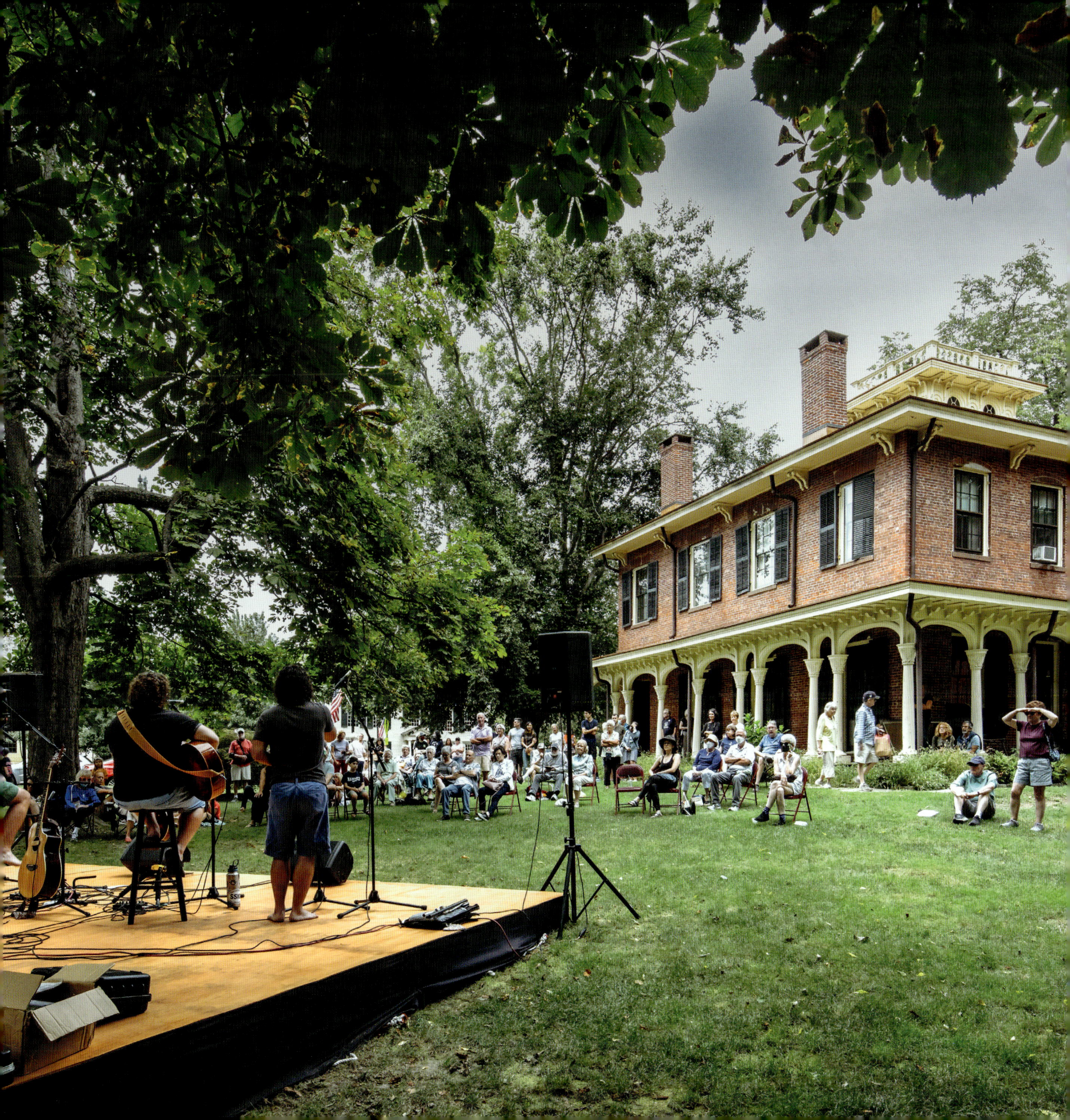

A SNUG HOME AND TAVERN AND FICTIONAL WITCH

Belden House and Tavern (Buttolph-Williams House)

— 249 Broad Street —

Before twentieth-century zoning required the separation of industrial and commercial uses from residential neighborhoods, most men conducted their business or trade at home. This was certainly true for licensed tavern keepers, whose homes also functioned as taverns where locals could gather for hard cider or rum, and travelers might find lodging for the night. It was not unusual for strangers to share beds with each other or a member of the keeper's family.

Tavern keepers were licensed with specific reference to their character and the location of their establishment. In 1673, John Belden (1631–1677) was "chosen ordnary keeper, for the entertainment of straingers and travillers, as the law requires." (Adams 1904) This was the location of what would become the Buttolph-Williams House that stands today.

The Belden House and Tavern — when acquired in 1949 by the Antiquarian and Landmarks Society (now Connecticut Landmarks), the house was straight sided. Two layers of clapboard removed during restoration revealed the original overhang and evidence of diamond-paned windows.

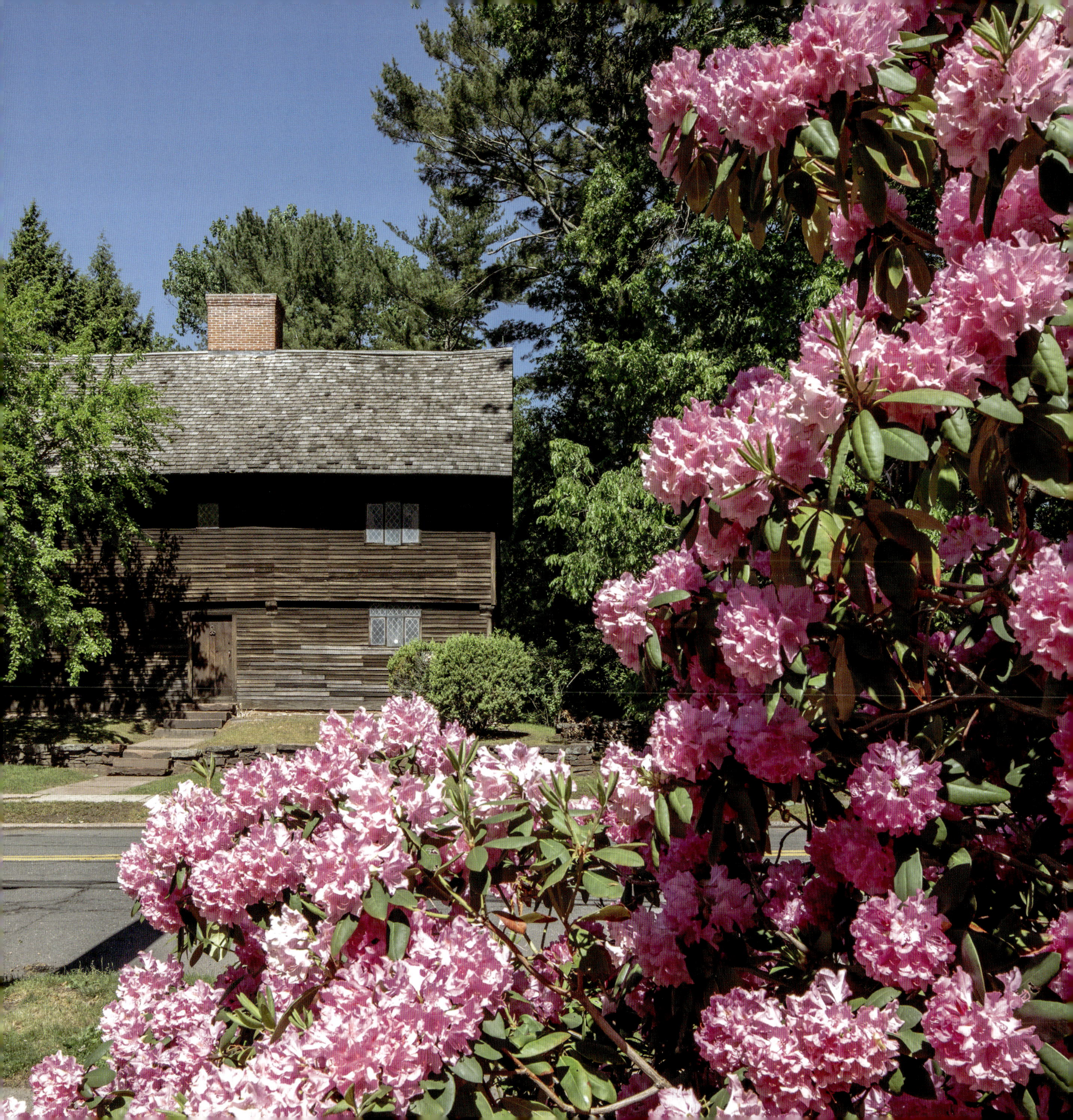

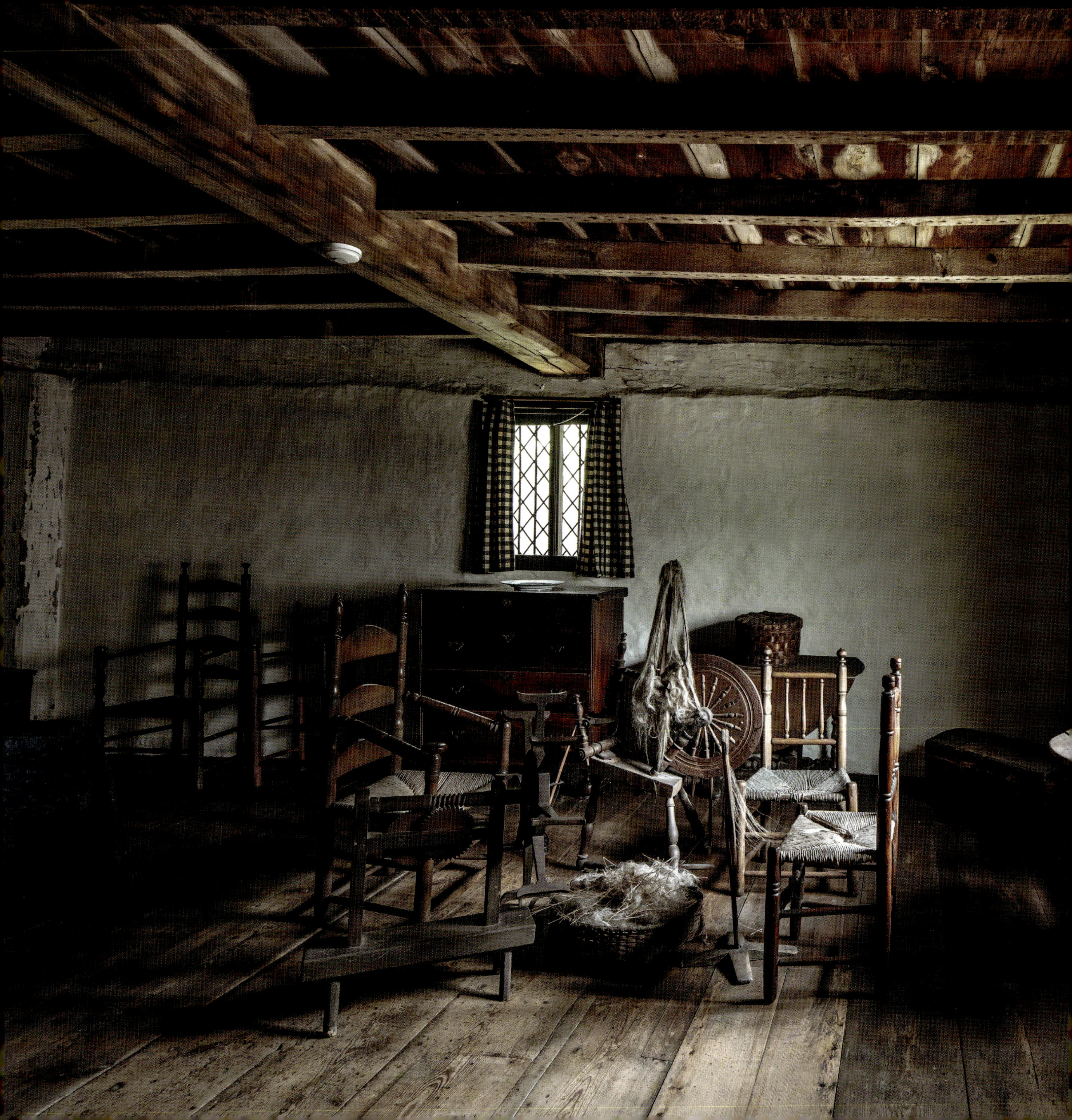

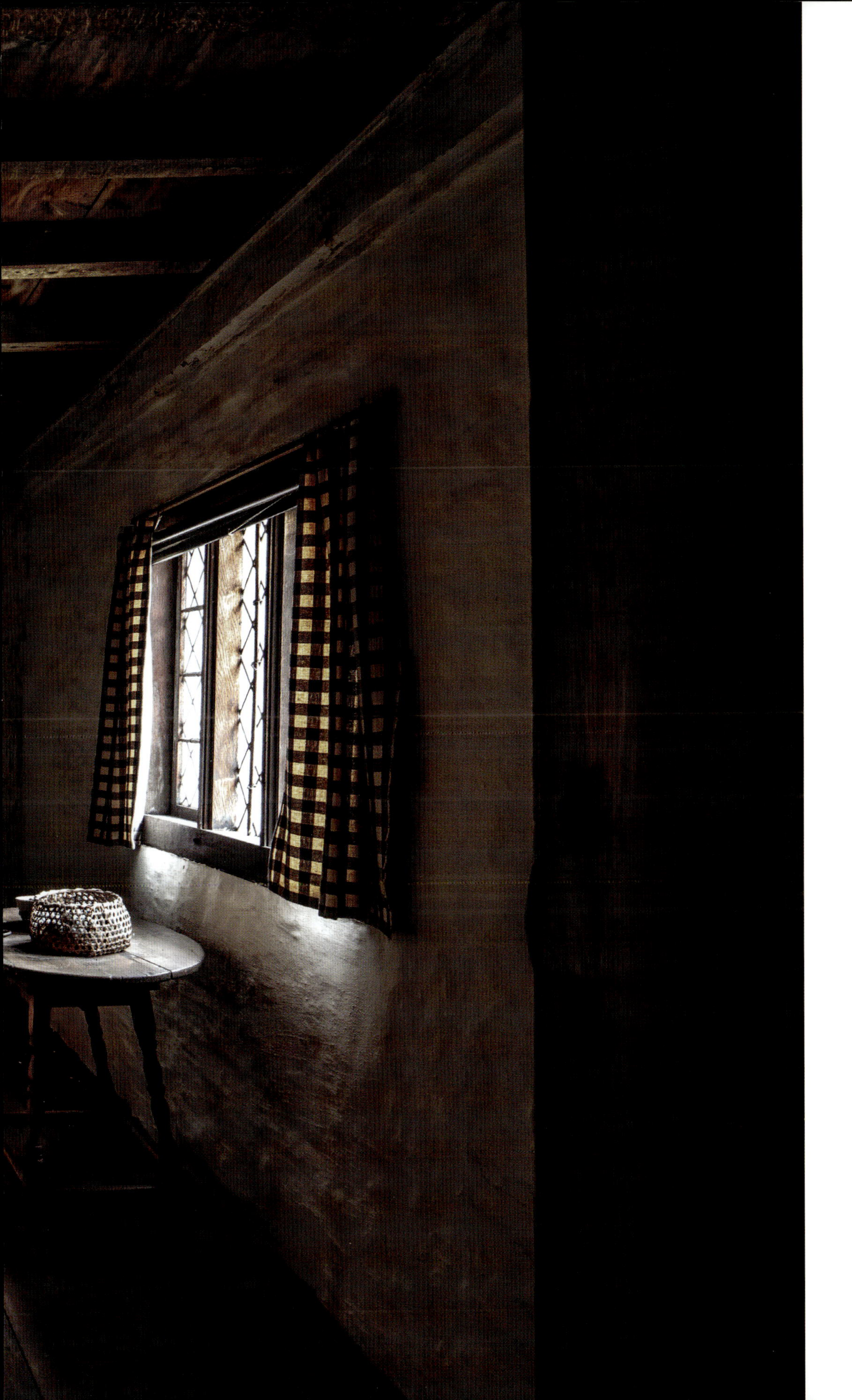

Looking into the north chamber.

Although precise ownership records are not available, there is documentation that David Buttolph inherited the property around 1692 and sold it in 1698 to Robert Turner. Subsequently, John Belden's grandson, Benjamin (1687–1741), purchased the property at 249 Broad Street from Turner in July 1711, returning it as the Belden family's home and to tavern keeping.

Benjamin Belden married Anne Churchill in January of 1714 and was licensed as a tavern keeper later that year, by which time he had presumably completed his house and established a new Belden Tavern. They had six children, who would have helped with the family business.

A view of the south hall with its period appropriate furnishings.

The Belden House and Tavern was framed in such a way that the steeply pitched gable roof projected beyond the walls of the second floor, and the front and side walls of the second floor projected beyond the walls of the first. The extended upper stories were reminiscent of the practice in English towns where the overhang sheltered the sidewalk from rain.

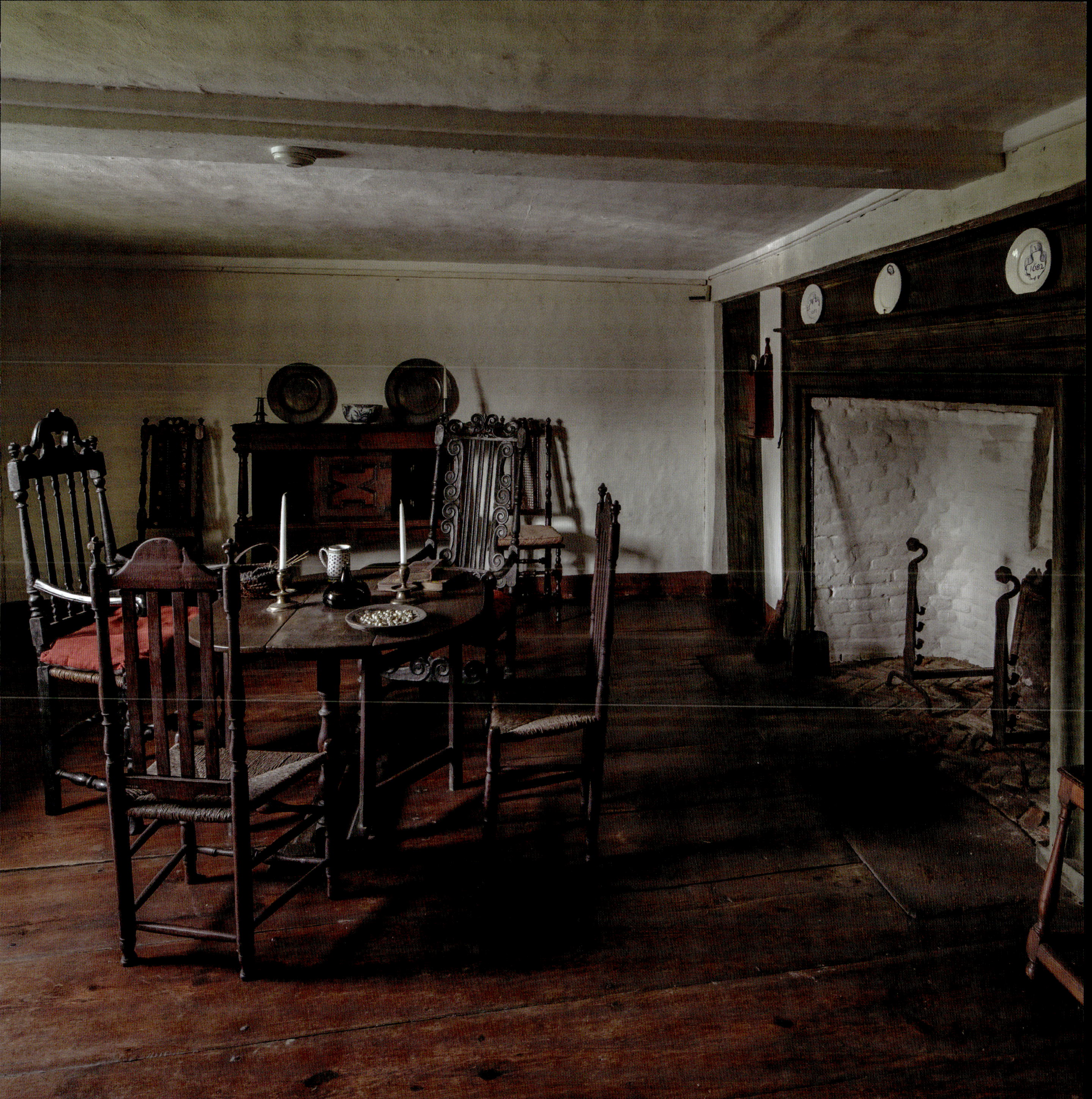

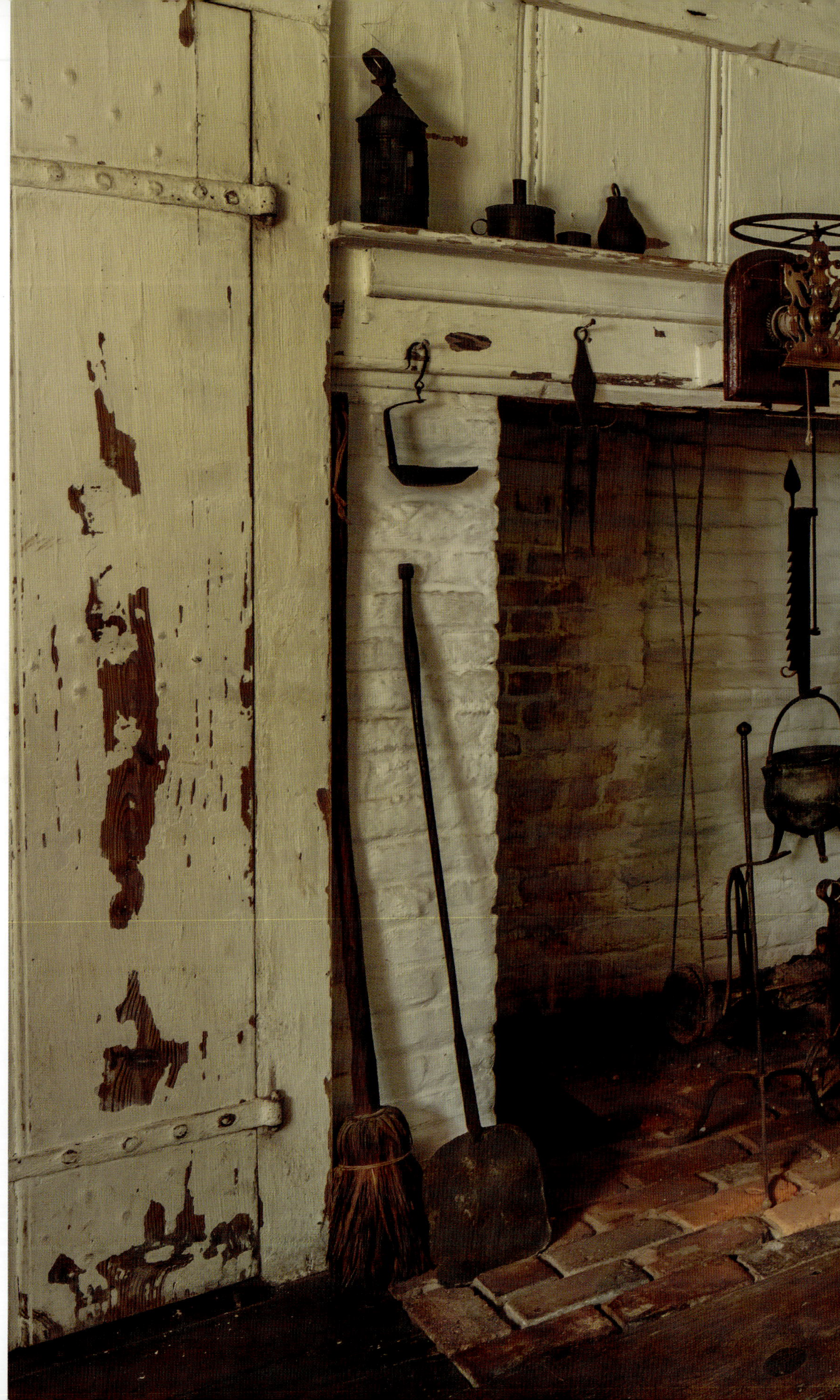

The kitchen fireplace and its equipment, including a clock jack to rotate a spit for roasting meat.

(following spread)
The whitewashed kitchen is furnished with an excellent assemblage of appropriate late seventeenth and early eighteenth-century furniture, and kitchen tools and vessels collected by Frances Phipps, author of Colonial Kitchens, Their Furnishings, and Their Gardens.

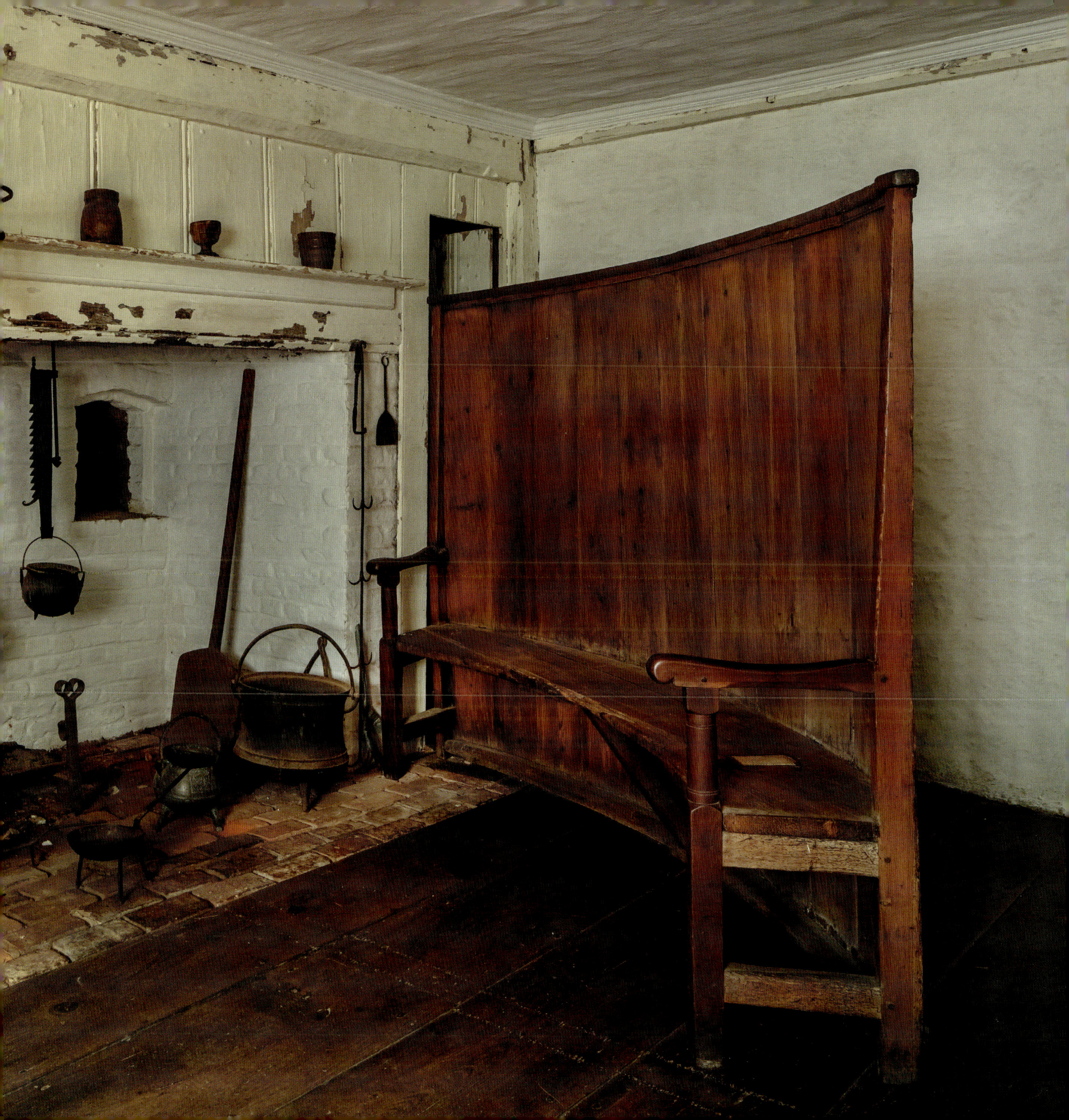

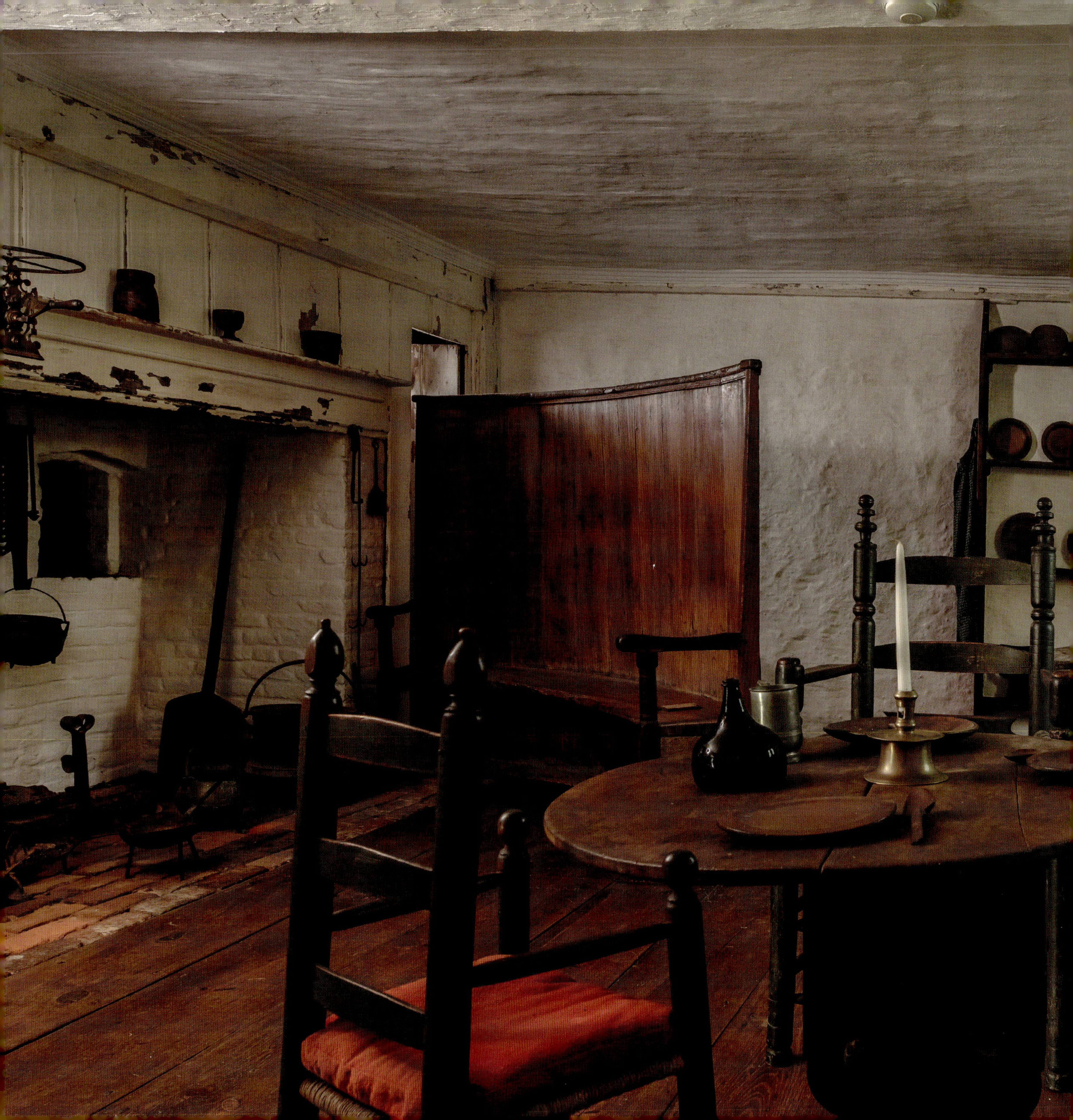

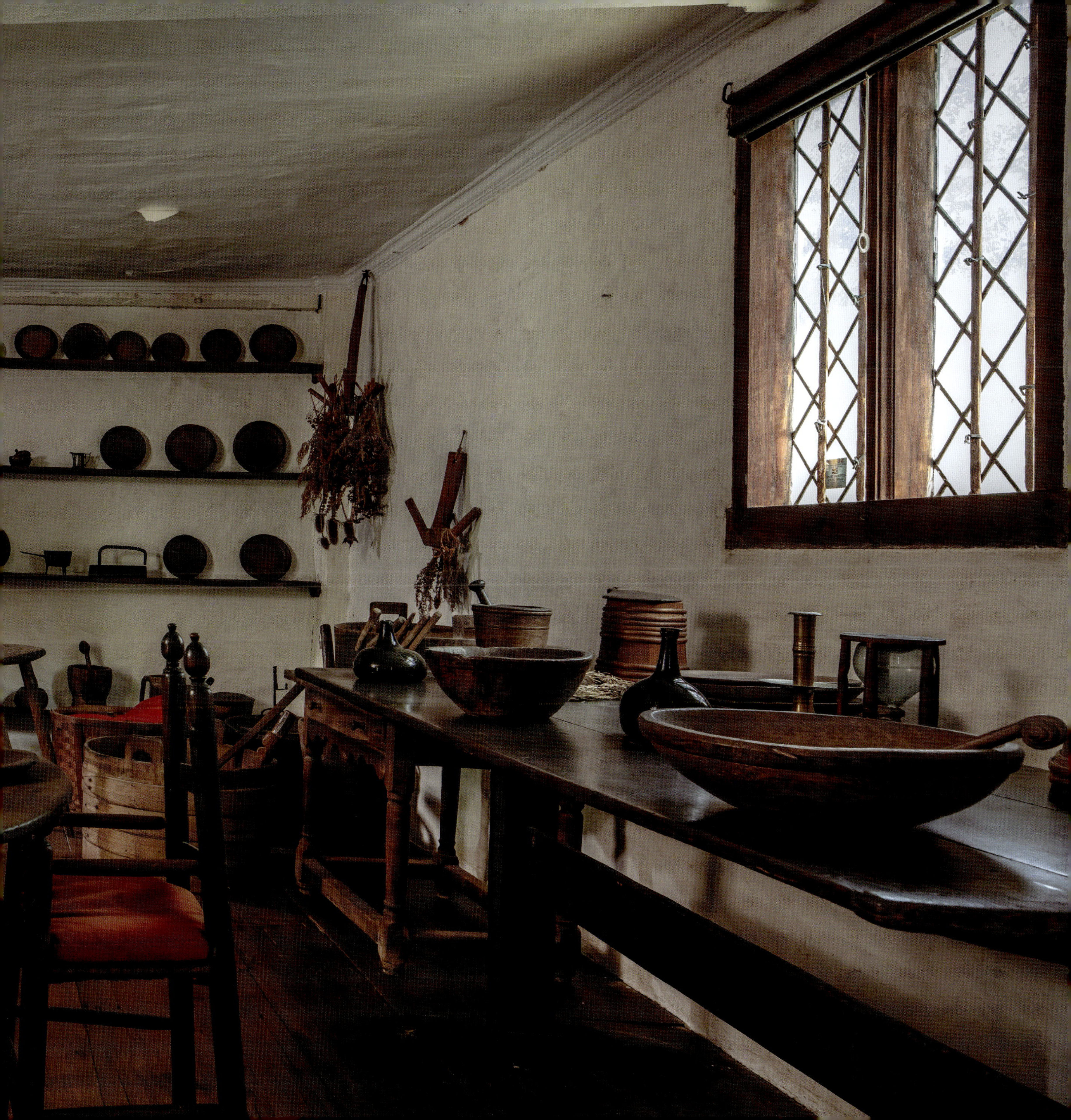

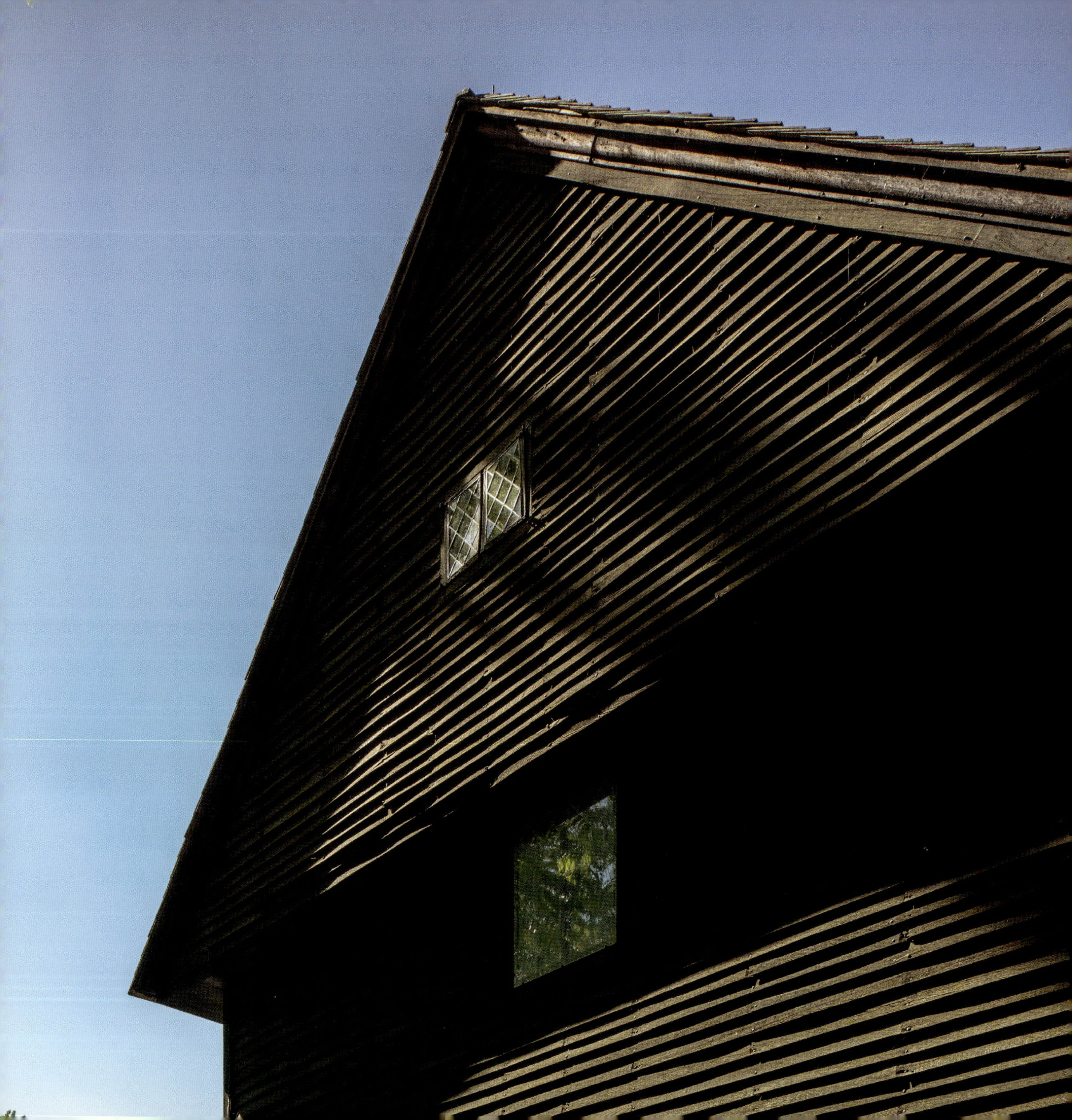

The north gable end showing the prominent attic overhang.

The corbeled chimney, steep roof, projecting upper floors, nail-studded board and batten door, and the diamond-paned casement windows are features of the Jacobean style. Belden's continued use of this style was a little retro; at a time when the Georgian style was already in vogue, his use of the older Jacobean style might have been a conscious attempt to retain the look and appeal of a traditional English tavern.

In 1721 Belden sold the property to Daniel Williams, who remodeled the house in the Georgian style. The lower floors were built out to conceal the overhangs, and the house was resided with long pine clapboards. The window openings were altered to accommodate double-hung windows paired on either side of the center doorway.

The south chamber's ambitious and handsome woodwork and the great bolection molding of the fireplace surround. Red is the original color.

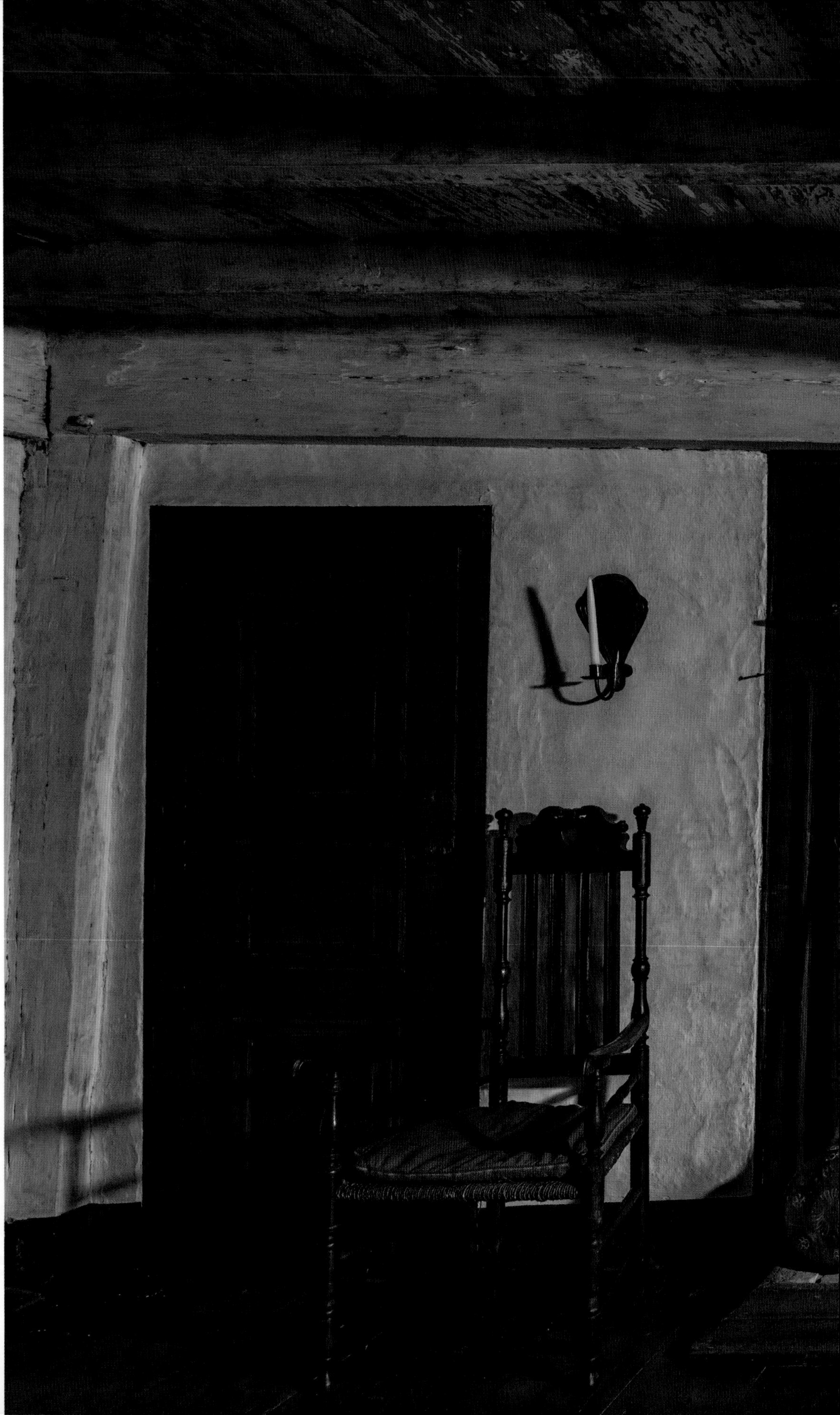

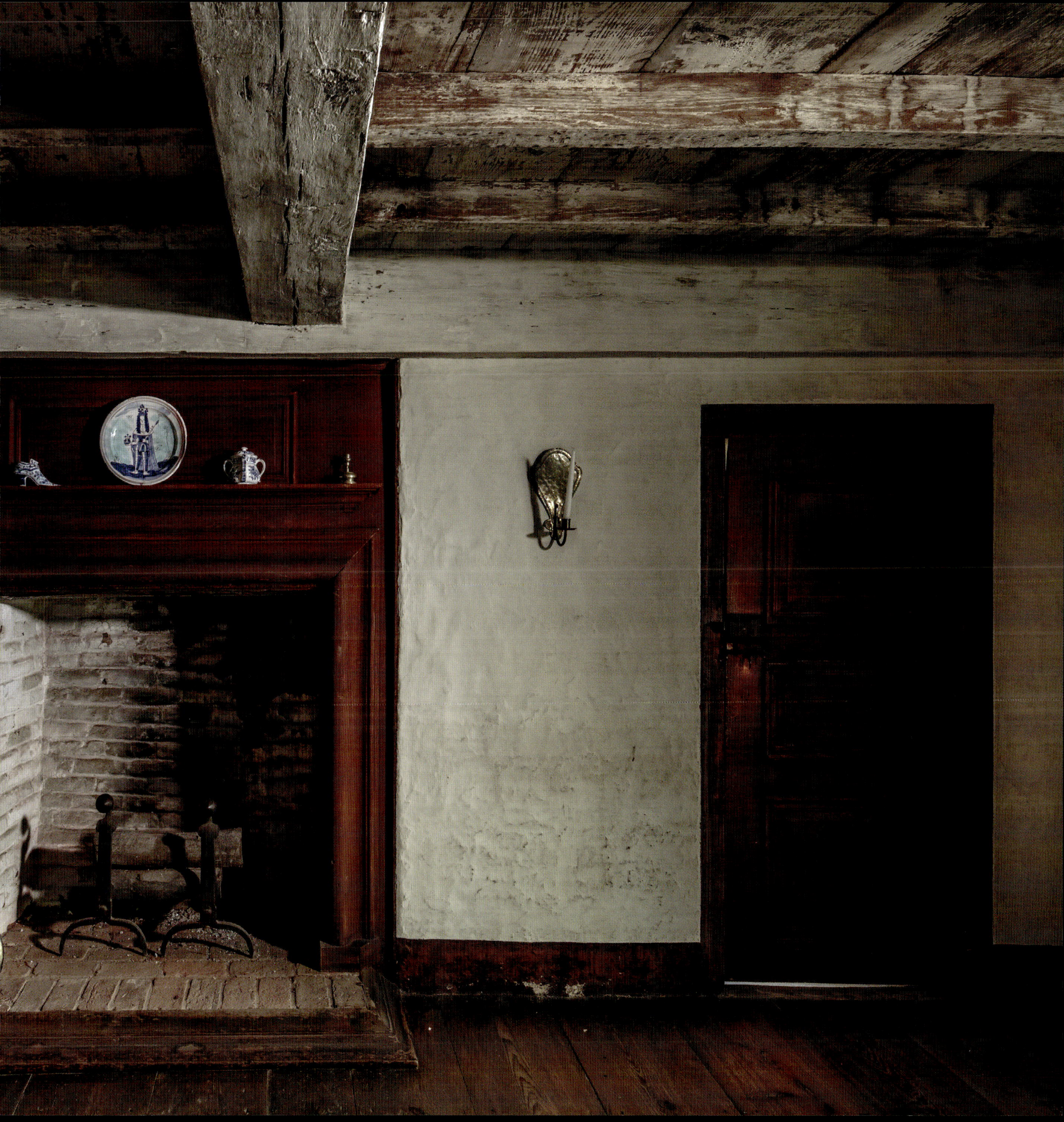

The Antiquarian and Landmarks Society (now Connecticut Landmarks) purchased the property in 1949 and decided to restore the house to Benjamin Belden's preferred Jacobean-style appearance. One of the organization's founding members, the preservation architect Frederic Palmer, supervised the structural investigation and restoration. His documented methodology established the highest professional standards for preservation in Wethersfield and across the state.

The crew took the Belden House and Tavern down to the frame, resided it with oak clapboards, and installed casement windows and reproduction board and batten doors. The interior of the house followed the two-room plan. The center chimney stack included a fireplace in each room. It is notable that the sides of the fireplaces were square with the opening taller than wide, as they were in England, rather than angled and wider than tall, as they were in houses built in America in the late eighteenth century. During this period, it was unusual to have a mantel, but in the Belden House and Tavern, all four fireplaces had them.

The south side of the house showing the bracketed overhang and the door into the south chamber.

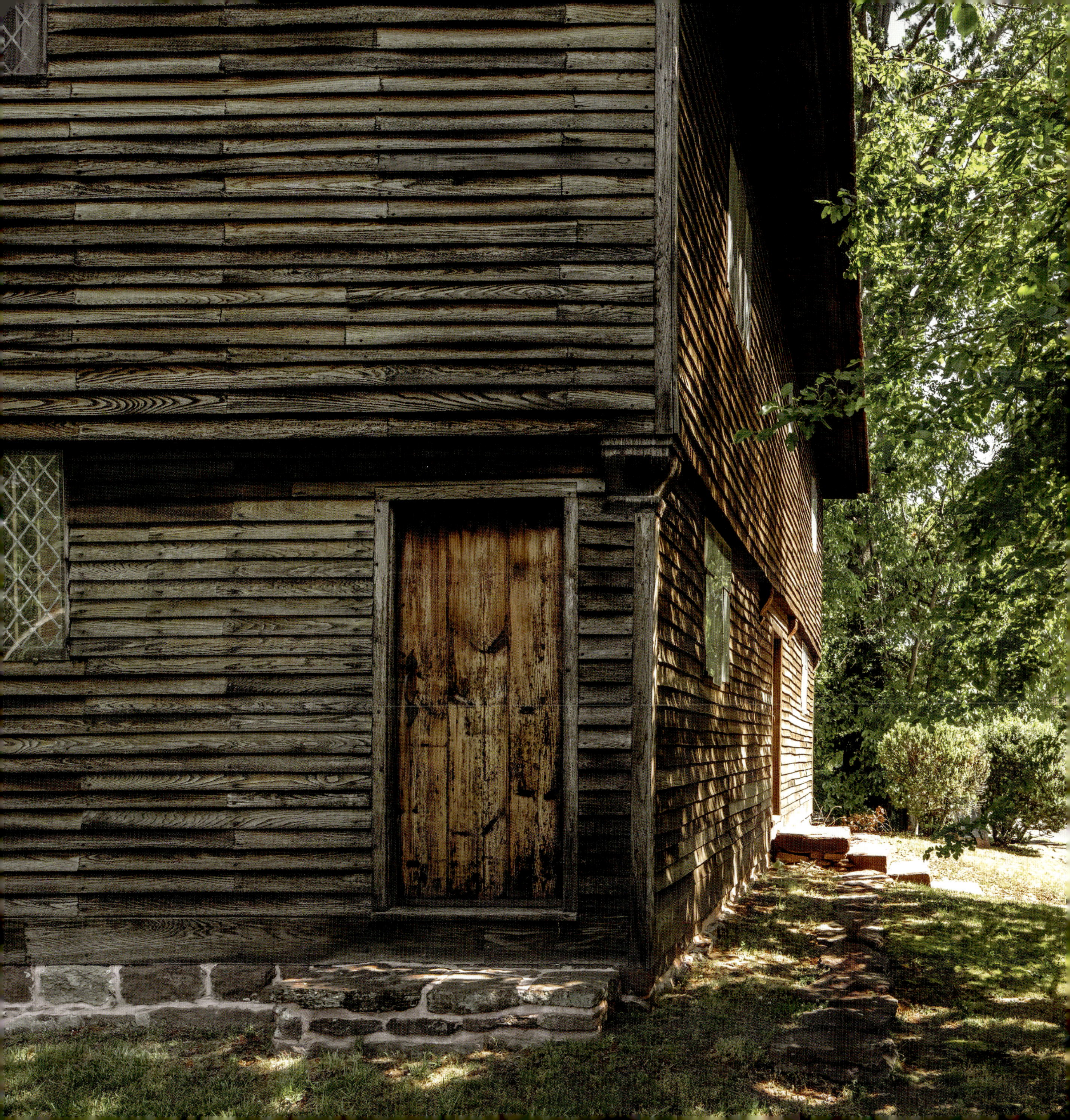

View of the façade with the second story and attic overhangs.

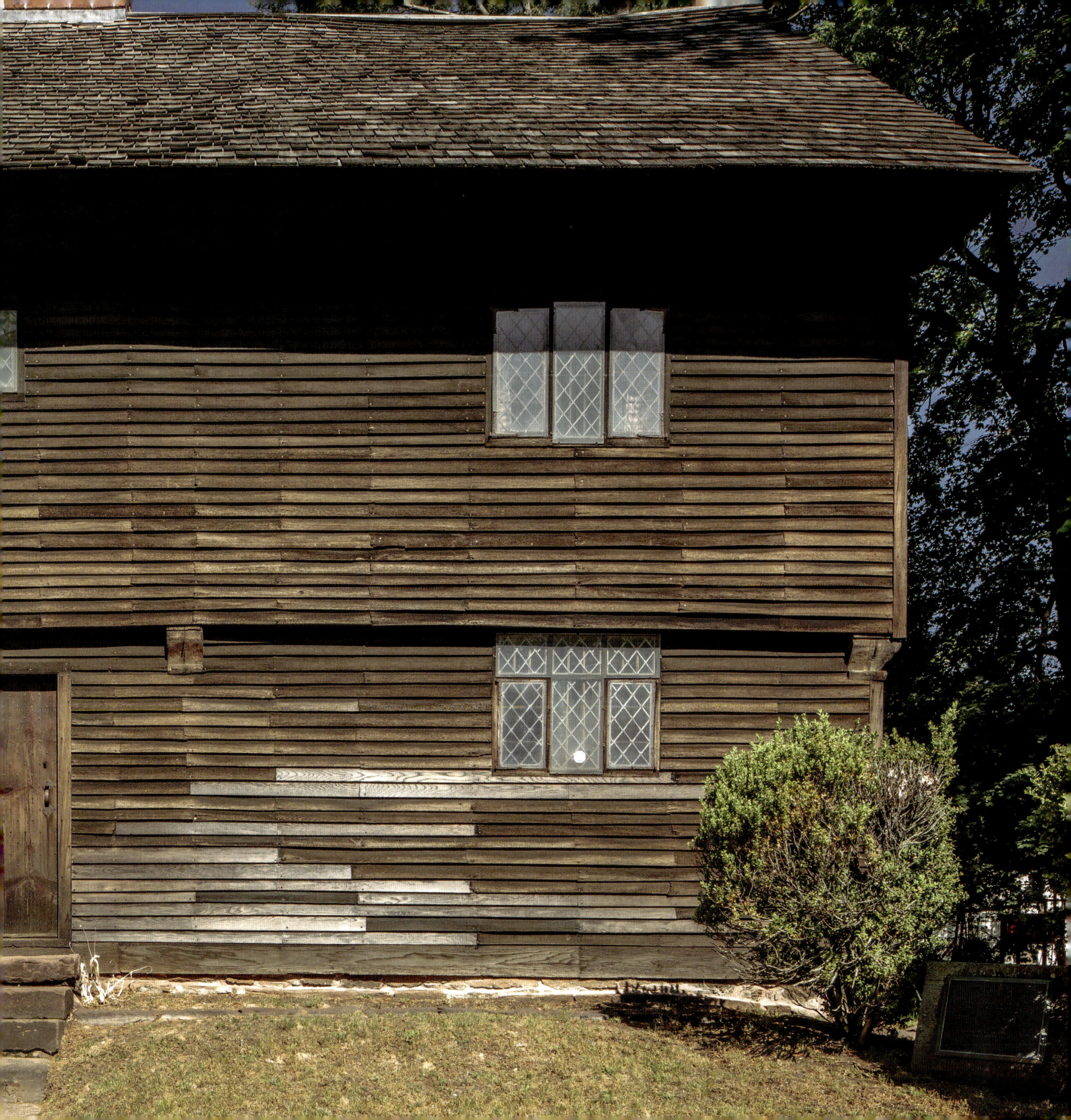

According to Palmer, the south room and its chamber contained "the most ambitious and handsome woodwork, so far as the fireplace surround and doors were concerned. . . . There are few counterparts — that is, in scale — existing in Connecticut of the great molding used on these two fireplaces." (Palmer 1956) The original bricks in the back wall of the fireplace were laid in a decorative diamond pattern. Apart from the woodwork around and above the fireplace, the rest of the fireplace wall, the three outside walls, and the ceiling were plaster. The coffin door on the south end of the house opened into the south room, which probably functioned as the tavern's public room.

View of the reproduction nail-studded board and batten door.

The fireplace in the north room included a bake oven in the back wall, indicating this room was the kitchen. Here the edges of the chimney girt, posts, and transverse summer beam had rather flat chamfers ending in lambs-tongue stops. The fireplace wall consisted of vertical sheathing with a decorative joint. Frederick Palmer described the joint as "having two quarter-inch beads with a double bevel between them — the whole rather resembling very deeply cut shadow molding." (Palmer 1956) This distinctive joint also appeared on the sheathing in the front entrance porch.

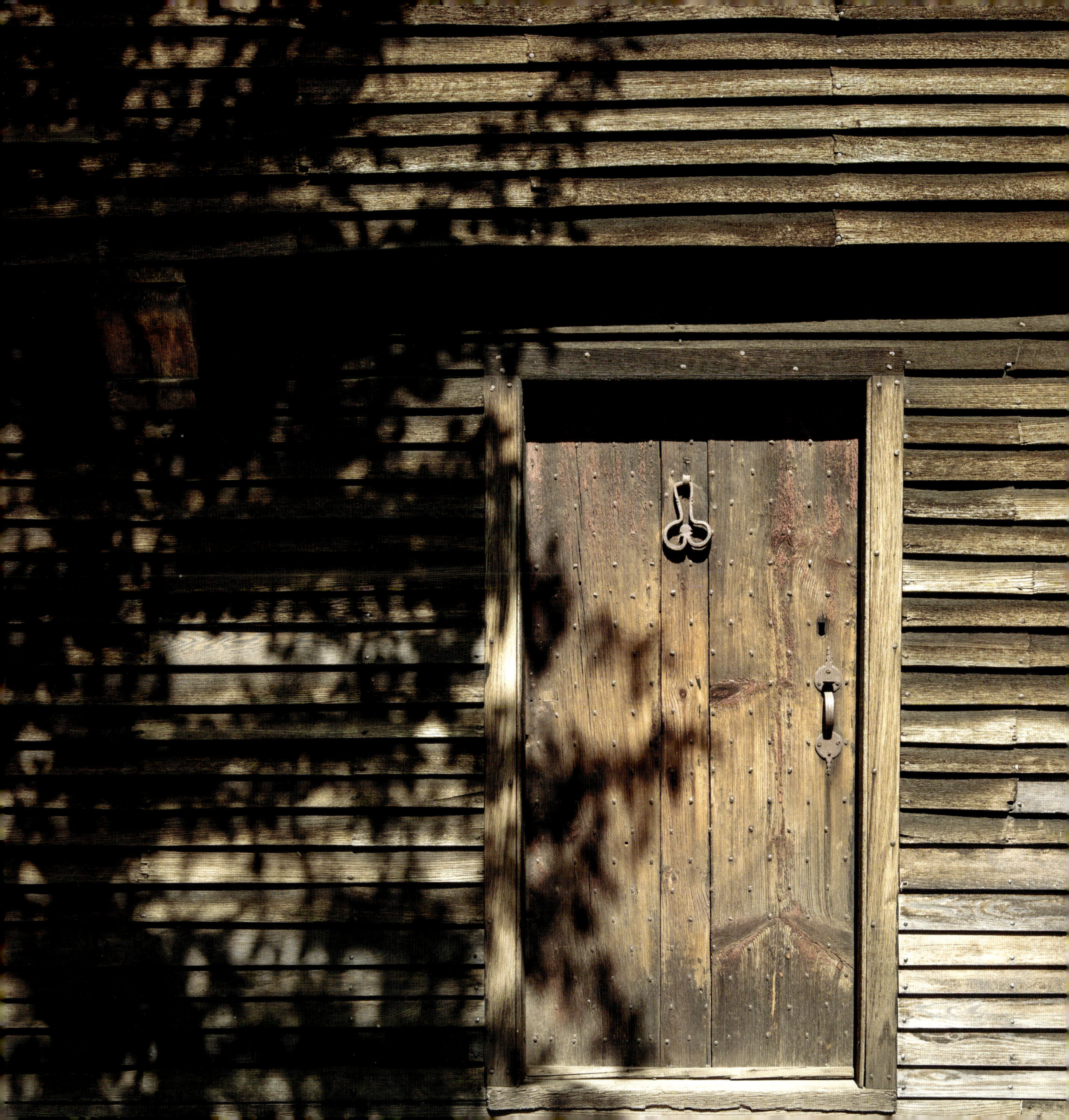

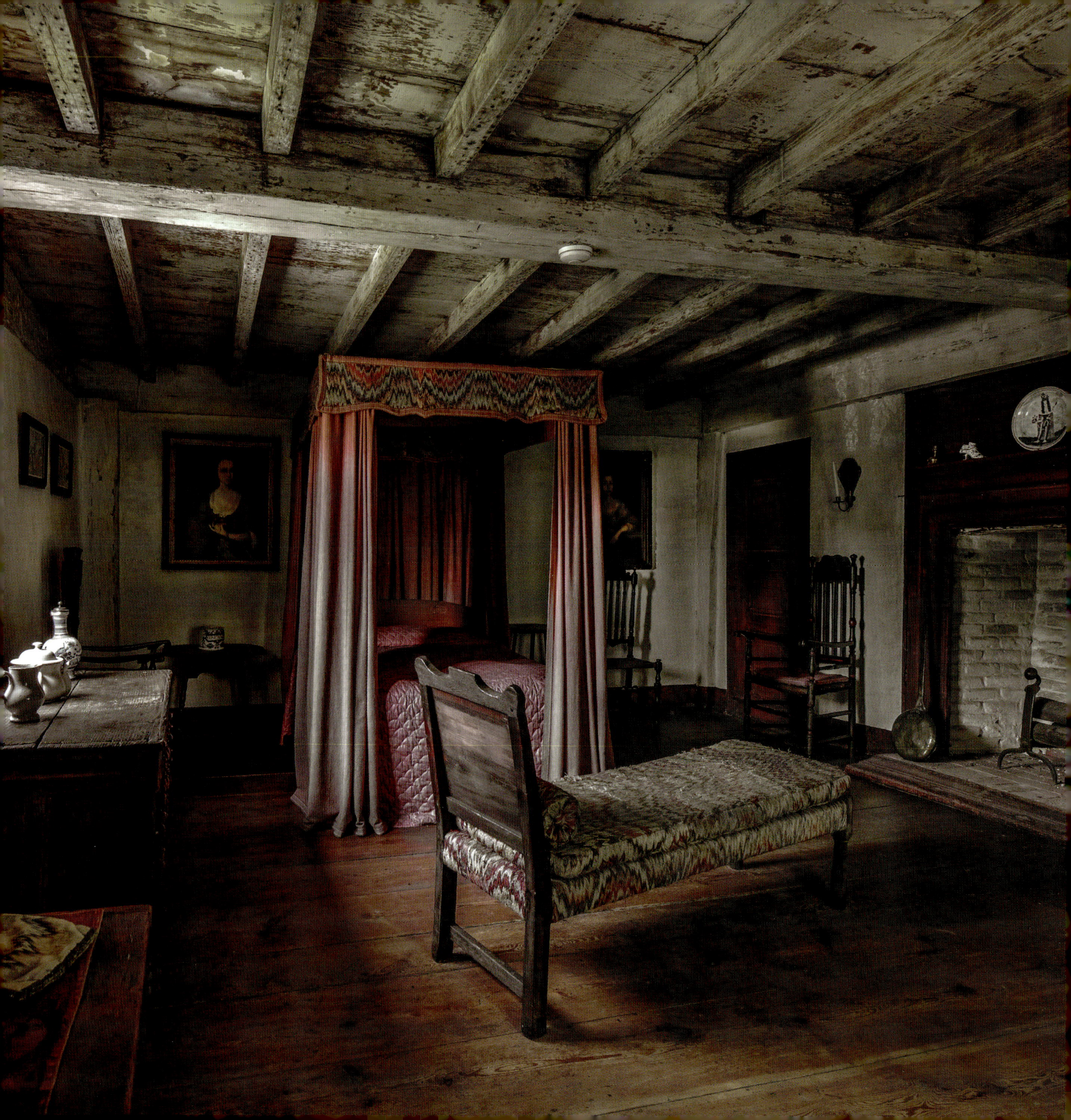

The other three walls and the ceiling of the kitchen were plastered. A painted strip around the base of the walls served as a baseboard. A crown molding delineated the transition from wall to ceiling.

The second-floor chambers retained their original features including the fireplaces, woodwork, and plaster walls. The ceilings were not plastered. It is interesting to note that the casement windows on the front wall were closer to the floor than the casements on the end walls. This might have been done to prevent the large overhang of the roof from blocking the daylight.

The south chamber with its original fireplace, woodwork, and plastered walls.

The Buttolph-Williams House was designated a National Historic Landmark in 1968. Meanwhile, the successful evocation of life in late seventeenth and early eighteenth-century Wethersfield inspired Elizabeth George Speare to use the home as the setting for her 1958 Newbery Award-winning novel, *The Witch of Blackbird Pond*. Due to that connection, the Buttolph-Williams House was designated a Literary Landmark in 2009. ♛

WASHINGTON DINED HERE AND SLEPT NEXT DOOR

Silas Deane House

— 203 Main Street —

The front of the Silas Deane House with the brownstone foundation of its original front porch, or piazza, the earliest known in Connecticut. By the time of its demolition, before it was bequeathed to the Colonial Dames, the porch's original columns had been replaced by late nineteenth century turned posts that confirmed the erroneous belief that the porch was not part of Deane's original construction. The Colonial Dames plan to restore the piazza to its authentic design.

The house at 203 Main Street was built for America's first diplomat, Silas Deane, in 1769. This four-bay gable originally included a front porch, or piazza, which was unfortunately removed in 1954 due to the mistaken notion that eighteenth-century houses did not have front porches. However, there is sufficient evidence to support an authentic restoration. The brownstone platform on which the piazza rested has survived, and the location and pitch of its roof can be ascertained from mortices in the beam where its roof rafters were once attached. An early photograph of the house with the piazza and research of contemporaneous or slightly later examples would provide a model for the porch posts and railing.

The top of the front door frame is flat because it was originally covered by the roof of the piazza.

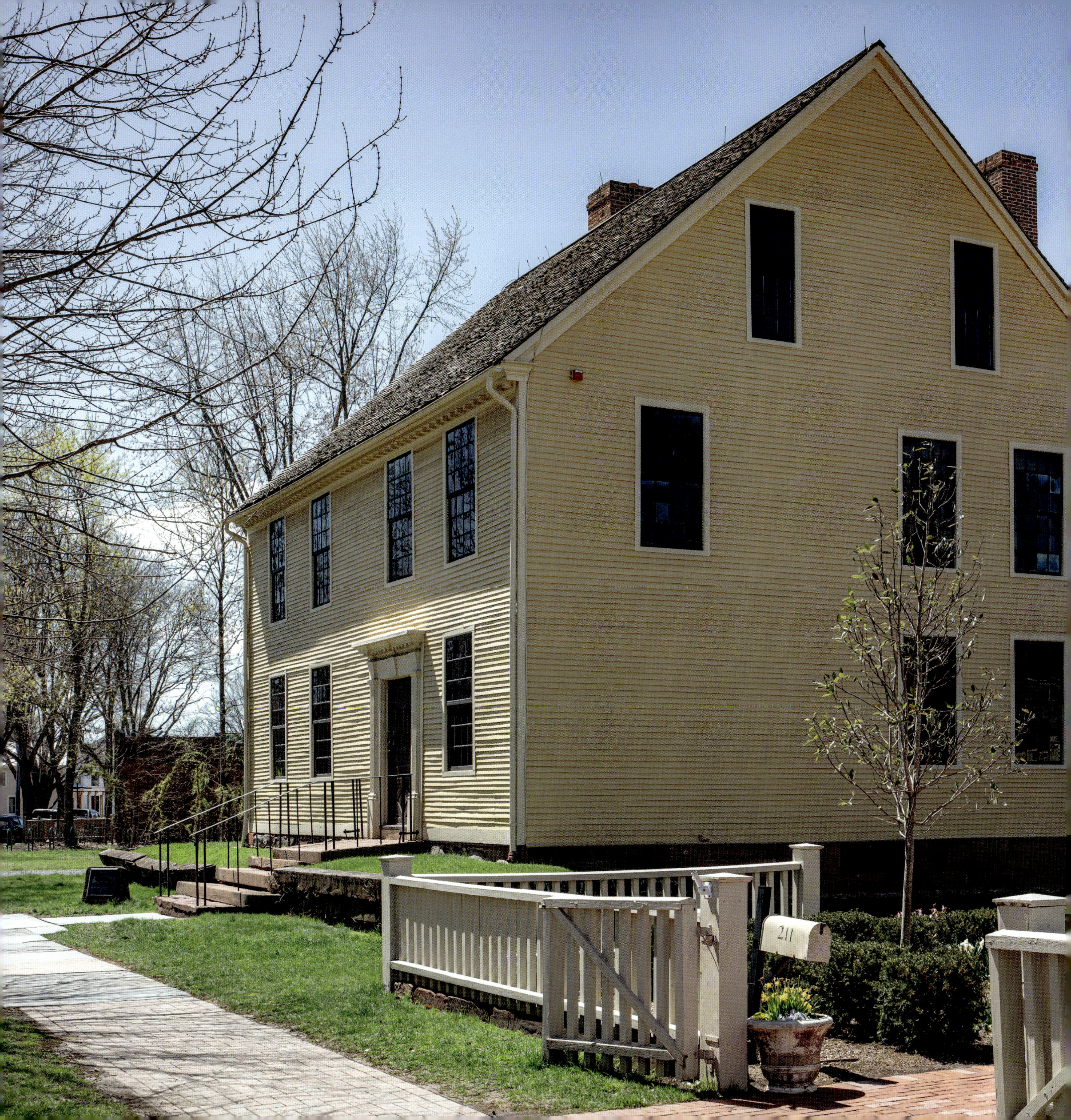
211

The Deane House was designed for entertaining. The house's four-bay façade, unique in town, allowed for a large, gracious stair hall with a coat closet, unusual for the time, under the stairs.

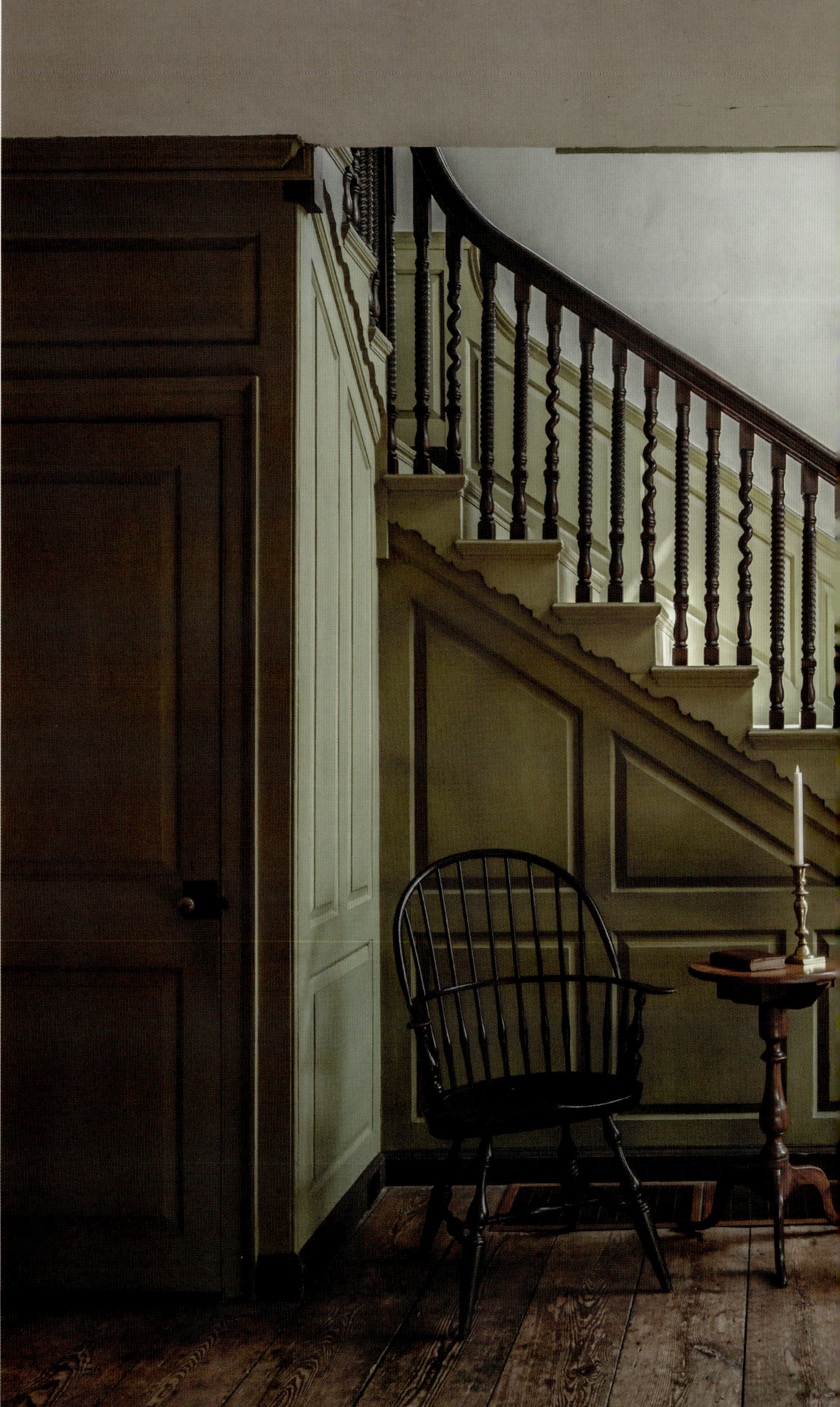

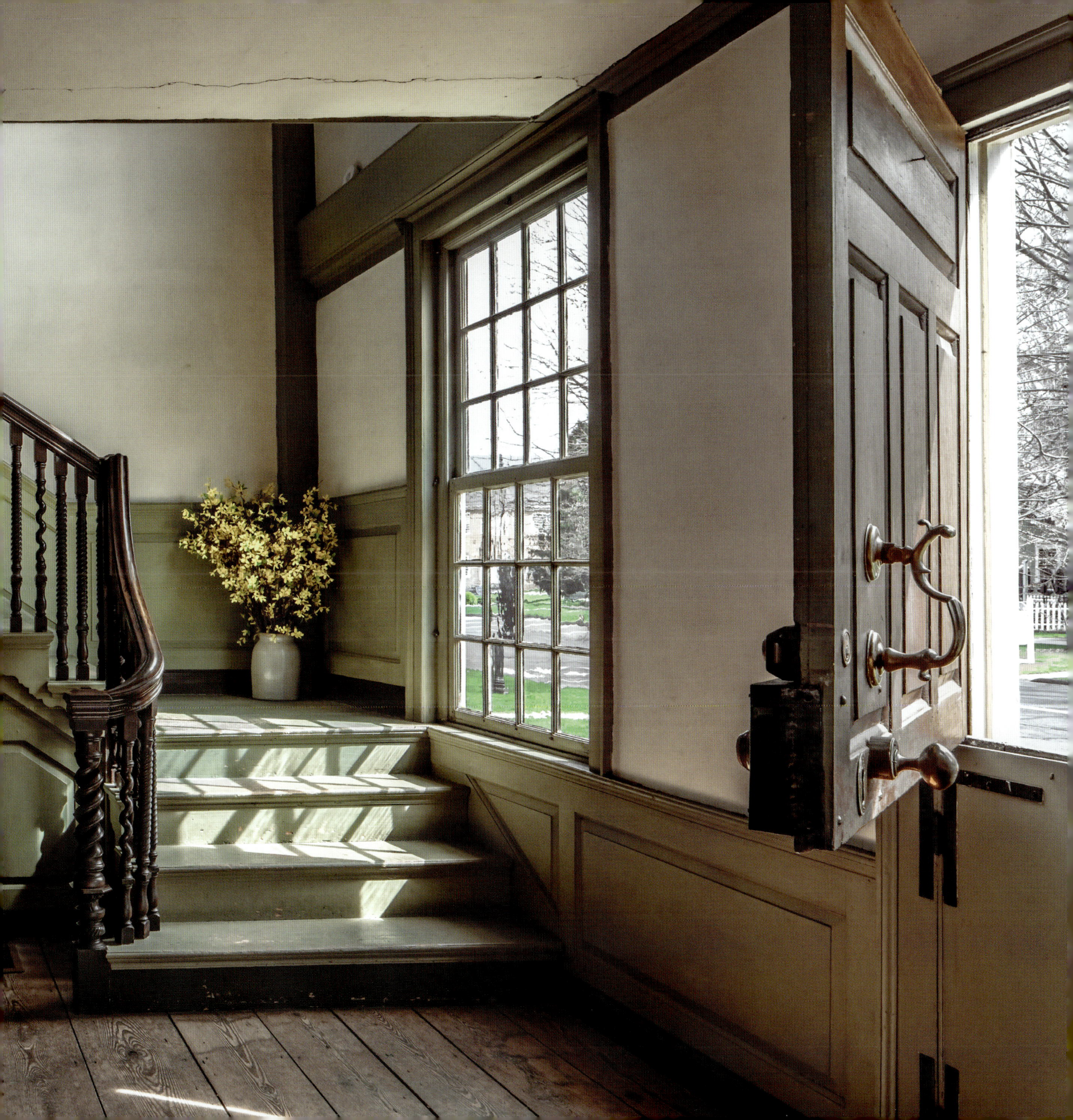

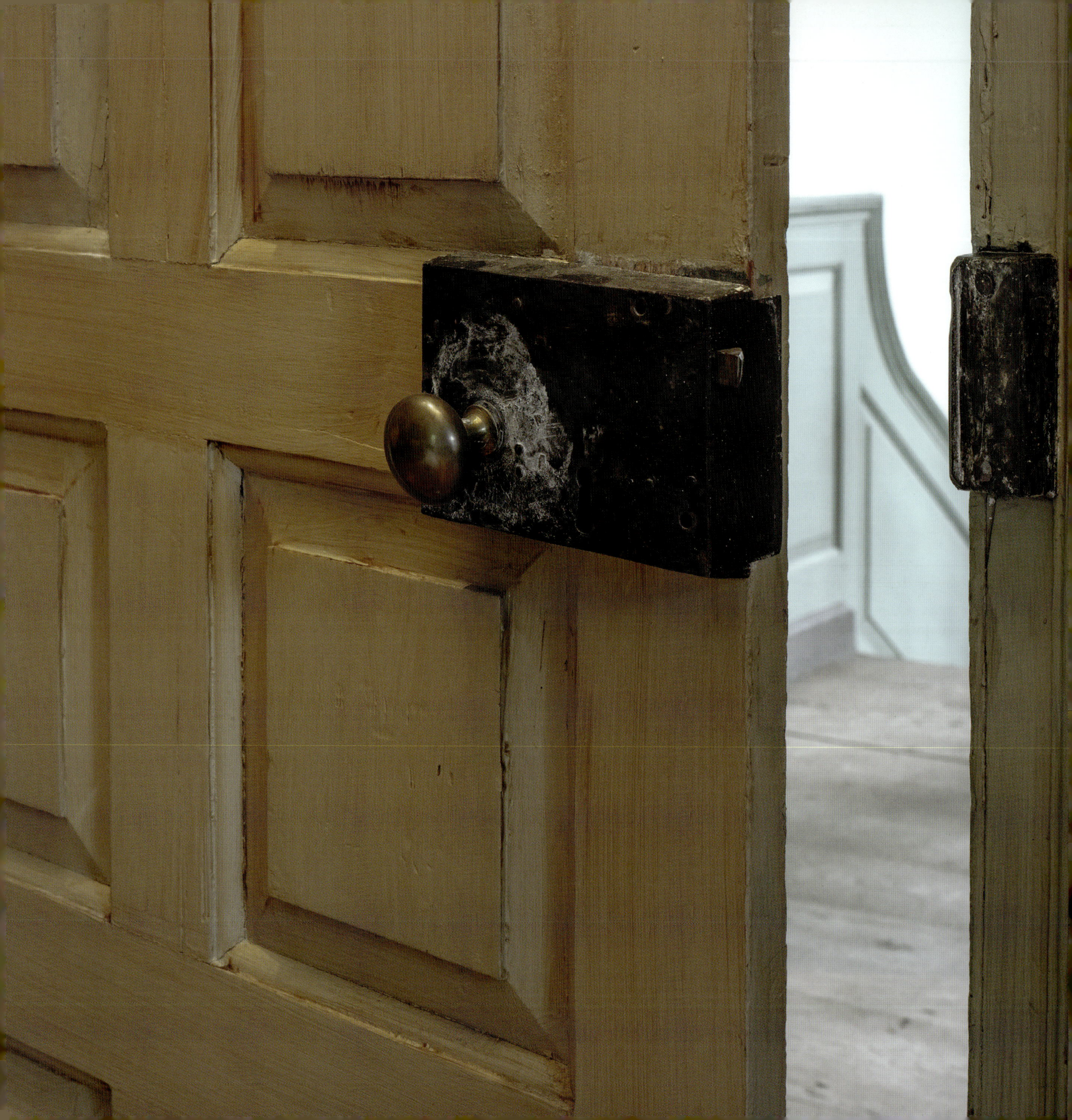

Silas Deane (1737–1789) was born in Groton, Connecticut, whose proximity to the open ocean made it a logical departure point for ships owned and manned by Wethersfield residents. The son of a blacksmith (a profitable trade that provided essential hardware for the home building and maritime industries) and a graduate of Yale College, Deane taught school in Hartford while he studied law. He passed the bar and opened a law practice in Wethersfield in 1761.

A detail of the view from the front chamber into the upstairs hall, showing the lock.

One of his first clients was Mehitable Webb (1732–1767), a twenty-eight-year-old woman. Her husband, Joseph Webb (1727–1761), had just died, leaving her to manage his mercantile business and raise their six surviving children. In those days, widows were expected to remarry. Mehitable wed Deane in 1763, and their son, Jesse, was born in June 1764.

The next year, they added a one-story ell to the back of the Webb House at 211 Main Street. One can assume Deane intended to live in that house with Mehitable and the seven children until Joseph Webb Jr. (1749–1815) would reach his majority in 1770 and inherit the Webb house, according to the settlement of the Webb estate for which Deane was executor. In anticipation of that eventuality, Deane purchased the property adjoining the Webb's southern boundary in 1765.

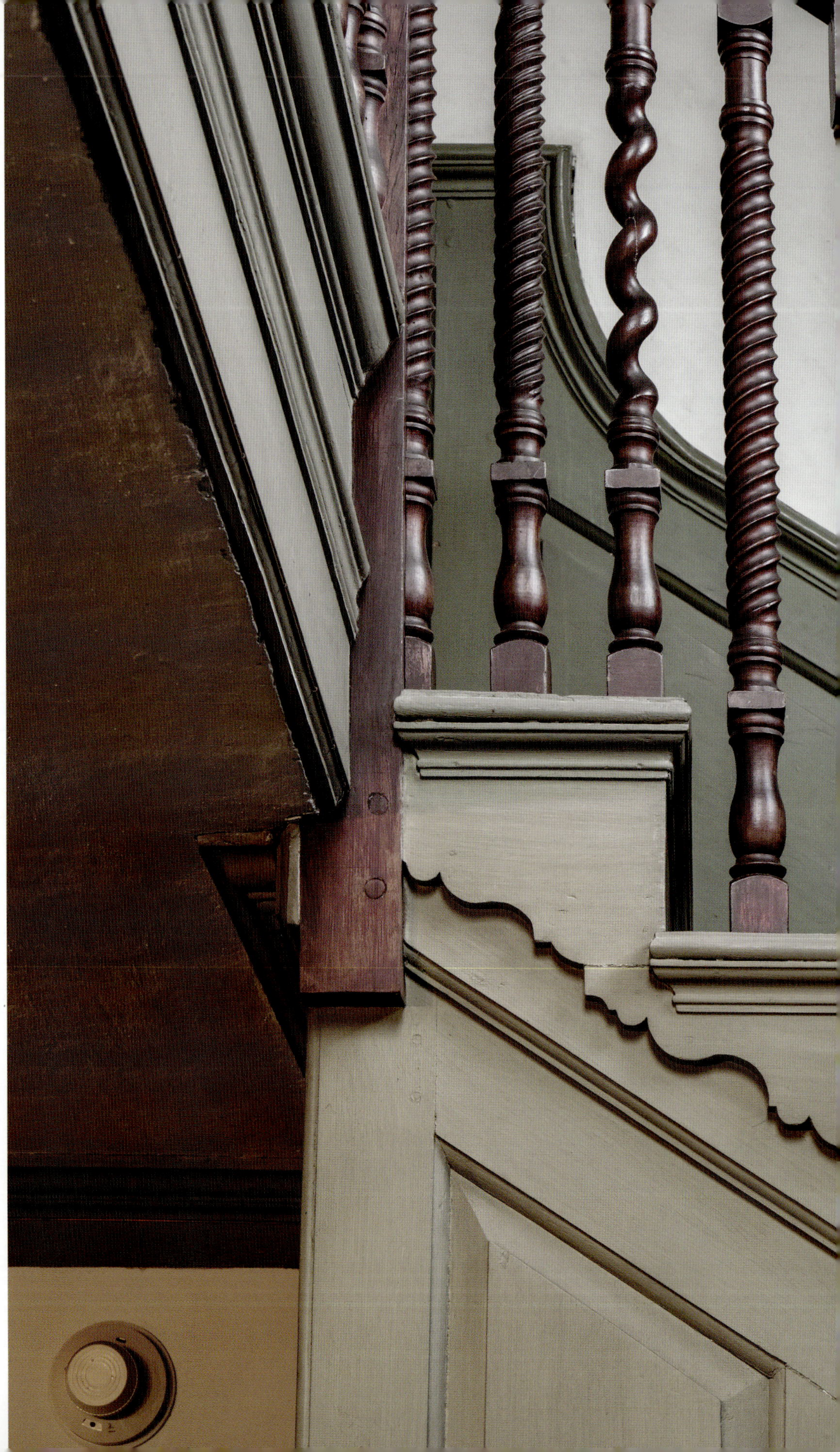

The stairs with alternating turned and spiral balusters, and molded handrail, is made of cherry.

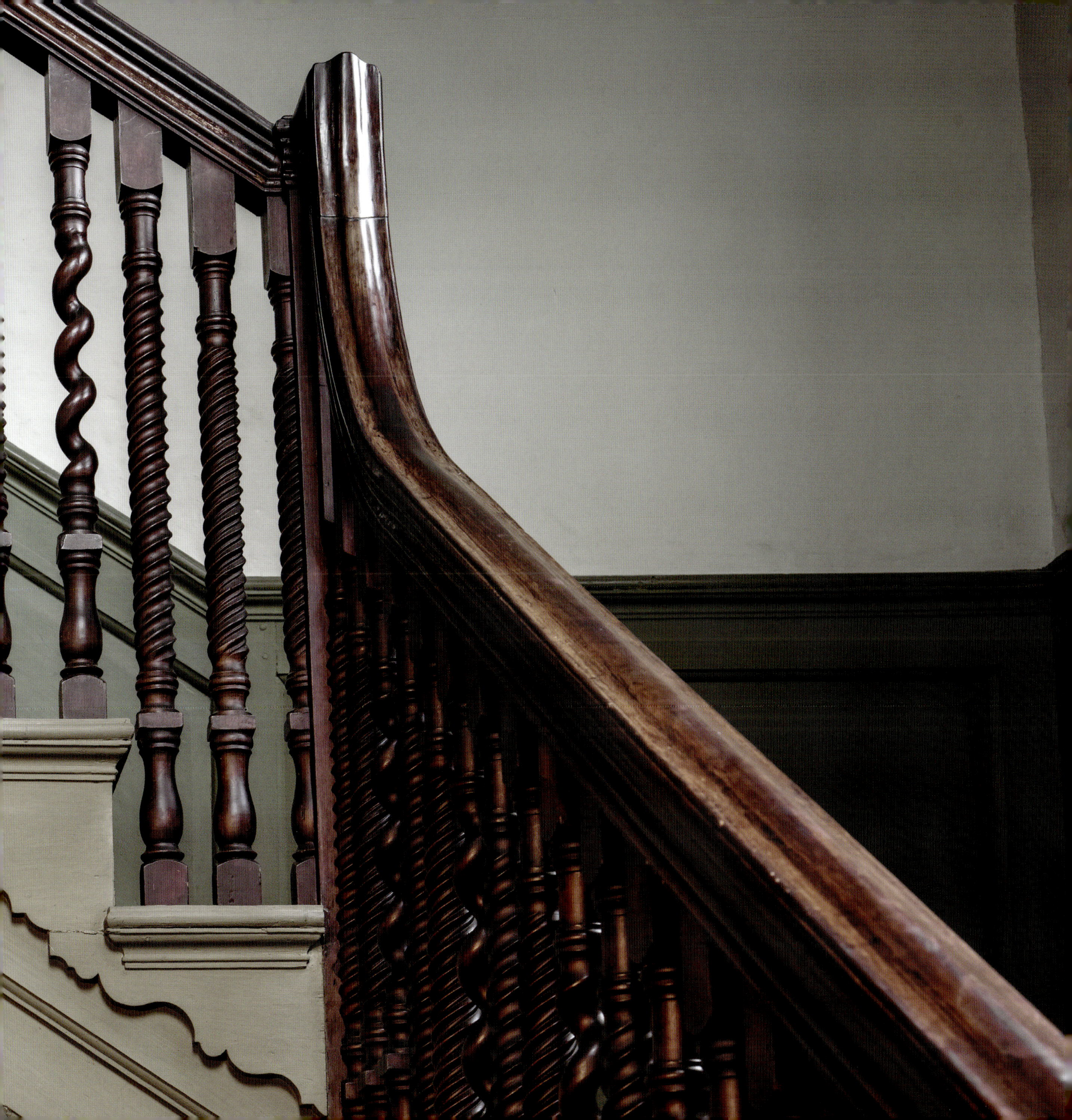

This handsome carved Portland brownstone fireplace surround is in the Deane House's front parlor.

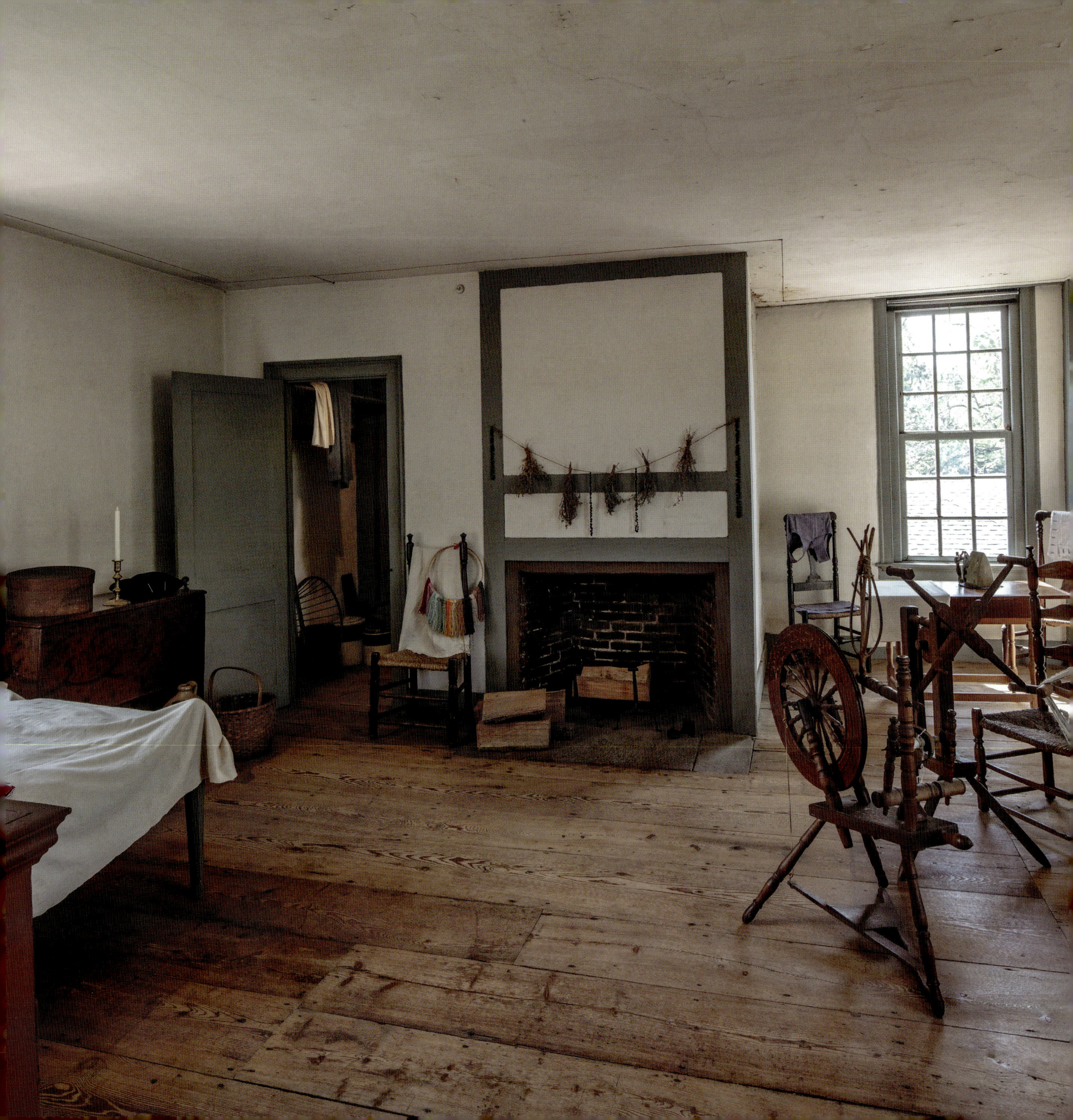

Deane's plans were altered by Mehitable's death in October 1767 at the age of 35. Deane asked his fifteen-year-old stepdaughter, Sarah Webb (1752–1832), to return home from finishing school in Boston, Massachusetts, to help care for her younger sisters and brothers. In a remarkable show of independence, she refused. Silas's thirteen-year-old sister, Hannah Deane (1754–1824), came up from Groton to help care for the younger Webb children: ten-year-old Mehitable (Hetty), eight-year-old John, six-year-old Abigail (Nabby), and three-year-old Jesse.

The chamber over the kitchen, whose chimney contains a smoke oven, is interpreted as the space where Hager and Pompeii, enslaved African Americans, lived and worked.

After Mehitable's death, Deane turned to politics and was elected to the General Assembly in Hartford in 1768. He married Elizabeth Saltonstall Evards (1744–1777), a widow and the granddaughter of a former Connecticut governor, in 1769. The new couple moved into the house Silas had just built. The youngest of the Webb stepchildren and Silas's son, Jesse, lived with them. Elizabeth also brought two enslaved African Americans, Pompeii and Hager, with her.

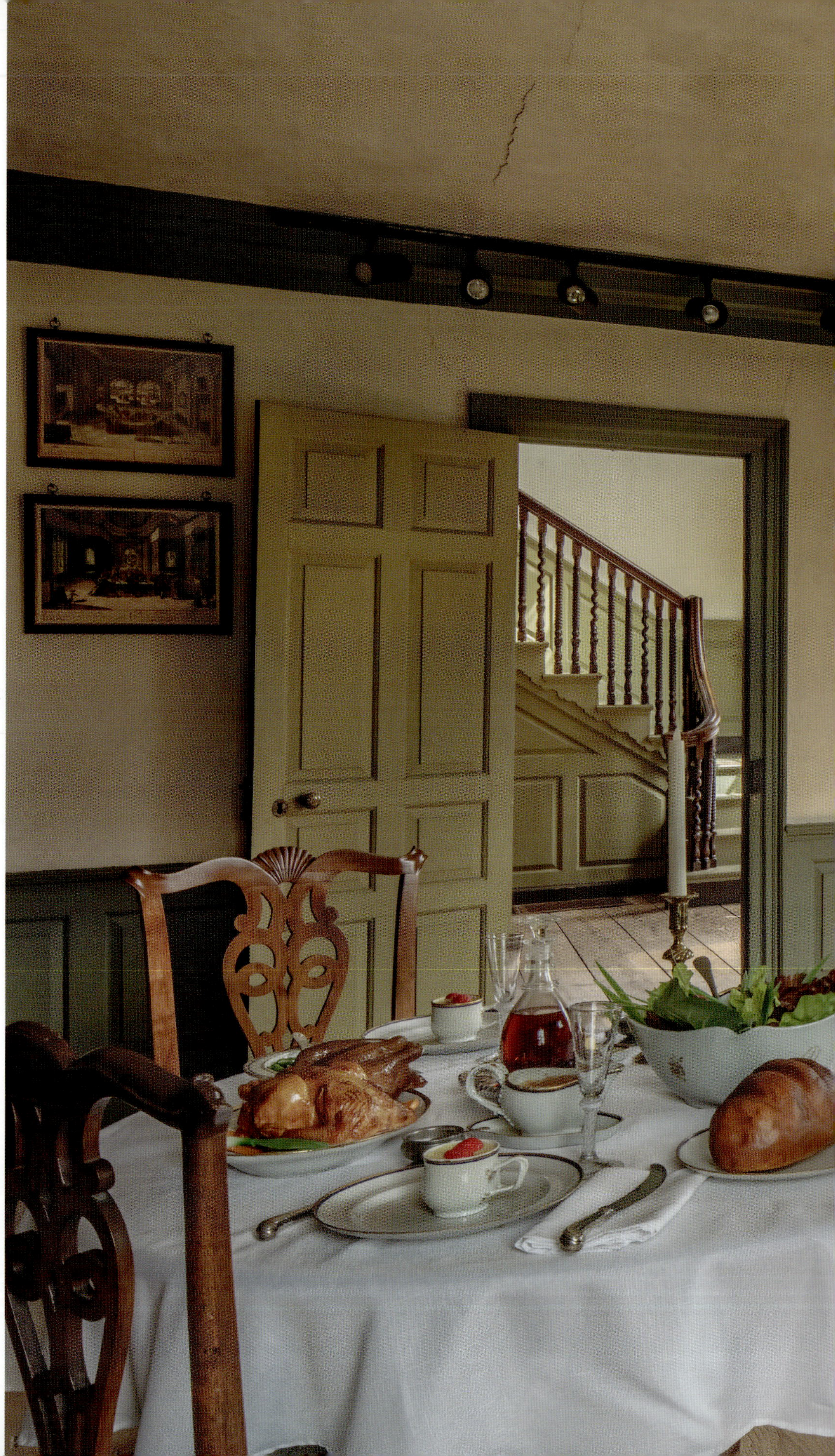

The front parlor — General George Washington dined at the Deane House in June 1775 with Major General Charles Lee and Jeremiah Wadsworth.

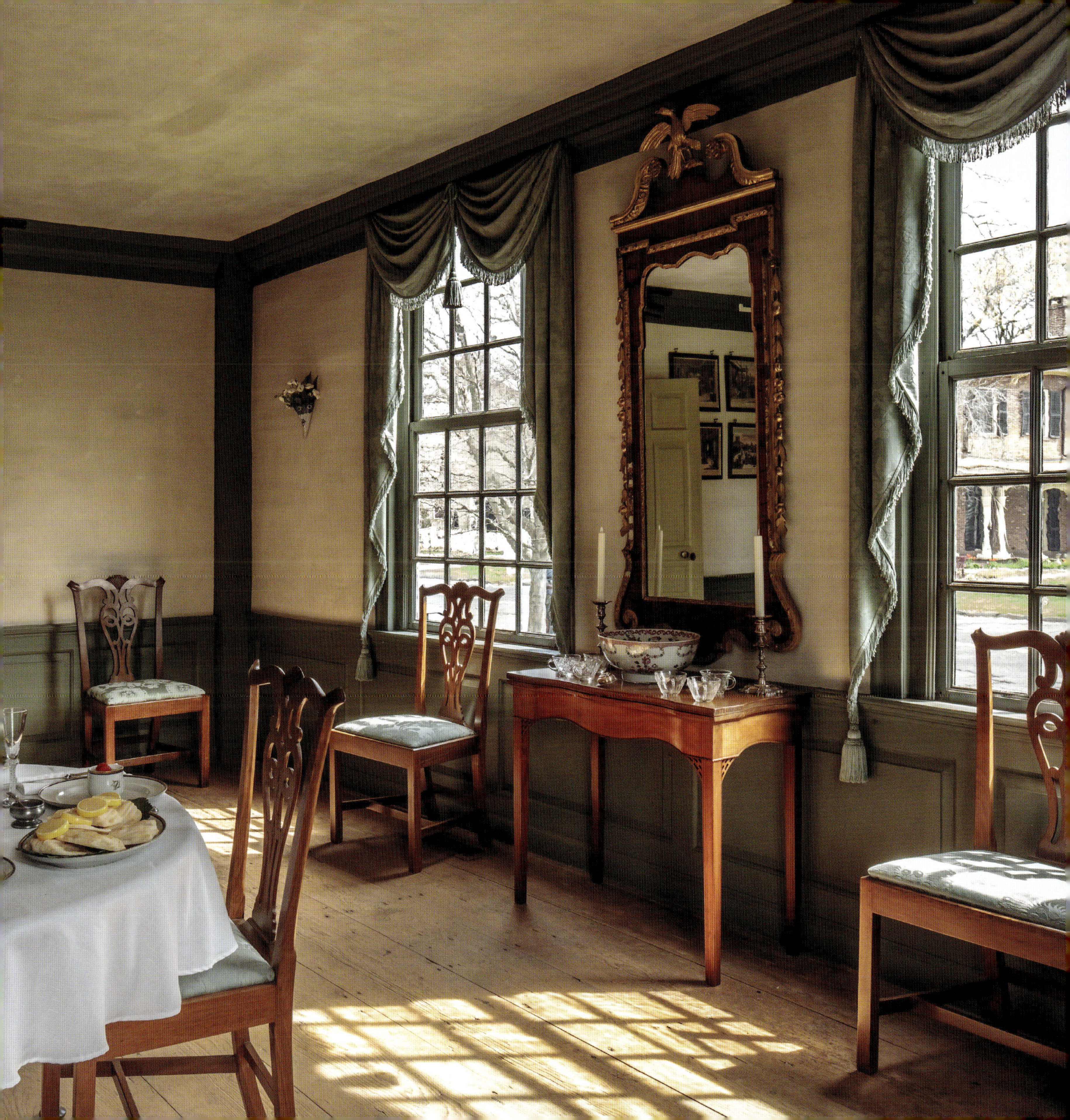

Silas was secretary of Connecticut's Committee of Correspondence and served as one of Connecticut's delegates to the Continental Congress in 1774. Shortly after reports of fighting in Lexington and Concord, Samuel H. Parsons, Samuel Wyllis, and Deane developed plans to capture the British canon in Fort Ticonderoga. They borrowed funds on their personal notes for a surprise attack on that western outpost. The Connecticut contingent, led by Benedict Arnold, met up with Ethan Allen and his Green Mountain Boys from Vermont. On May 10, 1775, under the cover of darkness, they stormed the fort and forced the British officers to surrender without firing a shot. By then, Silas Deane was back in Philadelphia for the opening of the Second Continental Congress. News of Fort Ticonderoga reached Congress, and Deane's associates named him "Ticonderoga Deane."

Having failed to be elected as one of Connecticut's delegates to the Second Continental Congress, Deane was sent on an undercover mission by the Secret Committee of the Congress. He left for France in March and arrived in Paris in June 1776. With the help of playwright Caron de Beaumarchais, he secured clothing and ammunition for the American army.

When Congress praised Beaumarchais for his services, he replied, "I testify that if my zeal, my advances of money, and my shipment of stores and merchandise have been acceptable to the august Congress, their gratitude is due to the indefatigable exertions of Mr. Deane throughout this commercial affair." (Beaumarchais 1778)

The importance of Deane's house and the role he played in the American Revolution was recognized during the Connecticut Tercentenary Celebration in 1935. Margaret Bacon Fenn (1868–1958), a member of The National Society of The Colonial Dames of America in The State of Connecticut, and her husband, U.S. Representative E. Hart Fenn (1856–1939), who owned the Deane House, were so respectful of its integrity that the only bathroom in the house was in the basement. In 1958, she left the Deane House to the Colonial Dames, who already owned the Webb house next door.

The Deane House was designated a National Historic Landmark in 1973. Today, the Deane House is part of the Webb Deane Stevens Museum at 211 Main Street. ♛

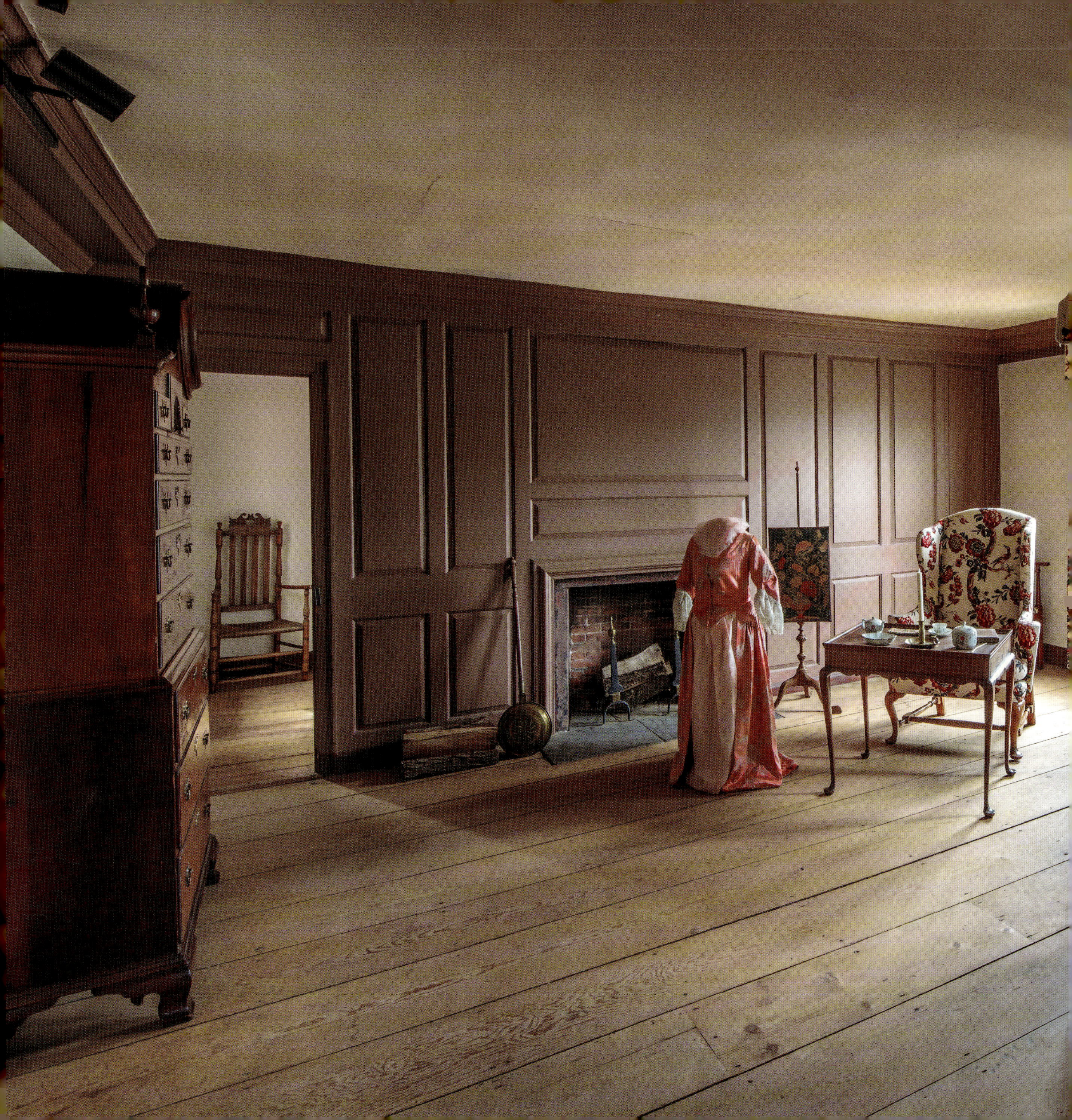

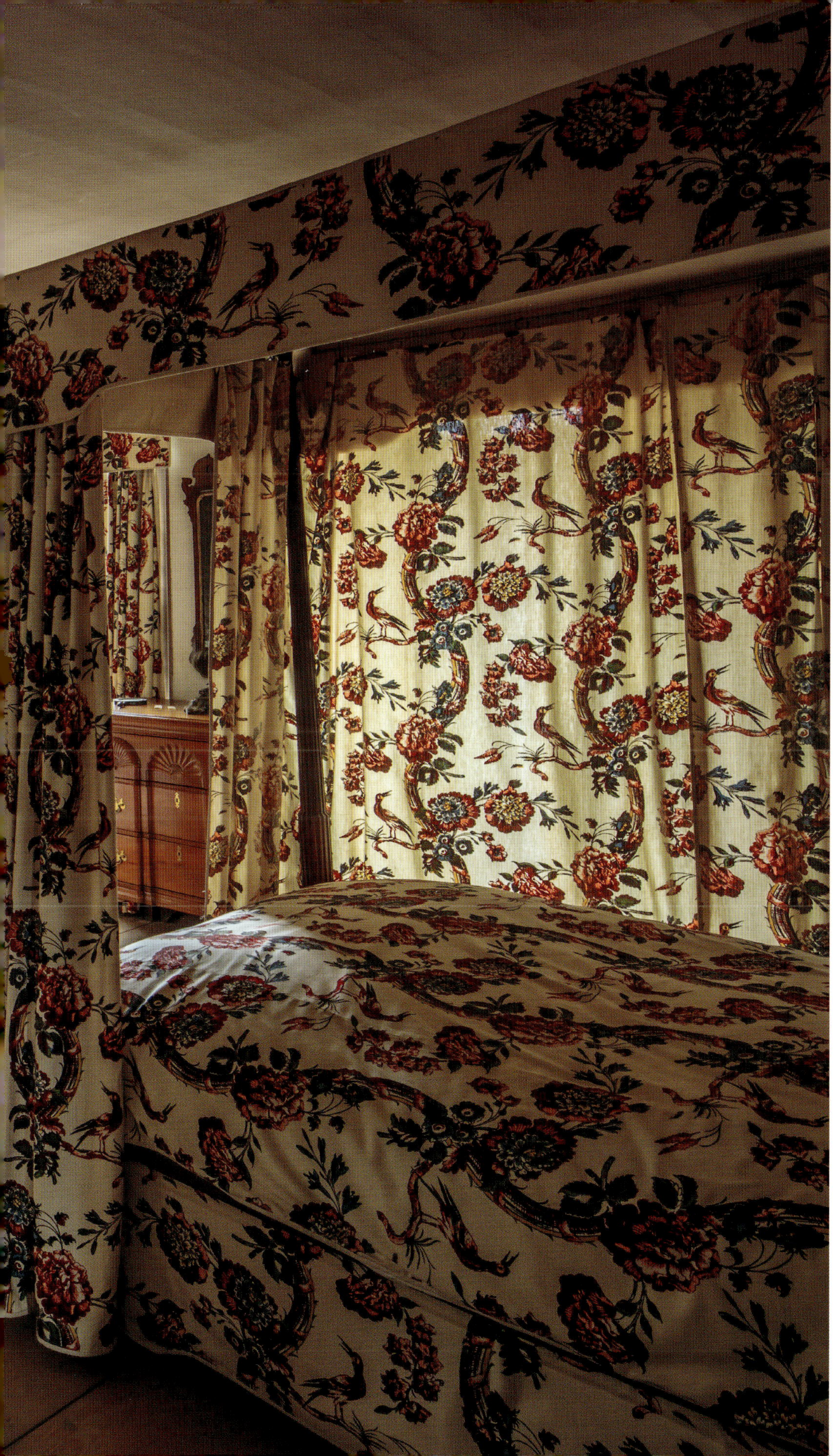

A view of the northwest chamber.

This front chamber is very unusual because it has no fireplace. There is evidence that it was heated by a stove, unlike any other room in town at that time. The floor's continuous unbroken run of boards has some spring, which supports the suggestion it was suitable for dancing.

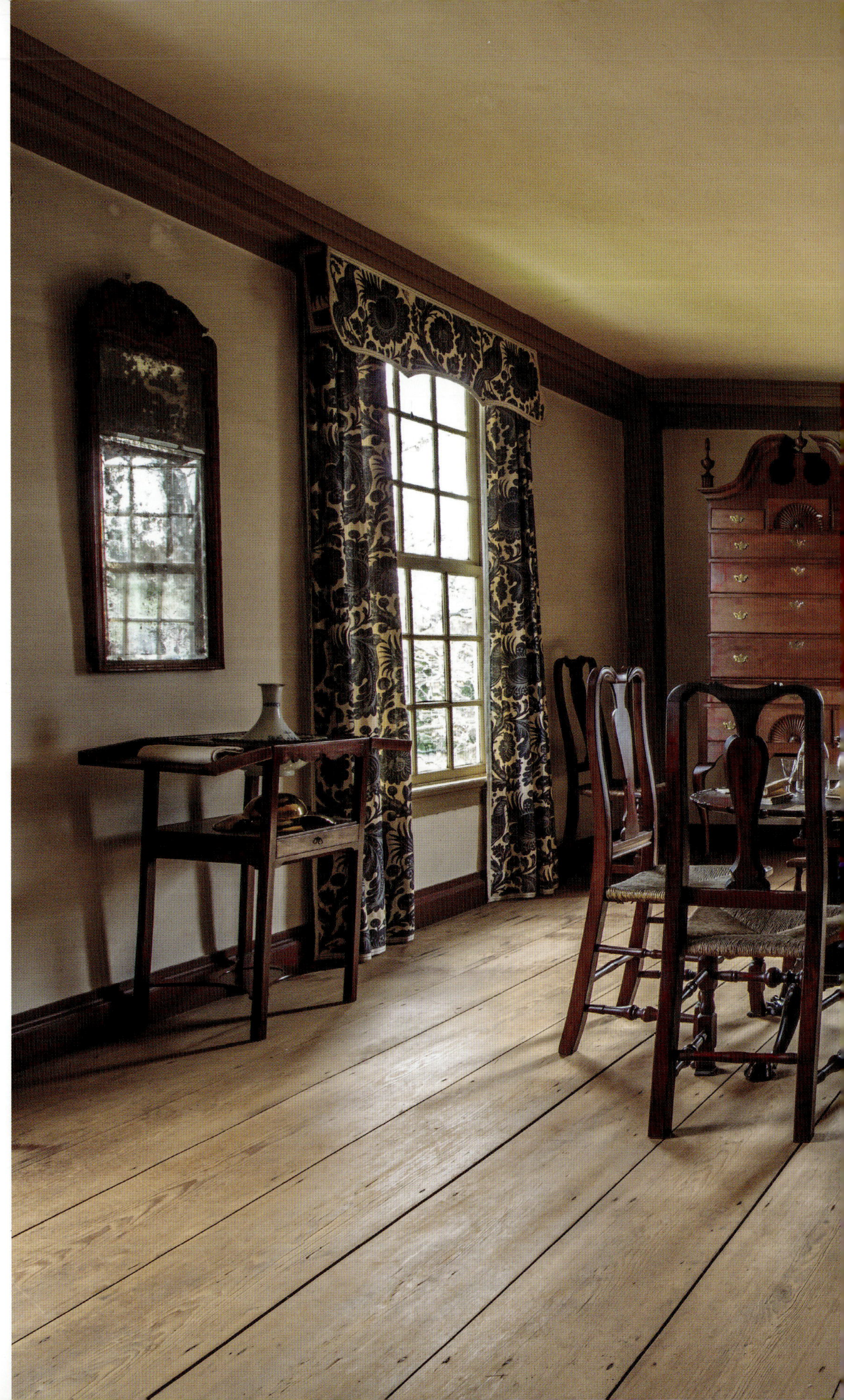

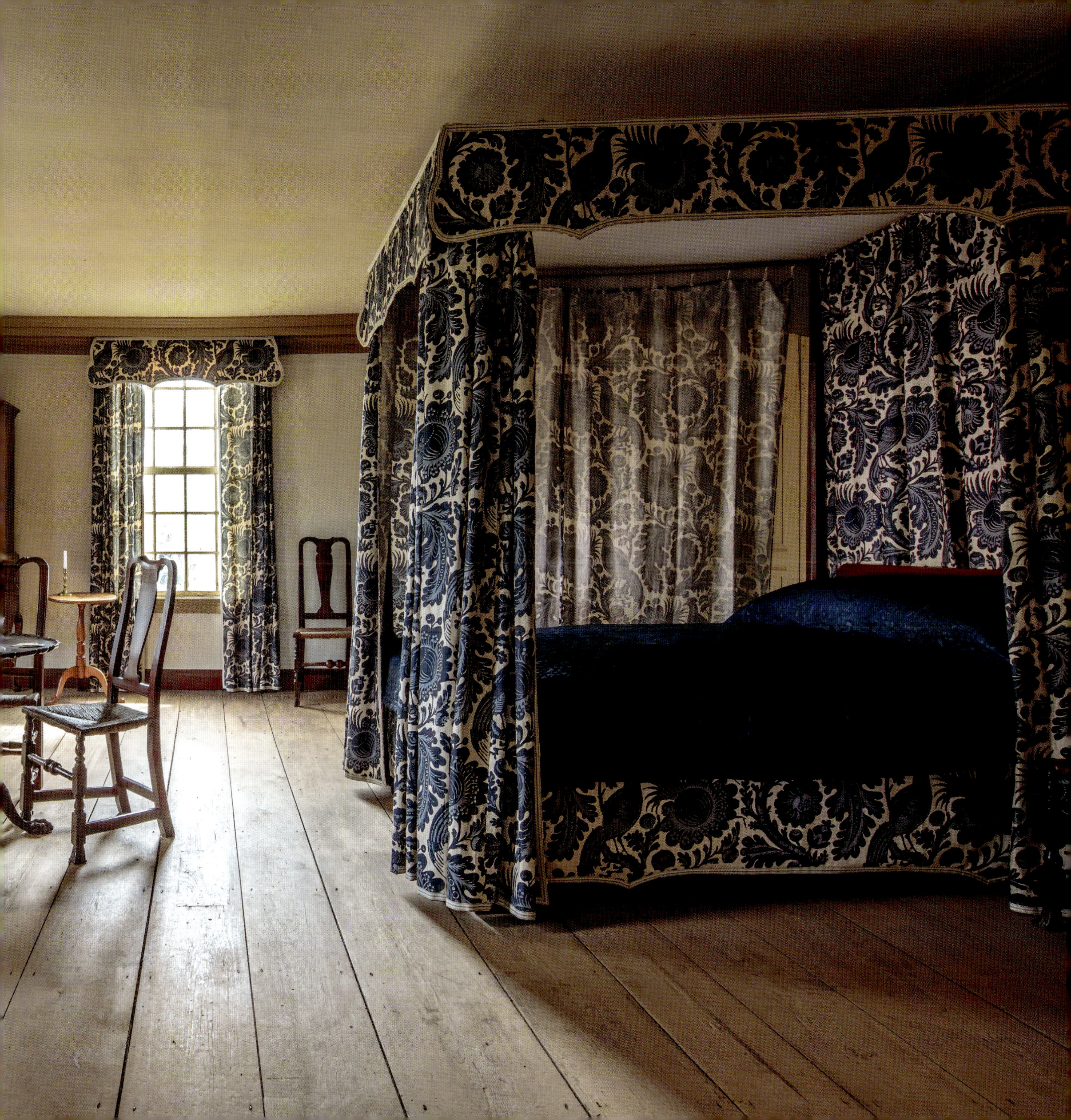

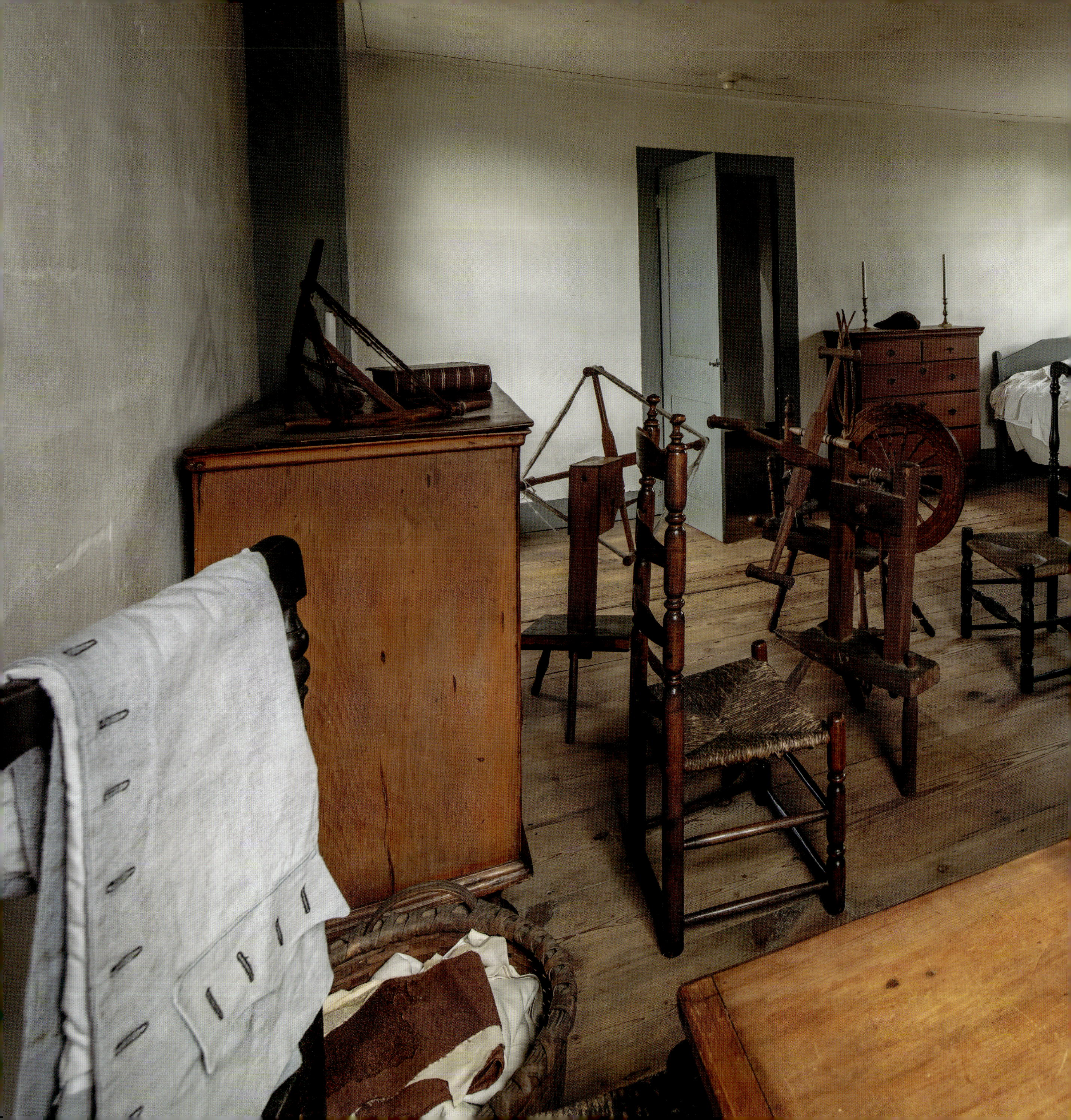

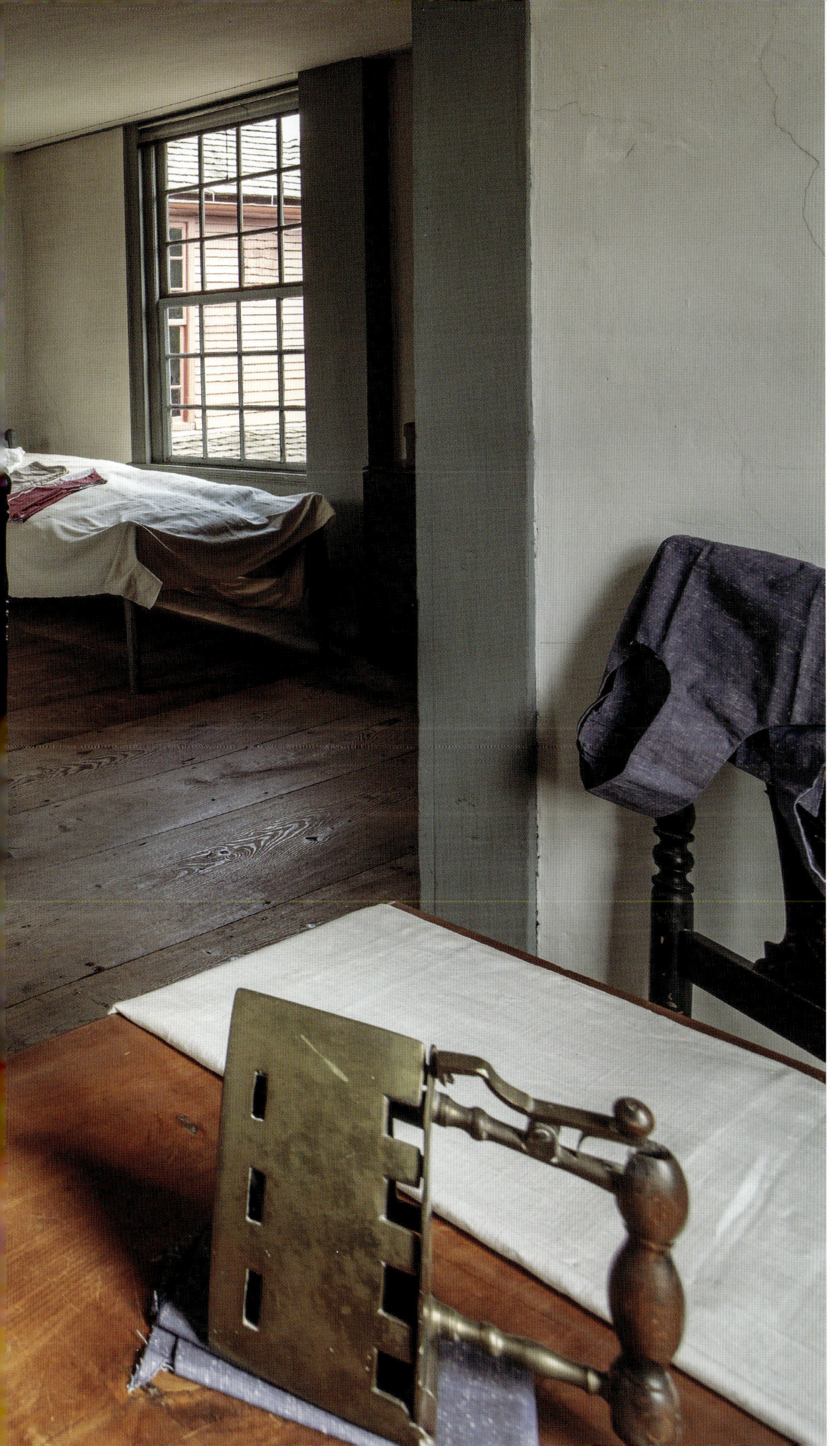

The kitchen chamber is reached by a back staircase from the kitchen.

A PRICELESS EIGHTEENTH CENTURY JEWEL — RESTORED

The Wethersfield Meeting House

— 250 Main Street —

Nothing reflects the urbanity and sophistication of the Wethersfield community during the colonial period as well as the brick Meeting House, built by the town at 250 Main Street between 1761 and 1764. The Wethersfield Meeting House was the only brick meeting house in the Connecticut Colony and is one of the finest examples of eighteenth-century church architecture in the state.

A view of the Meeting House with the glass connector allowing the ancient burying ground to be seen.

Wethersfield's First Society had begun discussing the need for a new meeting house in 1753. Colonel John Chester (1749–1809), Colonel Elizur Goodrich (1693–1774), and Captain Thomas Wells (1712–1787) were appointed as the building committee. Not surprisingly, given the fact that Goodrich owned a brickyard, they decided the new meeting house should be built of brick. The building would be eighty feet wide and fifty-two feet deep with stairs to the galleries located in the steeple and porch, so the worshippers would not be disturbed by people coming and going.

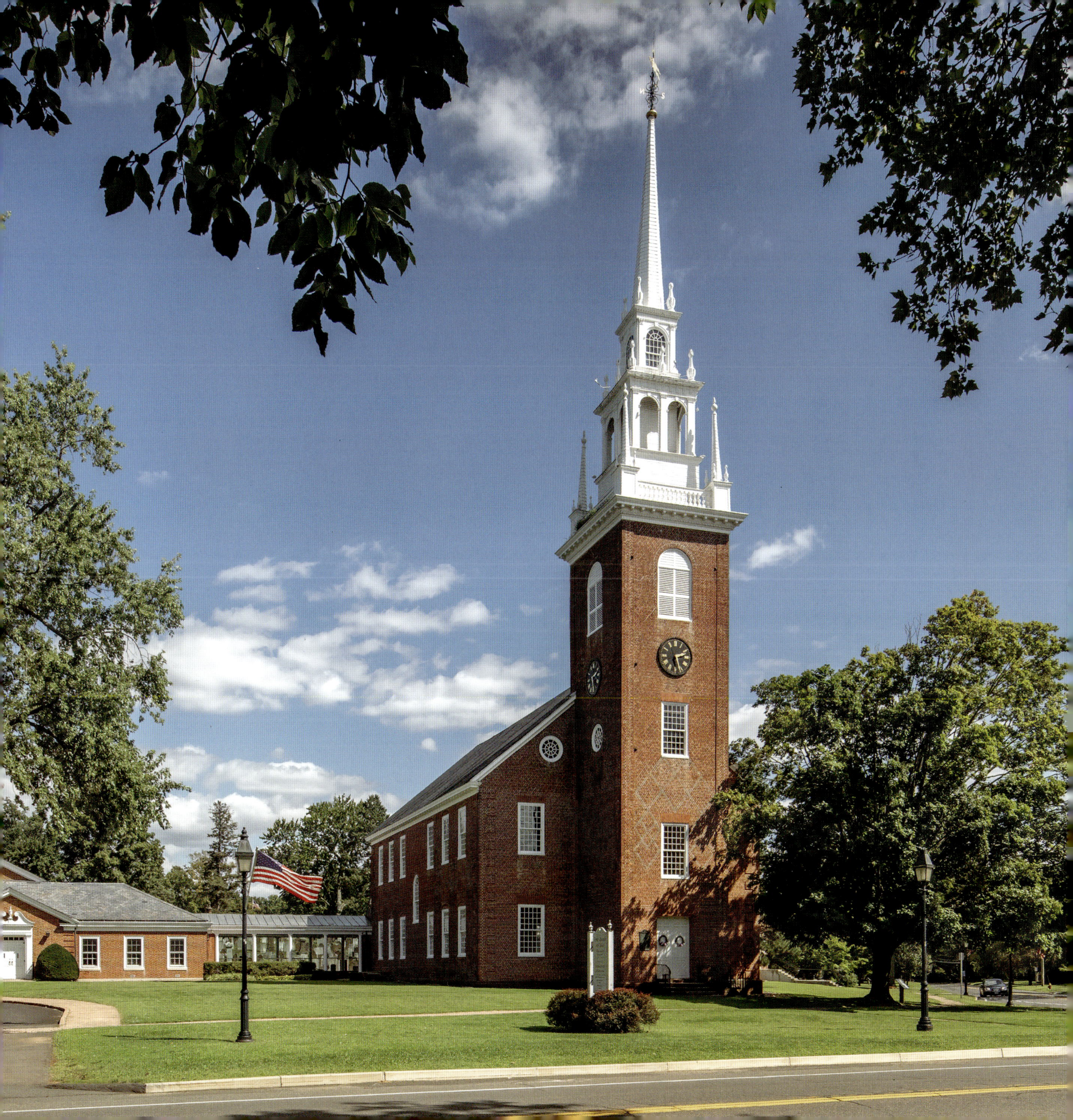

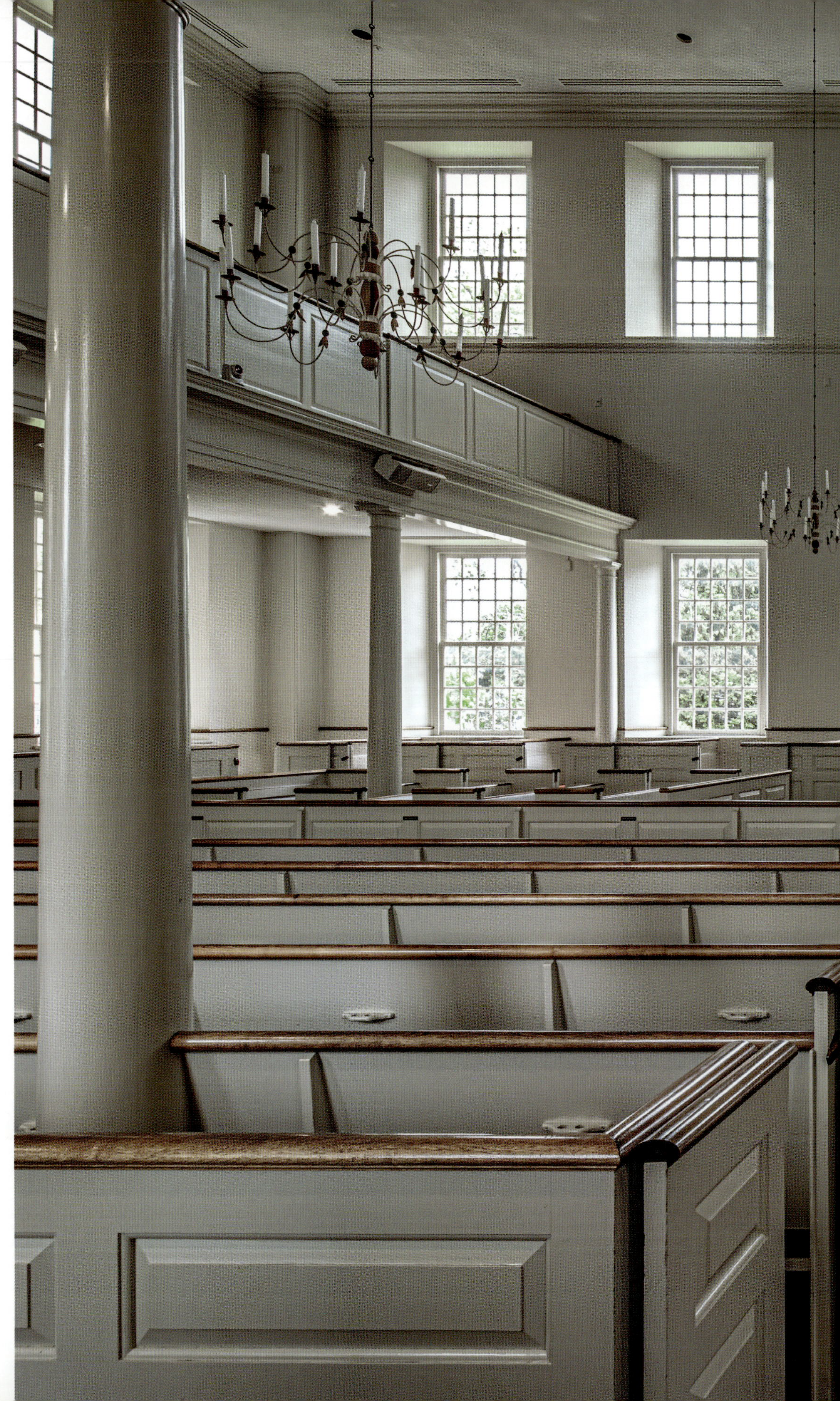

The interior after the 1972–1973 restoration, flooded with light after the removal of the 1882 two-story-high stained-glass windows, and the replication and restoration of the original windows.

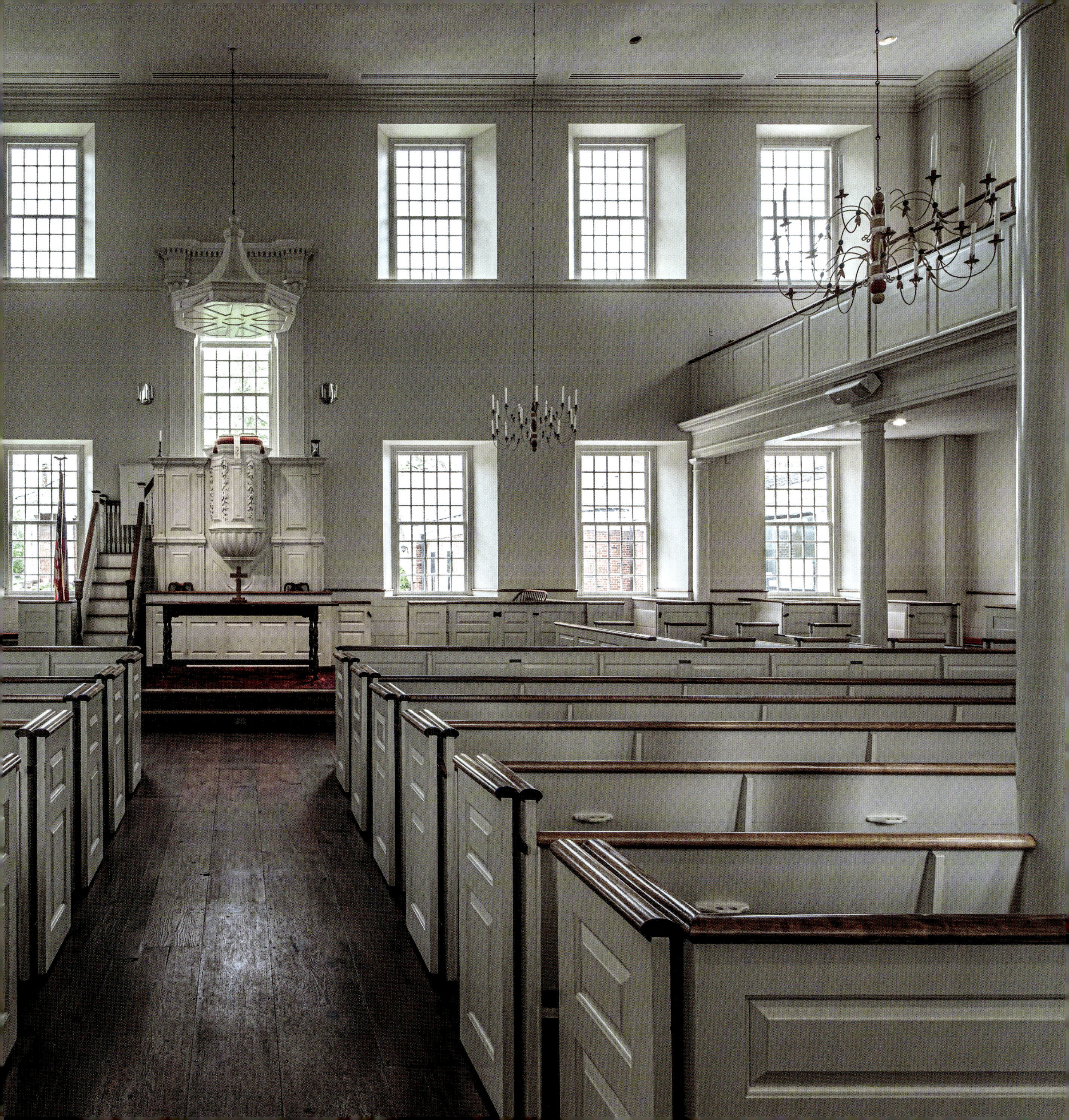

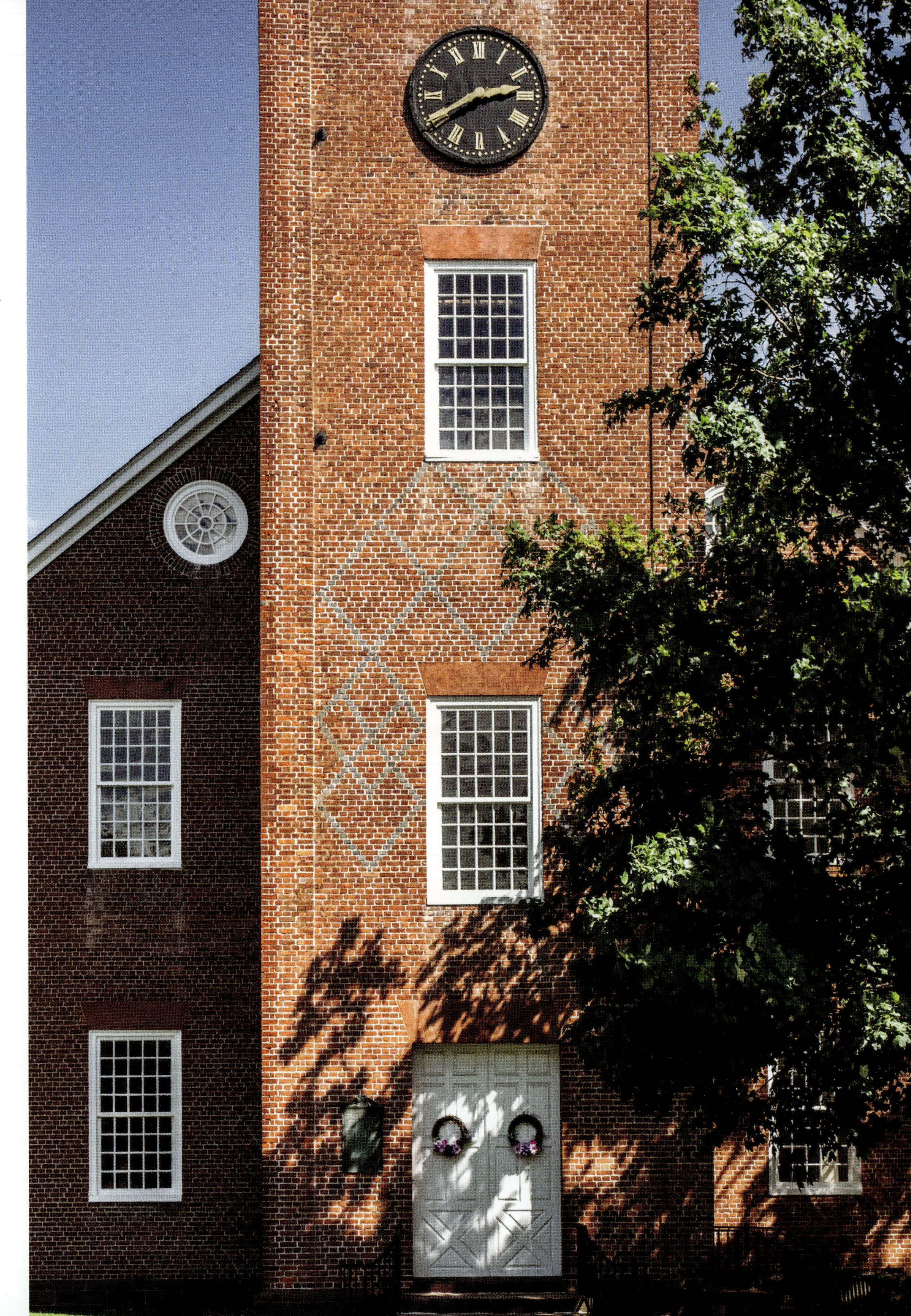

The steeple showing the diaper pattern of black brick headers.

The floor plan followed a pattern adopted by Protestant dissenters from the Church of England, following the Toleration Act of 1689, with the pulpit positioned along one of the long walls and the communion table relocated to a central position. From 1690 onward, Presbyterian and Unitarian Chapels and Quaker Meeting Houses in England followed this arrangement. The similar architecture, with clear window glass, whitewashed walls, and polished dark-brown pews, perfectly reflected the faith of those who worshiped there.

The Wethersfield Meeting House was a light-filled space, a symbol of the enlightenment that would inform the American Revolution to come.

The adherence to Puritan tradition did not extend to the design of the Meeting House lantern and steeple. They closely resembled those of two Episcopalian churches: Christ Church, built in Cambridge, Massachusetts in 1723, and Trinity Church, designed by Richard Munday (1685–1739) and built in Newport, Rhode Island, in 1725. The designs of their steeples were inspired by the work of British architect Sir Christopher Wren (1632–1723). At the height of his career, Wren was responsible for the reconstruction or replacement of over fifty churches that had been destroyed during London's Great Fire of 1666. By the time of his death in 1723, Wren's classically inspired designs were no longer fashionable in London.

The east porch, overlooking the Ancient Burying Ground, is entirely original, including the staircase.

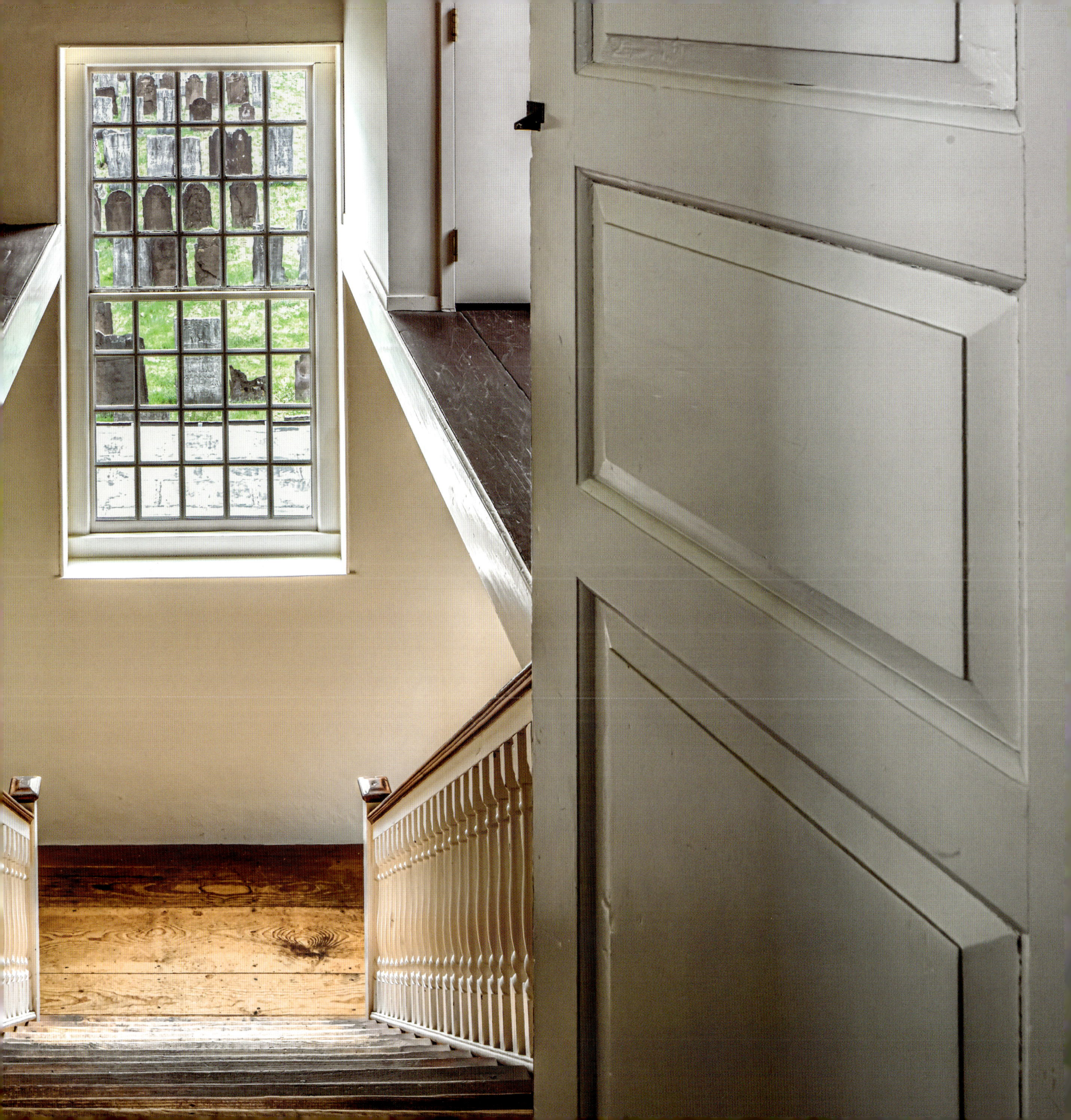

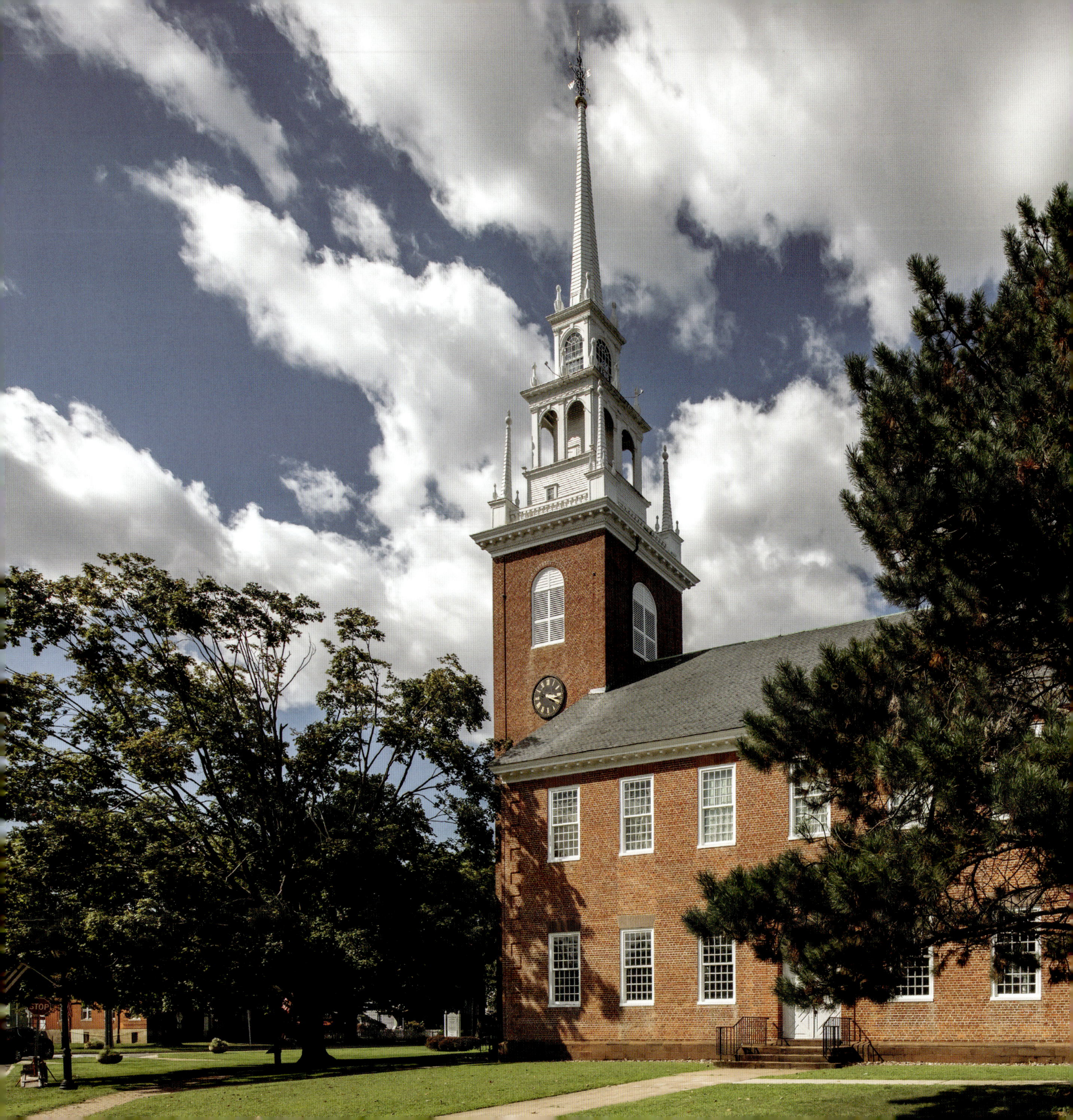
STOP

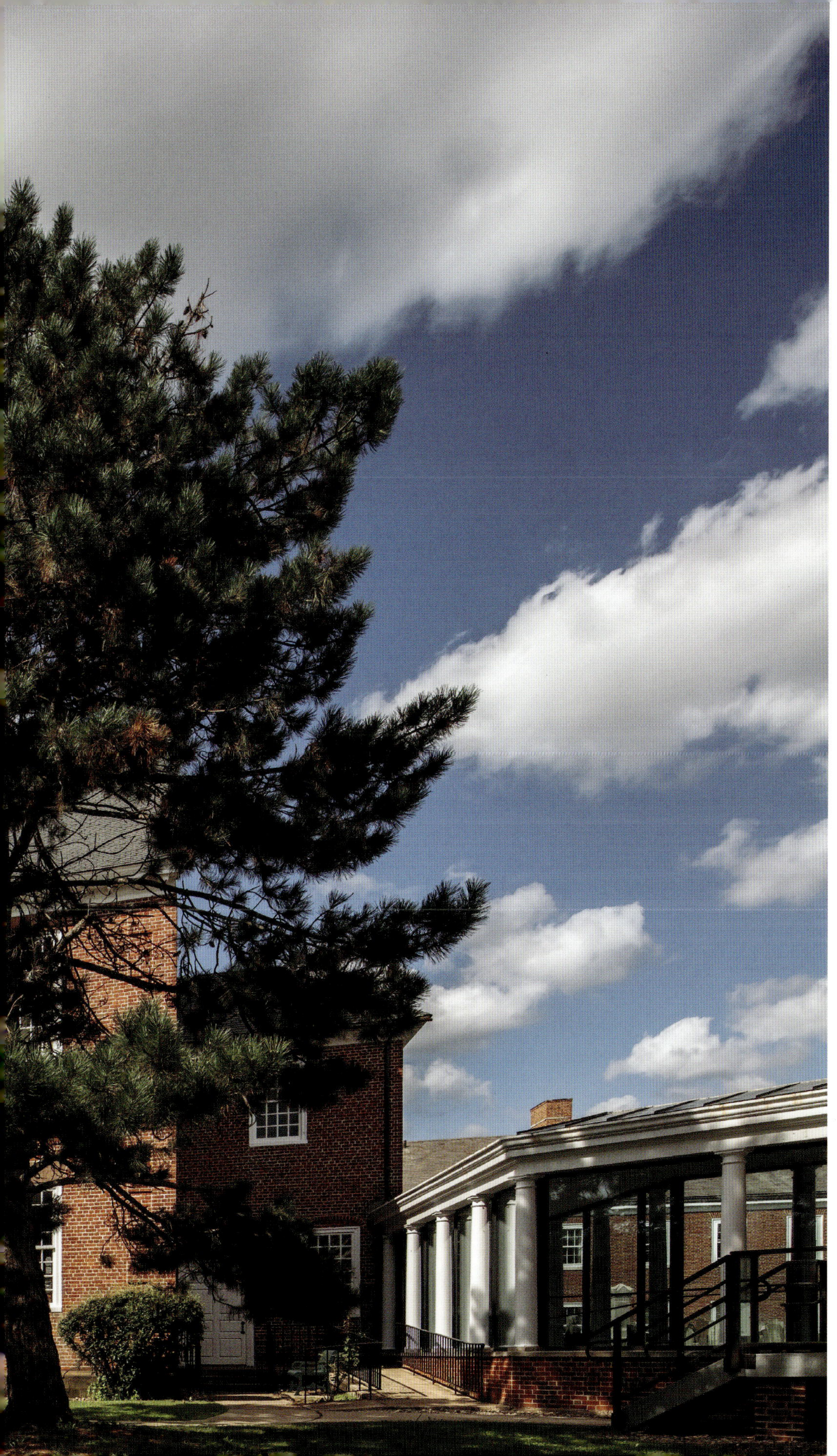

The view from Marsh Street showing the south connector.

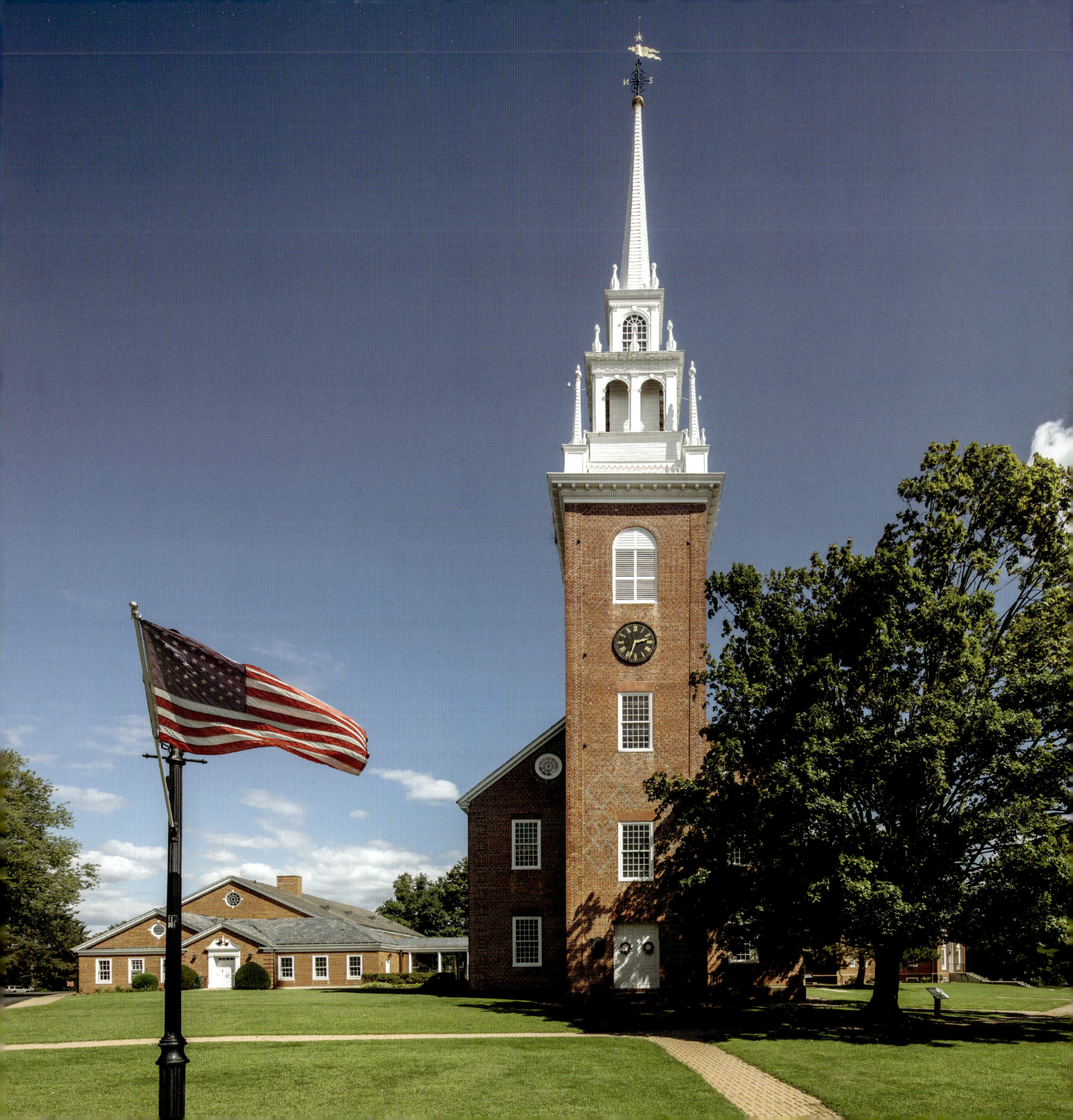

A view of the Meeting House steeple, inspired by the work of Sir Christopher Wren.

Architectural historian Norman Isham (1864–1943) hypothesized that Christ Church (also known as Old North) may have been built from Wren's plans for St. Ann Blackfriars, a church that was never built but whose plans may have been "in some way secured." (Downing 1967) While admitting there was no documentation for Isham's theory, Antoinette Downing and Vincent Scully Jr., authors of The Architectural Heritage of Newport, Rhode Island, 1640–1915, considered it plausible. Their research identified an agent with the motivation and opportunity to transfer Wren's plans from England to its New England colonies.

A London-based group of Anglicans called "The Society for the Propagation of the Gospel in Foreign Parts" was committed to offering moral and financial support to America's fledgling Episcopal Churches, including Christ Church in Massachusetts and Trinity Church in Rhode Island. Downing and Scully suggested a member of that Society could have obtained and sent a Wren design to the minister of Christ Church, who then turned it over to the Boston engraver William Price (1684–1771). Price developed the working drawings for Christ Church, which was certainly the inspiration for Munday's design for Trinity Church, although Munday introduced the use of circular-headed windows.

The interior restoration of the Meeting House included the balcony, the box pews and the reinstallation of the original pulpit that had been removed in 1882.

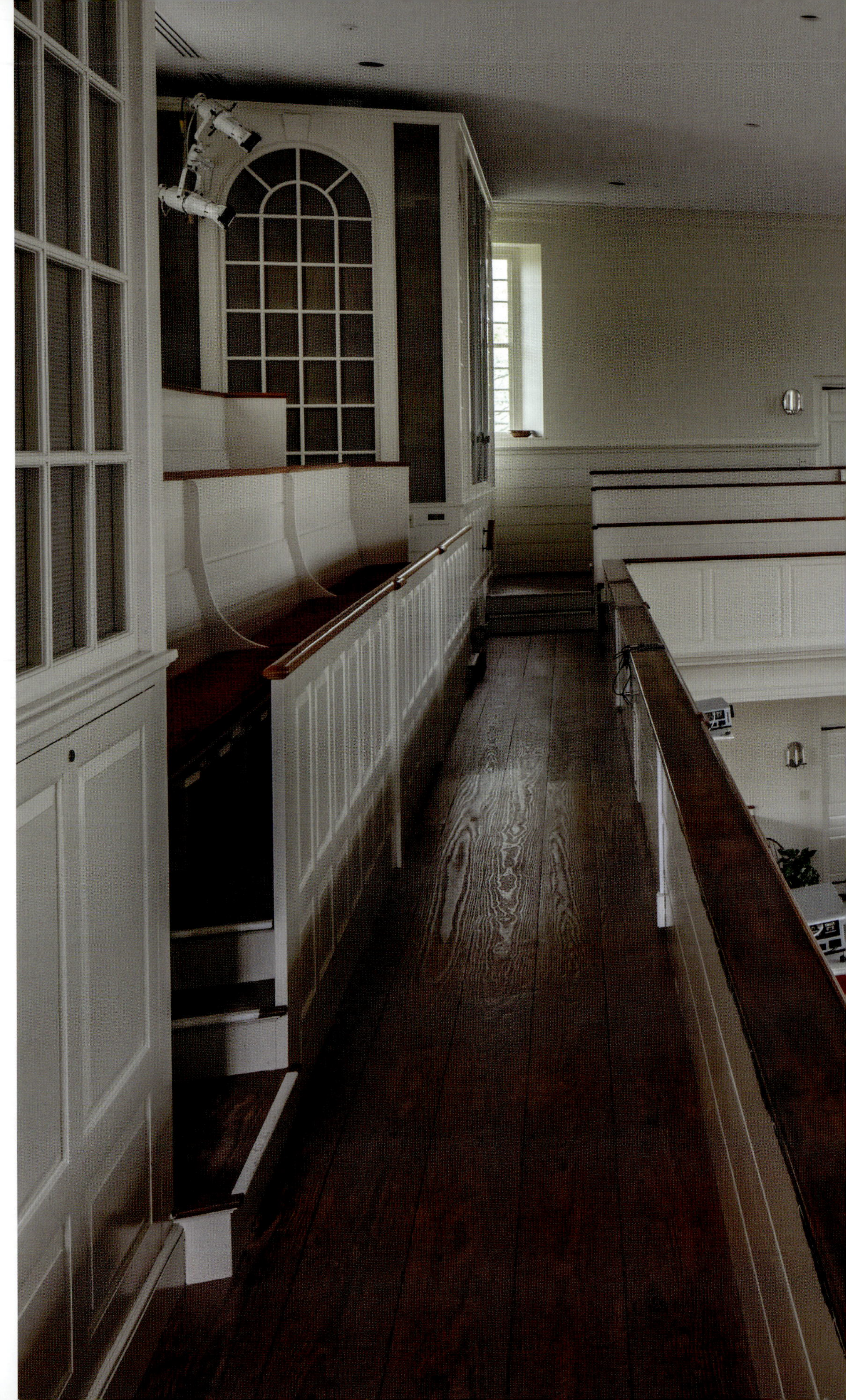

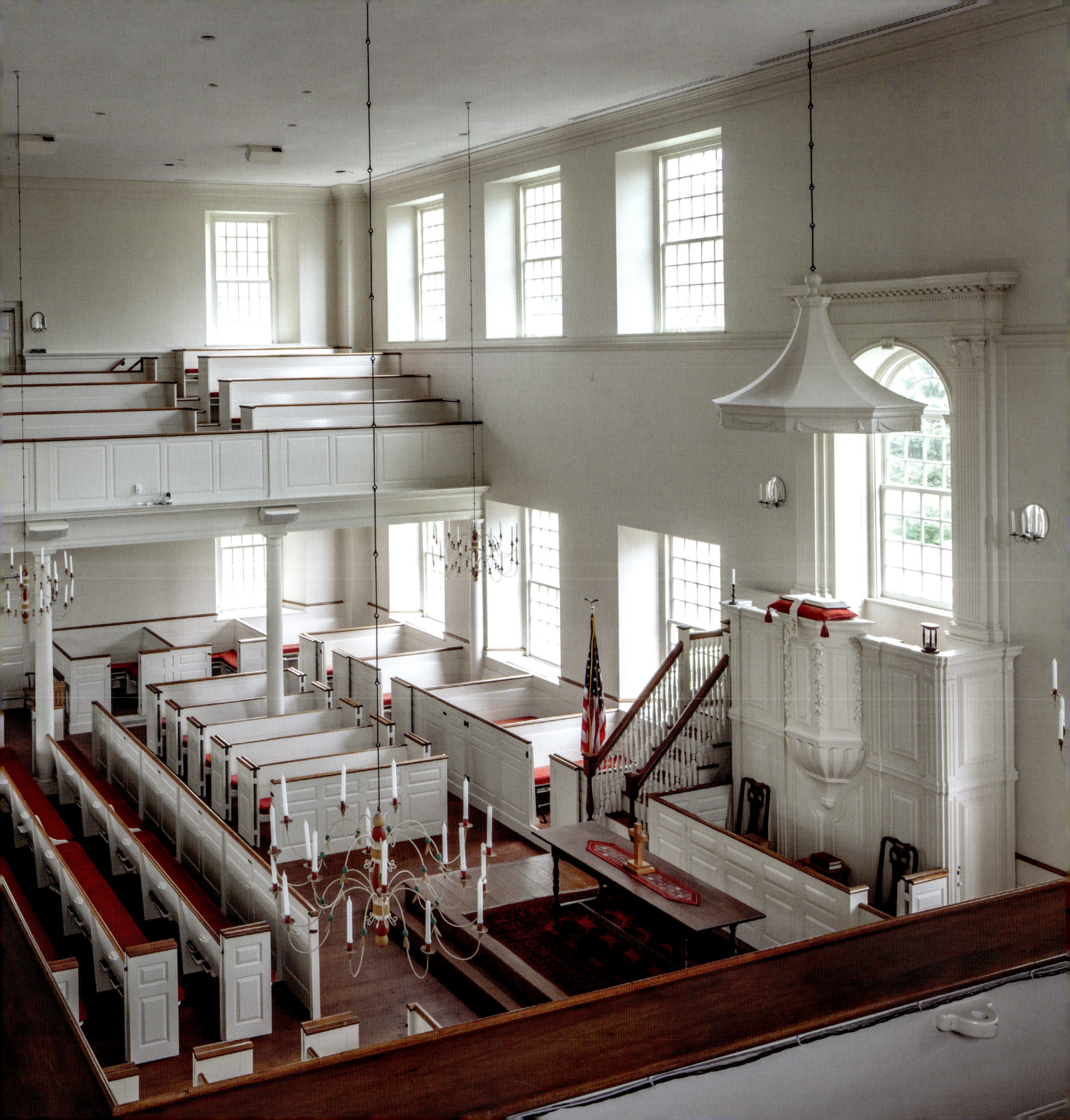

One feature that does not appear in either Christ Church or Trinity Church is the distinctive diaper pattern of black brick headers on three sides of the tower. This type of decorative brickwork may reflect the influence of the Dutch in New York.

First Society meeting minutes mention the names of only two tradesmen involved in the actual construction: a blacksmith named Hezekiah Crane (1748–1800) and a joiner named Amasa Adams.

Amasa Adams (1708–1790) was also a shipbuilder. He worked on the sloop Lark in 1743 and the sloops Dove and Dolphin in 1754. In 1760, he purchased a quarter interest in the Chester Mill, which by then included a lumber mill. During the construction of the Meeting House, he contributed £24-14s-01d in materials or labor.

He also assisted in the construction of the house for Reverend James Lockwood in 1767–1768. Lockwood (1714–1772) was the minister when the Meeting House was built. He had been Wethersfield's minister since 1738. He declined offers to be president of both Princeton and Yale colleges and continued his ministry in Wethersfield until his death.

View from the connector into the east porch where the original pulpit was displayed after its removal in 1882, and before its reinstallation in 1972.

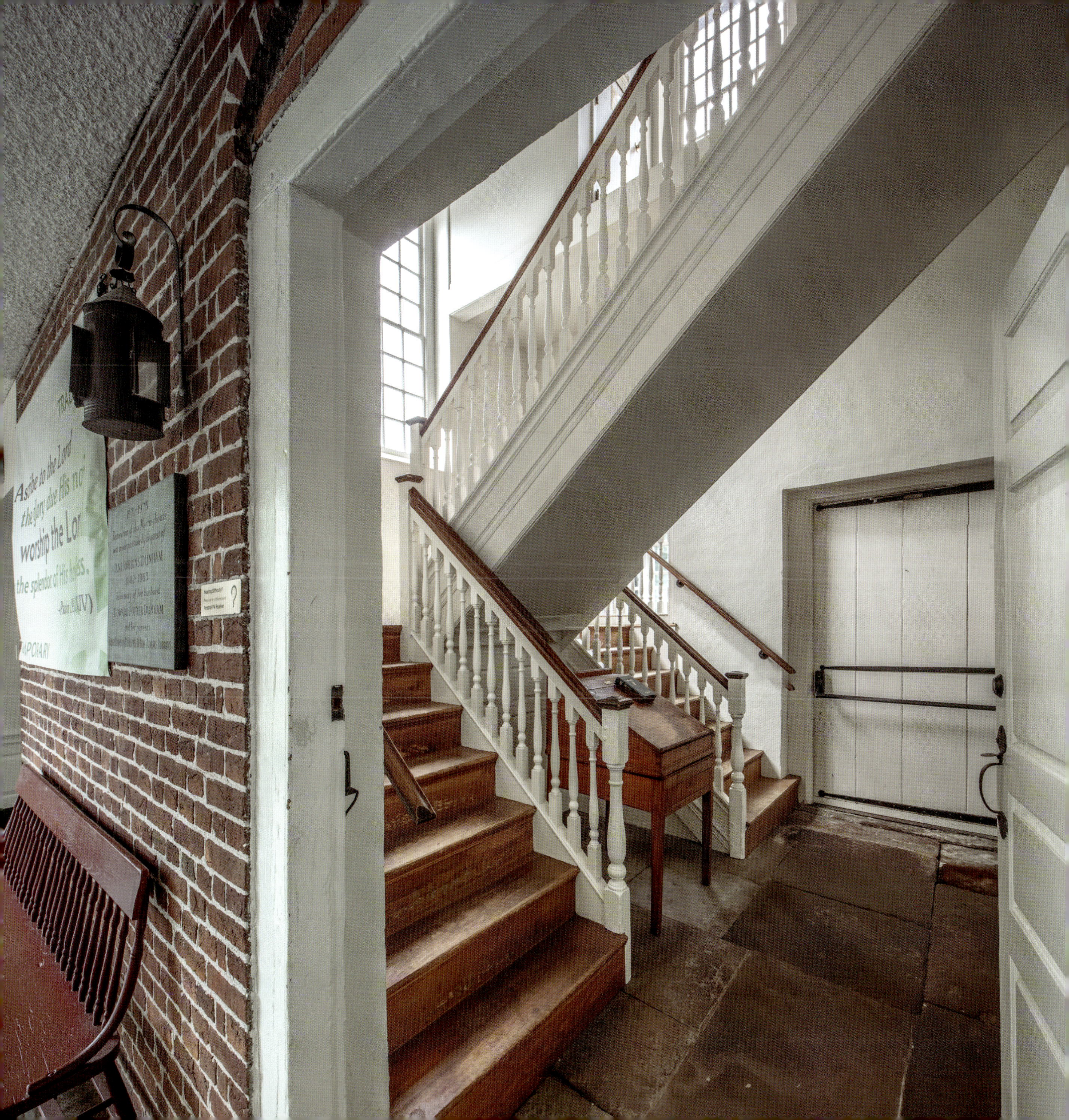
1971–1975
Hearing Difficulty?
Personal PA Receiver

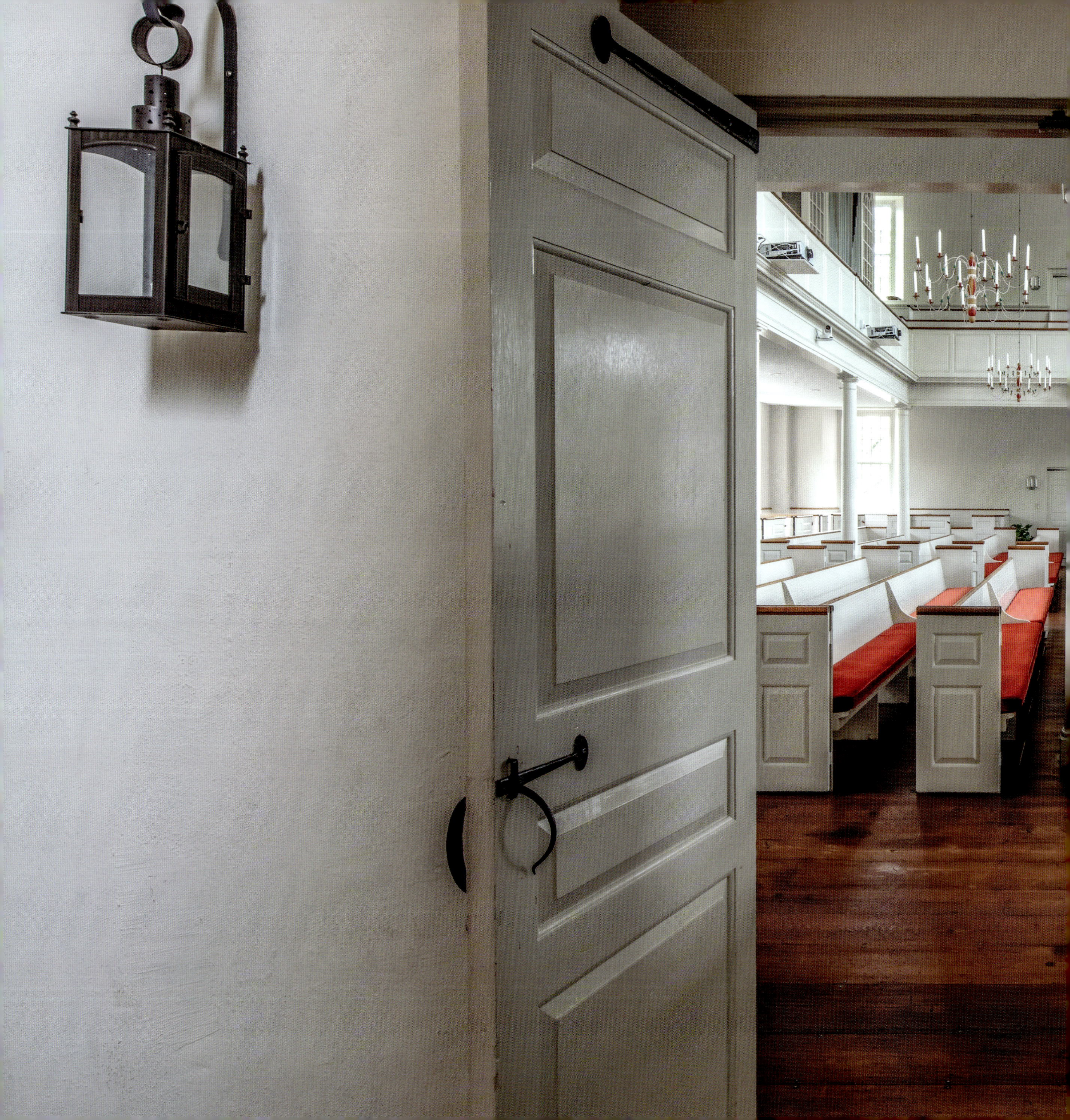

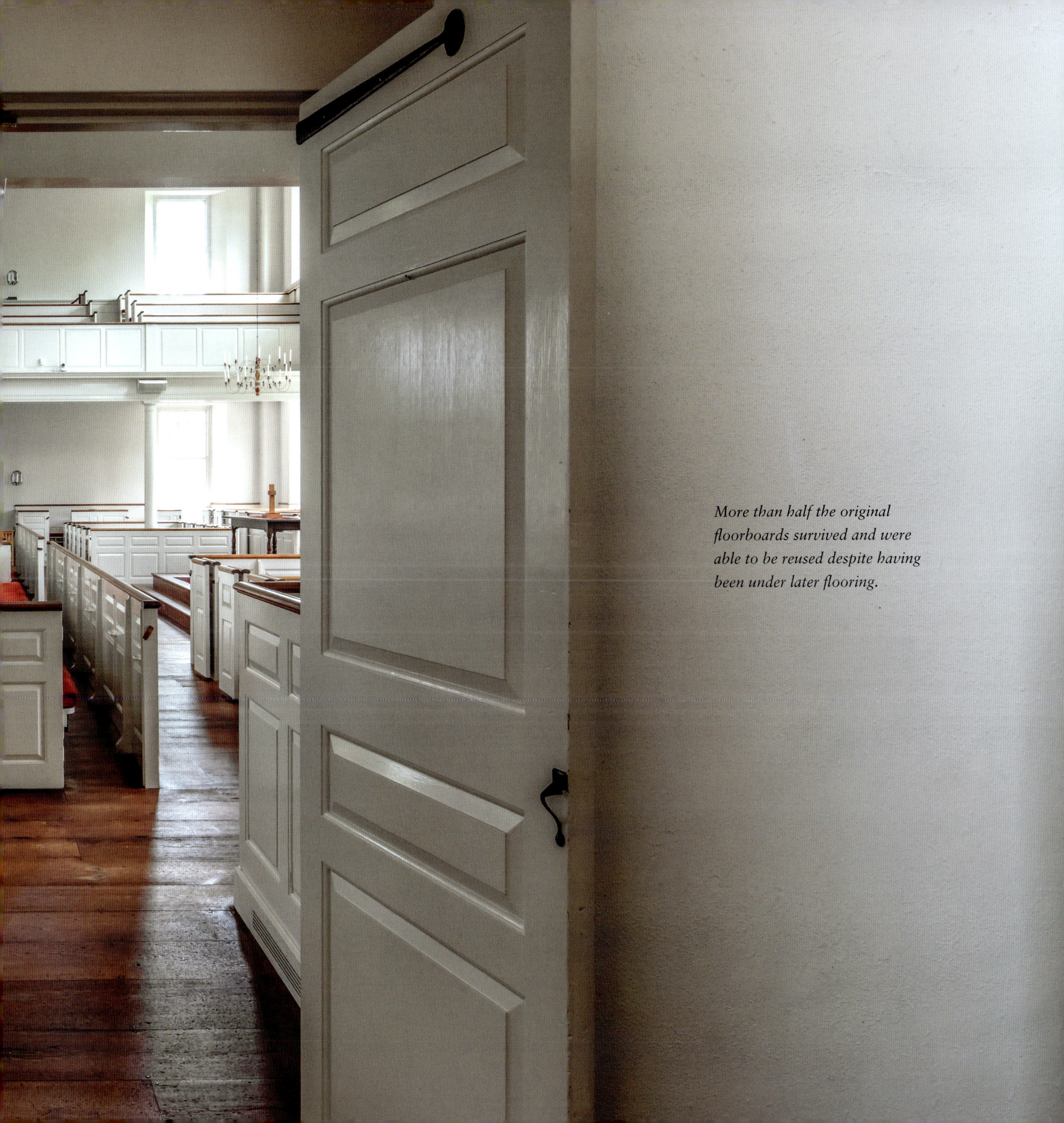

More than half the original floorboards survived and were able to be reused despite having been under later flooring.

Following Lockwood's death, the congregation invited a graduate of Harvard College to serve as its minister. Reverend John Marsh (1742–1821) came to Wethersfield in 1773 and married Ann Grant of East Windsor, Connecticut, in December 1775. They had seven children.

Marsh served as Wethersfield's minister for forty-seven years. In that time, he married 723 couples, baptized 1878 persons, and buried 1466. He continued to wear a wig, cocked hat, and cape when they were no longer fashionable.

The north side showing it restored after removal of the 1882 entrance porch and the two-story-high stained-glass windows.

Although their house next to the Meeting House was torn down in 1916, antiquarian Wallace Nutting (1861–1941) salvaged a corner cupboard and a fireplace wall from the Marsh House and installed them in the southwest room of the Webb House.

During the 1880s, Silas W. Robbins (1822–1910) paid to have the Meeting House extensively renovated, including a new entrance porch on the south side, replacement of the original clear windows of the Meeting House with two-story-high stained-glass windows, and the removal of the original interior to completely remodel it in golden oak. In her will, Silas' granddaughter, Jane Robbins Dunham (1884–1963) left funds for the First Church of Christ to restore the Meeting House to its eighteenth-century appearance.

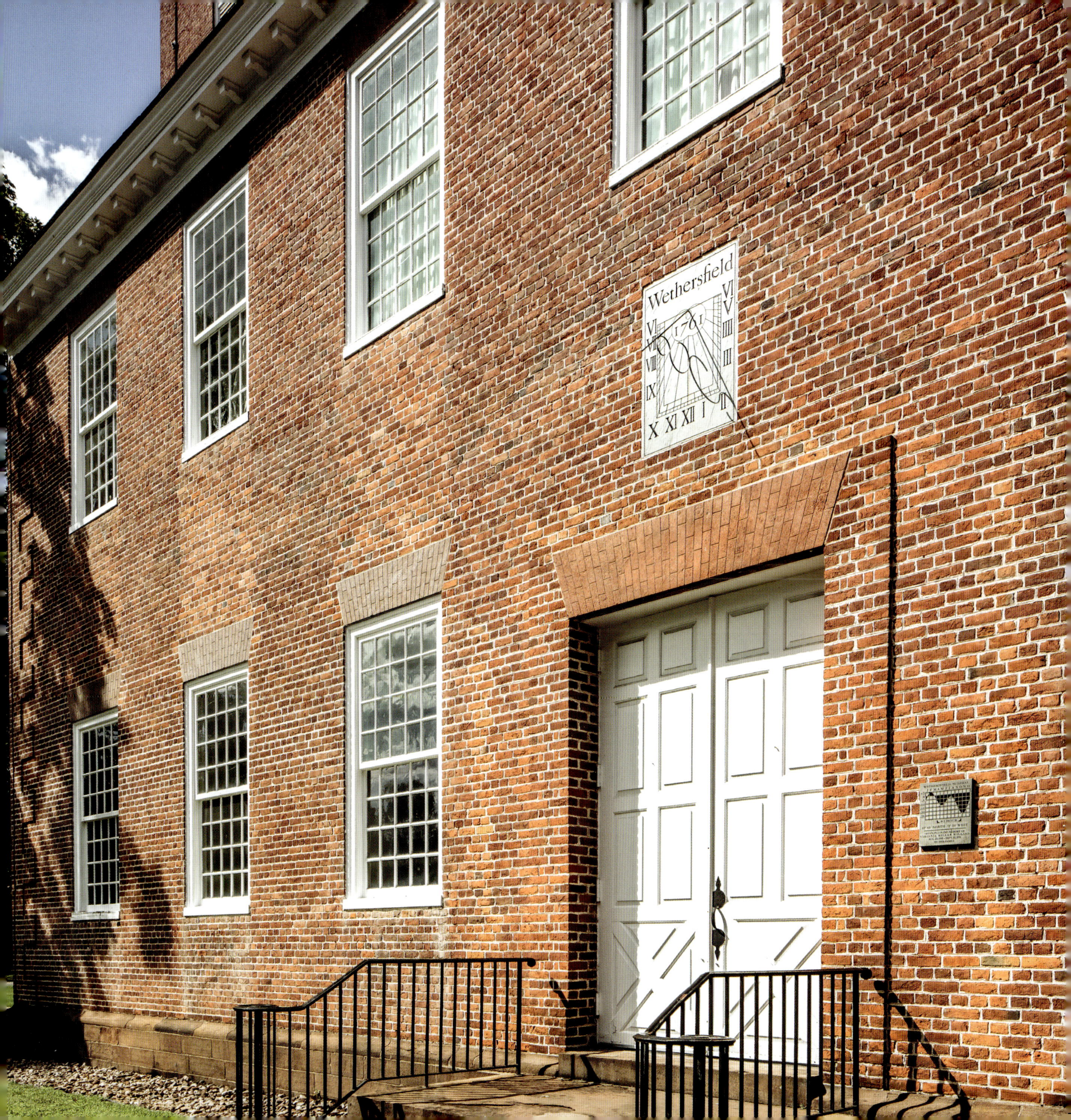
Wethersfield
1761

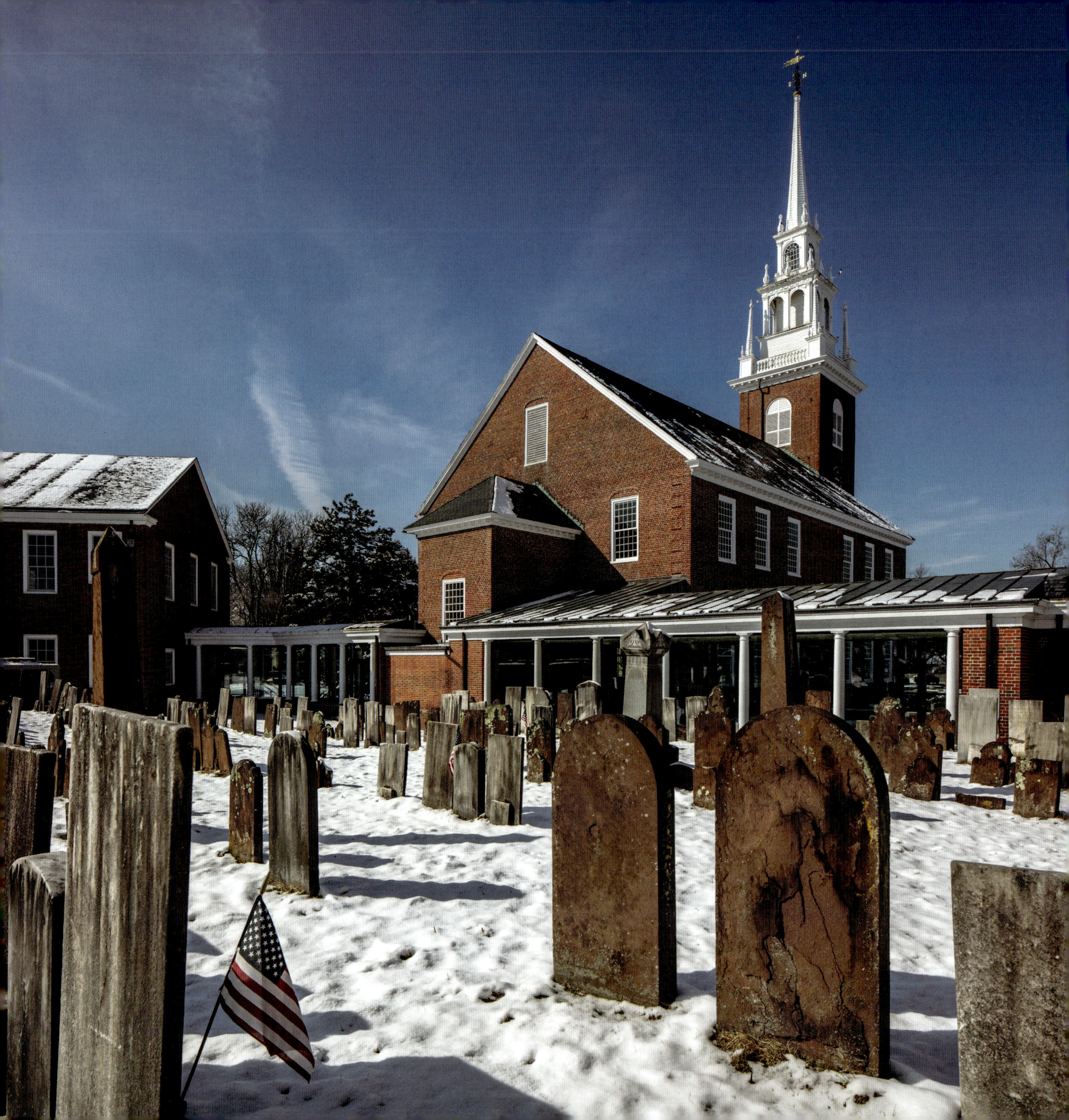

The Ancient Burying Ground — the enclosed connectors in the background between the Meeting House and the parish houses were glazed to preserve the view of the burying ground from Main Street.

First Church of Christ engaged Jeter, Cook & Jepson Architects to design and supervise the restoration of the Meeting House in 1972. The project included the creation of enclosed walkways between the Meeting House and the south and north parish halls.

The Historic District Commission did not approve of the initial design of brick connectors, because it offered no visual distinction between the historic eighteenth-century structure and the proposed additions. The commissioners suggested, and ultimately approved, a design consisting of a covered colonnade with plate glass walls that not only separated the Meeting House from the parish halls but also preserved views of the Ancient Burying Ground from Main and Marsh Streets.

The Commission allowed the church to tear down the Victorian chapel attached to the north side of the building and to restore the brickwork and windows on the north wall. The wider north connector has become a popular location for receptions. ♕

A RARE BRICK COLONIAL, RECLAIMED AND REVIVED

Dr. Daniel Hooker House

— 471 Main Street —

The Dr. Daniel Hooker House at 471 Main Street is one of the earliest brick structures in the state, the oldest surviving brick structure in the Wethersfield Historic District, and the earliest surviving house to have two free-standing chimneys.

Daniel Hooker (1679–1742) graduated from Harvard College in 1700. He and his wife, Sarah Stanley of Waterbury, Connecticut, were married in 1707 and moved to Wethersfield by 1708, where their daughter, Susannah, was baptized at First Church. Hooker might have come to Wethersfield to study medicine with Dr. Gershom Bulkeley. Hooker served as an army surgeon for the Canadian campaign of 1711.

The Dr. Daniel Hooker House showing the 1976–77 addition on the left.

The John Blackleach estate sold the three-acre homestead at 471–481 Main Street for £200 in 1710 to Hooker. He built this house as a one-story gambrel around 1725; in 1733, he and his son sold it to Caleb Griswold (1706–1754) for £400. The brick house remained in the Griswold family for more than four generations.

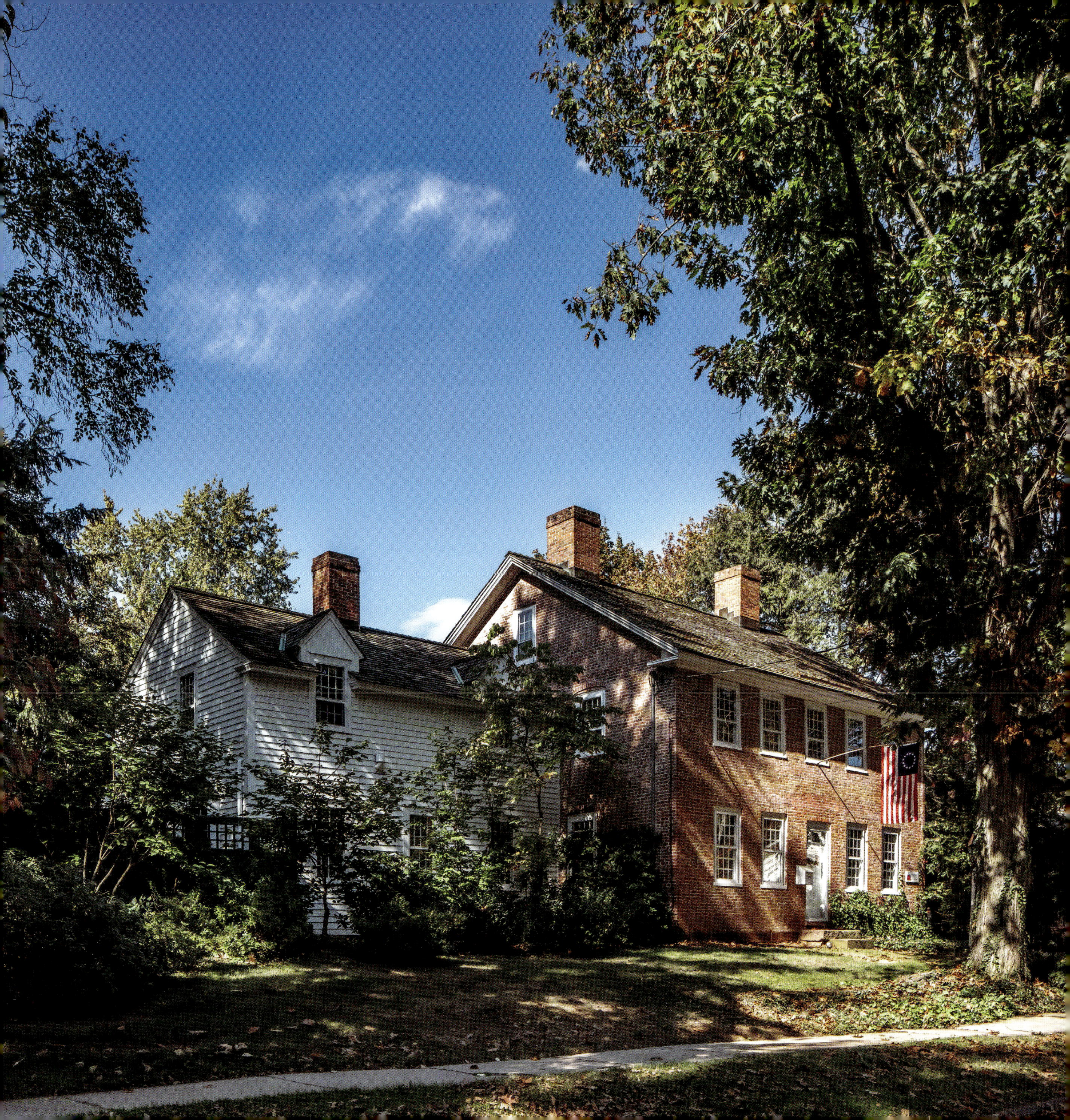

The dining room was the house's original kitchen. The cooking fireplace was removed in the early twentieth century.

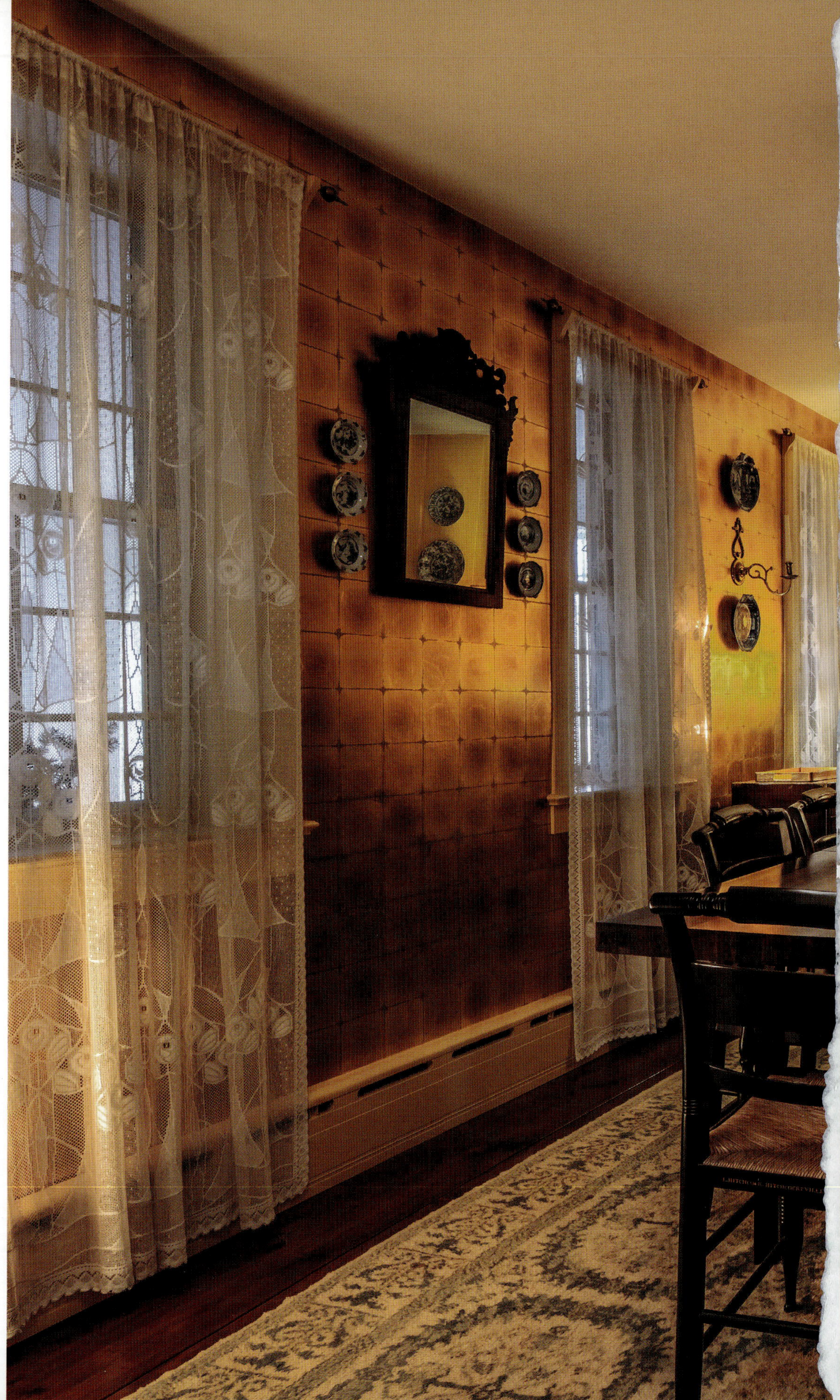

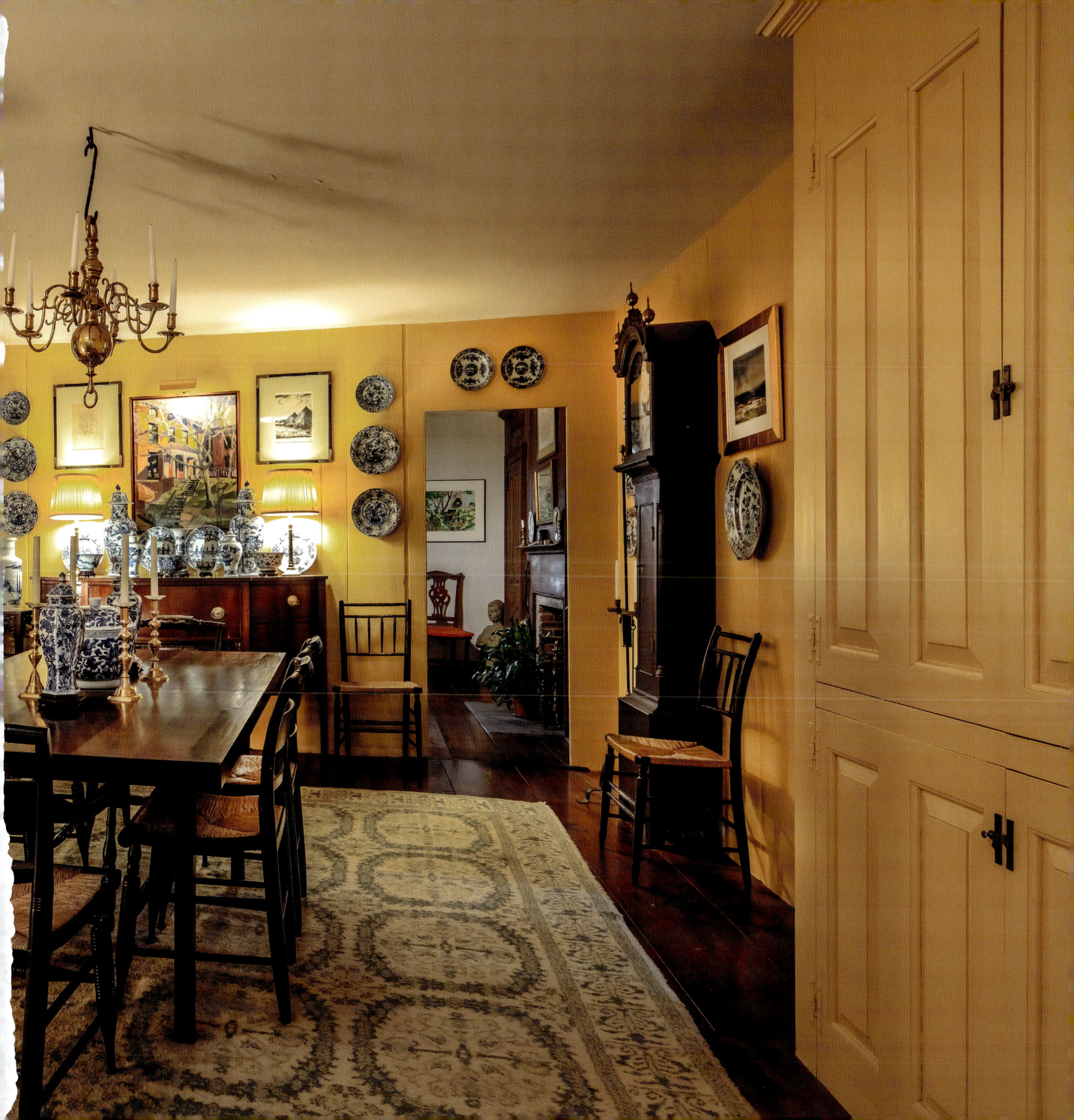

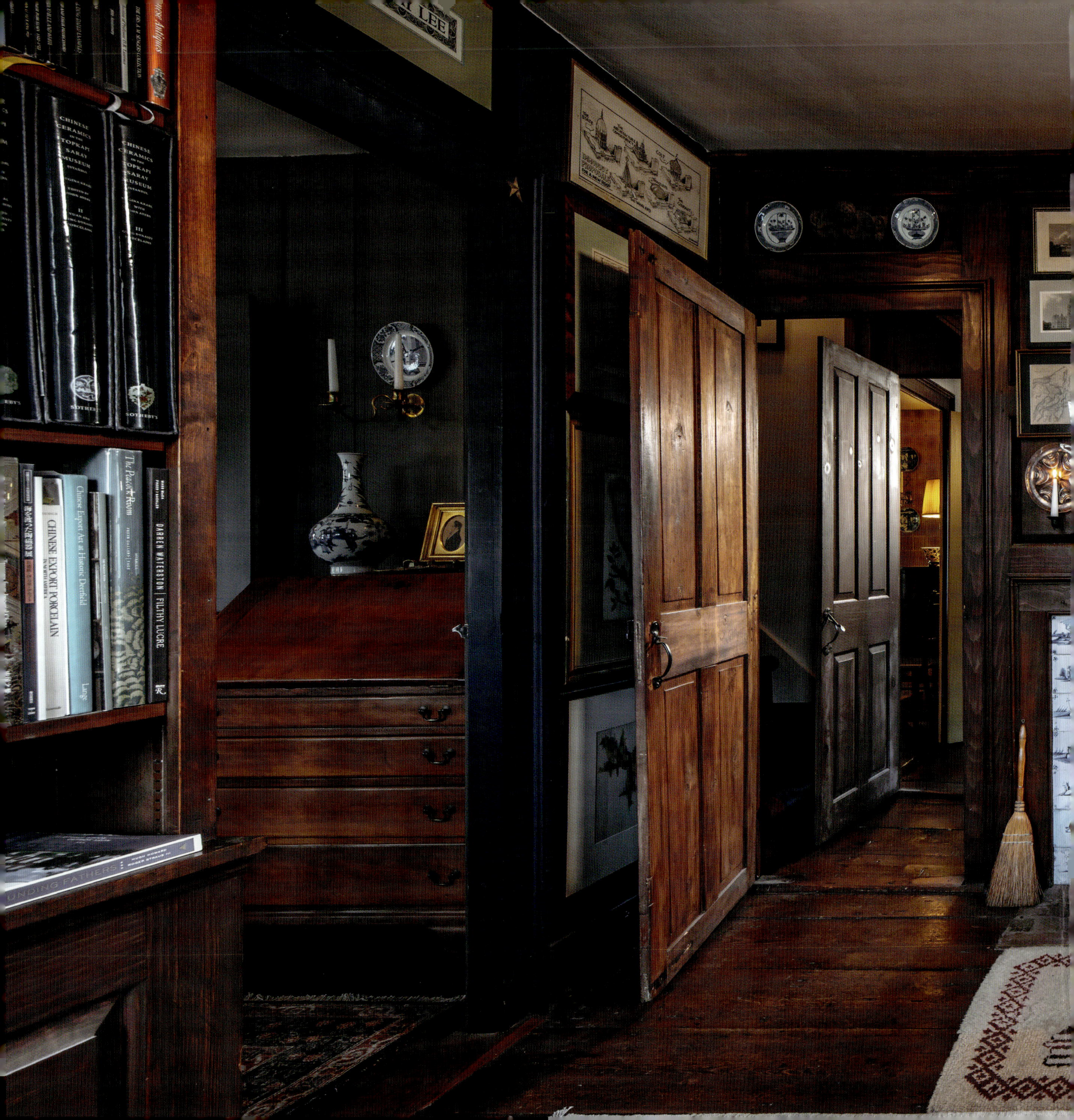
CHINESE CERAMICS IN THE TOPKAPI SARAY MUSEUM
SOTHEBY'S
SOTHEBY'S
The Peacock Room
Chinese Export Art at Historic Deerfield
CHINESE EXPORT PORCELAIN
DARREN WATERSTON
FILTHY LUCRE

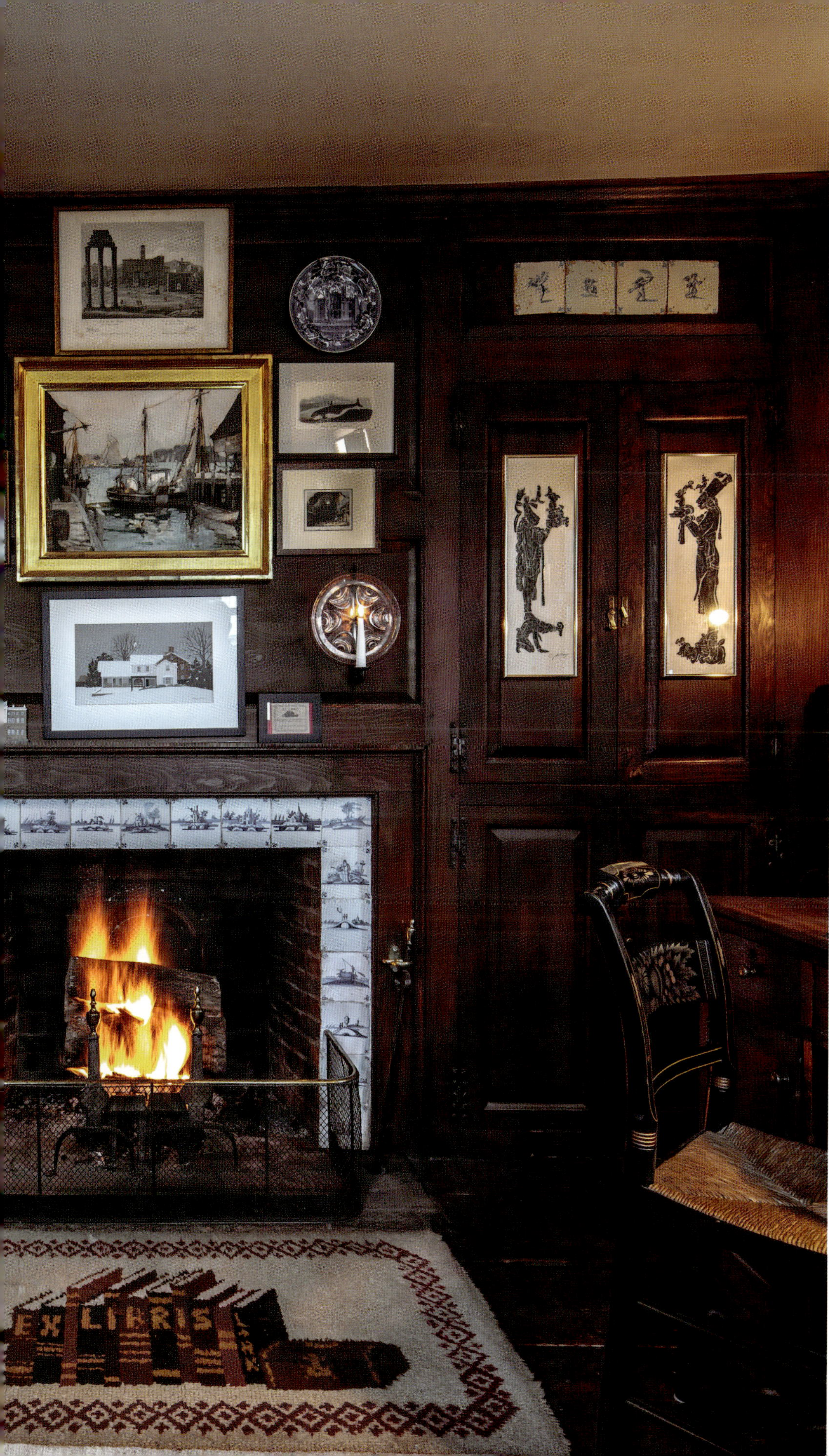

The northeast room — the original chimney stack and the paneling were removed in the early twentieth century. The evidenced based restoration includes some older materials. The floorboards are original.

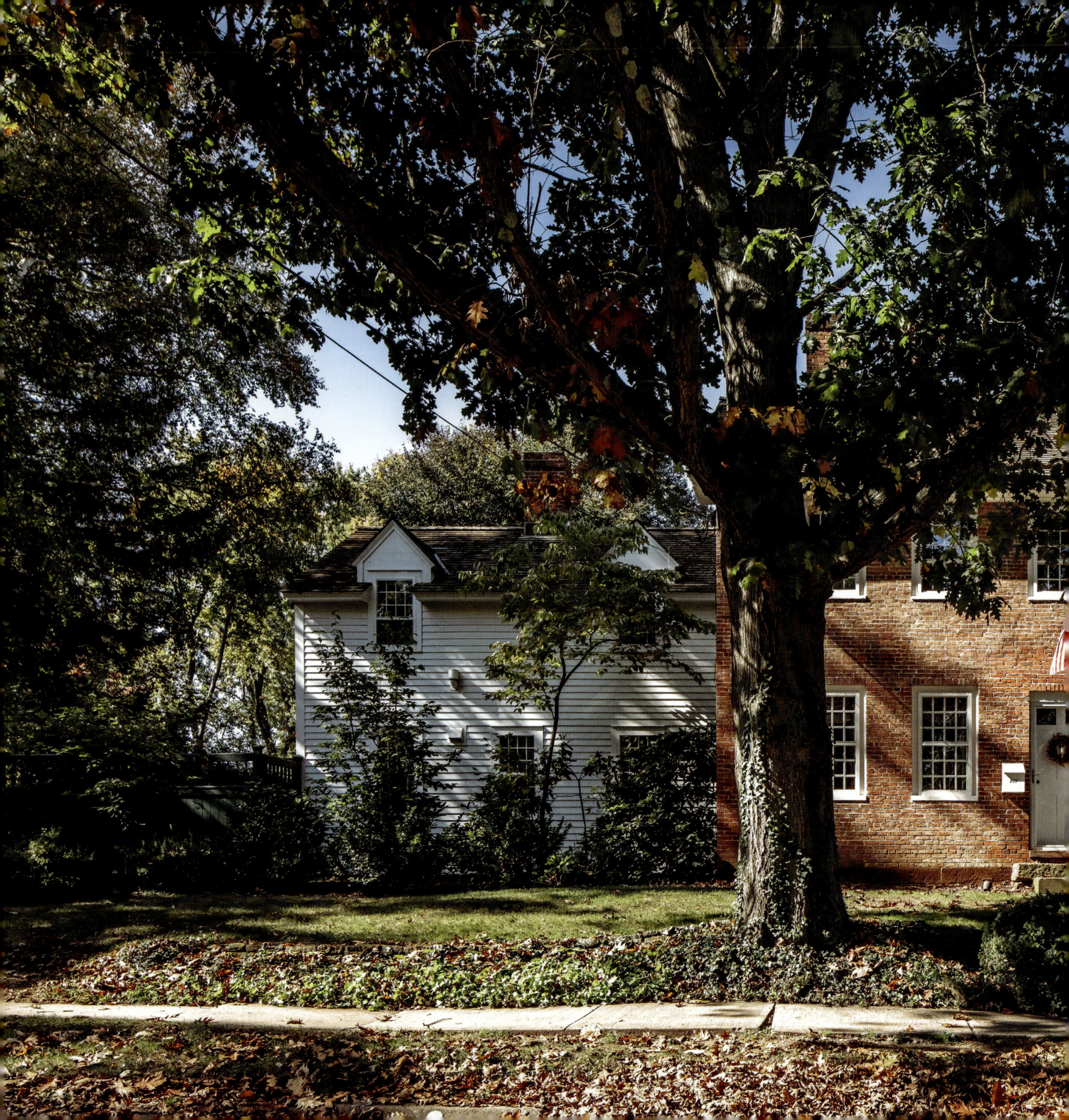

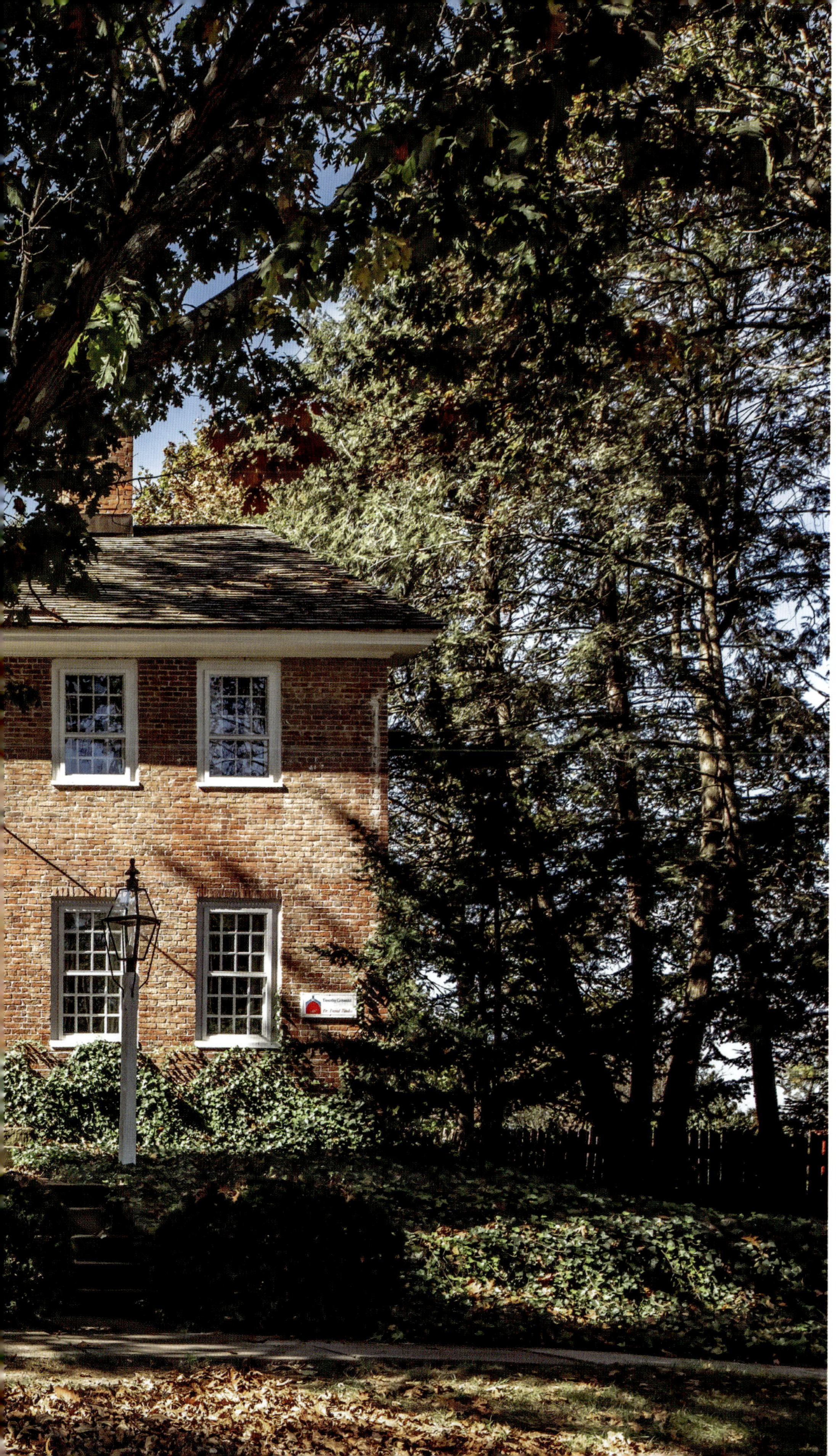

The front of the house after the Griswolds enlarged the original gambrel roofed structure to a full two stories under a gable roof.

Caleb Griswold's great-great-grandson, Timothy Griswold (1795–1837), purchased the home from his father in 1823. Timothy married Laura Standish (1796–1838) in 1821, and in October 1827, they took out a $2,100 mortgage to finance the remodeling of the over one-hundred-year-old brick house. They enlarged it to a full two stories under a gable roof with new windows in the front and back walls and an attic. The beams that had supported the break in the original gambrel roof were reused to support the new roof, and the beaded boards that had lined the sloping walls of the second floor became the floor of the new attic. Traditional 12/8 sashes in the new second-floor windows were used to match the old ones in the end walls.

The northwest room after the northern chimney and fireplaces were rebuilt — the fireplace wall of paneling was restored using old wood. Only about a quarter of the paneled wall is original.

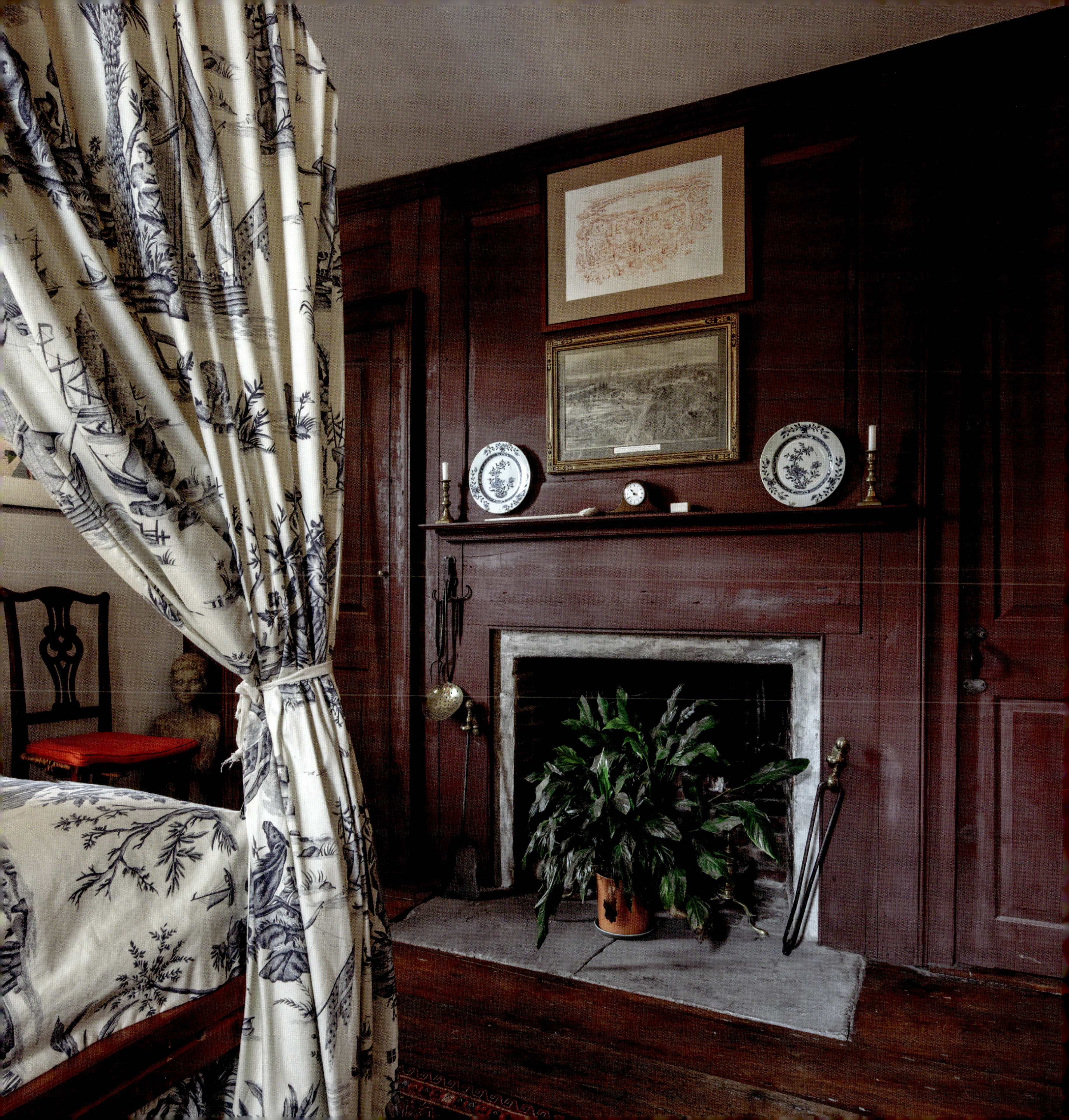

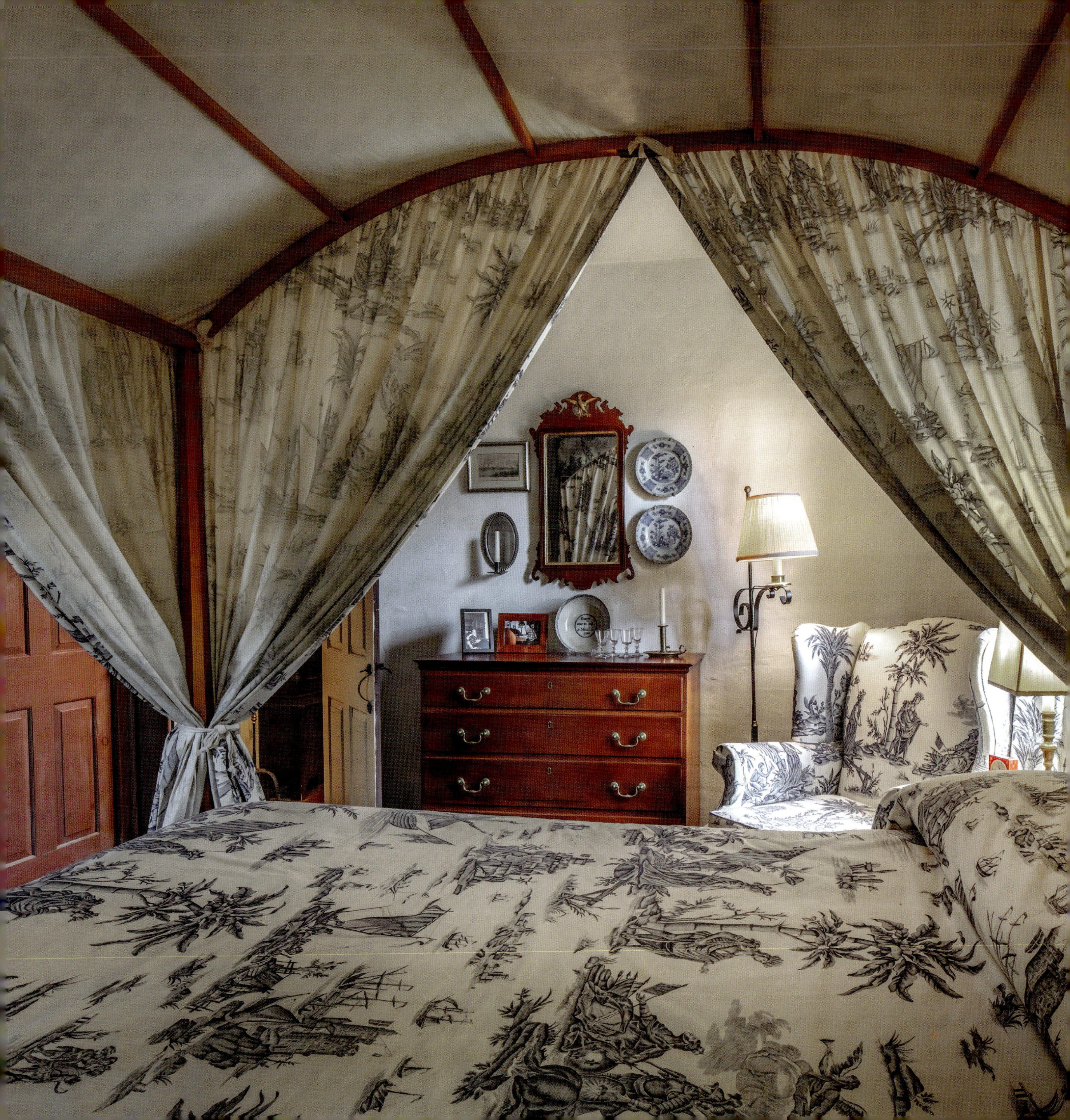

A view of the northwest room.

The Griswolds were evidently unable to pay off the mortgage, so a second cousin, Caleb Griswold Jr. (1799–unknown), who had grown up in the house at 451 Main Street, purchased it in 1833. Caleb and his wife, Mary Willard, had seven children, five of whom lived to adulthood. Caleb Griswold sold the house to the Deming family in 1848. During the Deming's ownership, the overhang of the roof was extended, a belvedere was added to the rooftop, and a bracketed portico was built over the front door. These Italianate-style features were removed during the Colonial Revival period.

Lee and Anne Kuckro purchased the house in 1968. The first thing they did was restore the wood shingle roof. They later replaced the chimney that was removed in the early twentieth century and restored the other to its original size. They stripped the painted brick and restored the 12/12 sashes on the ground-floor windows in 1971.

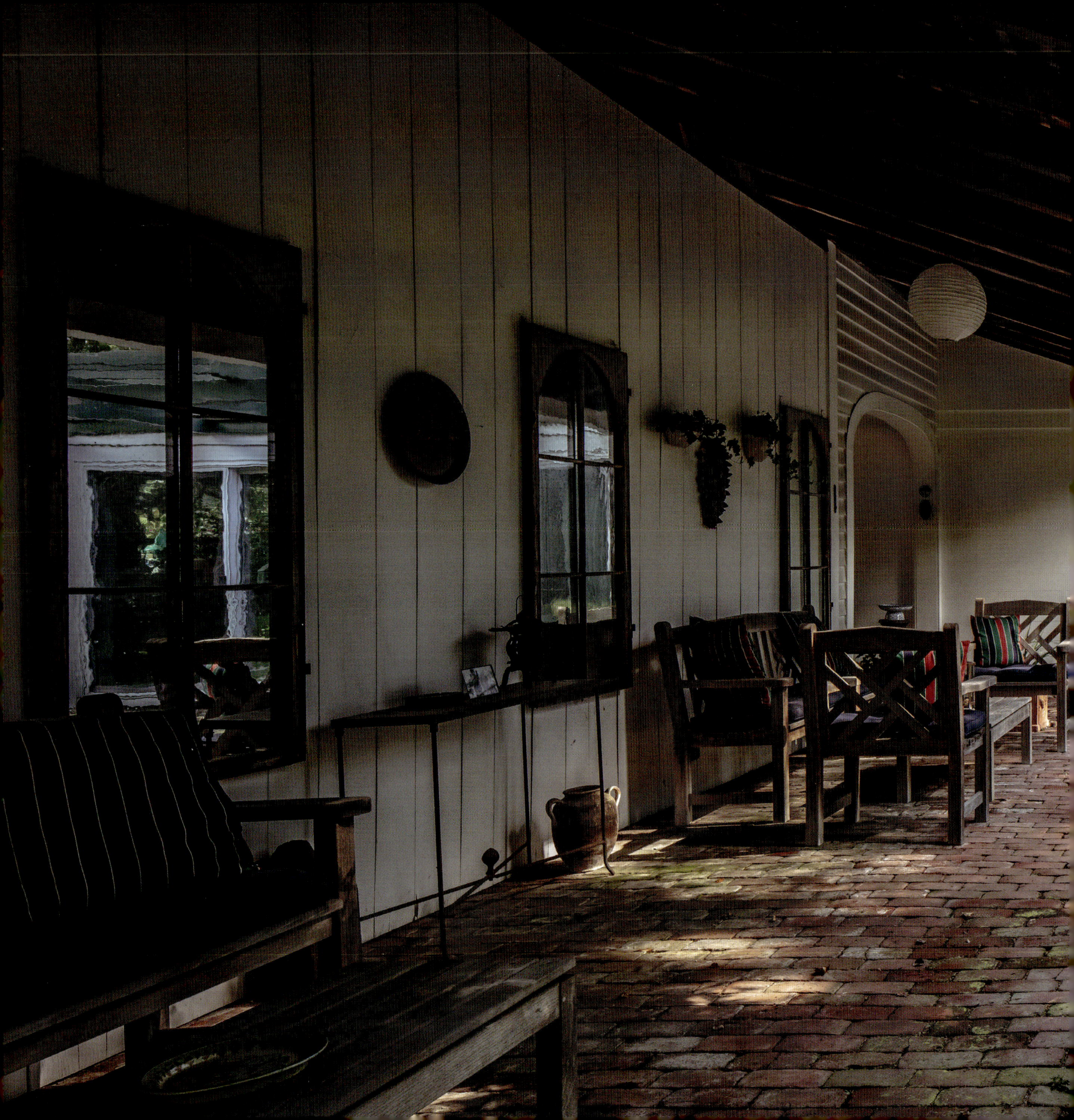

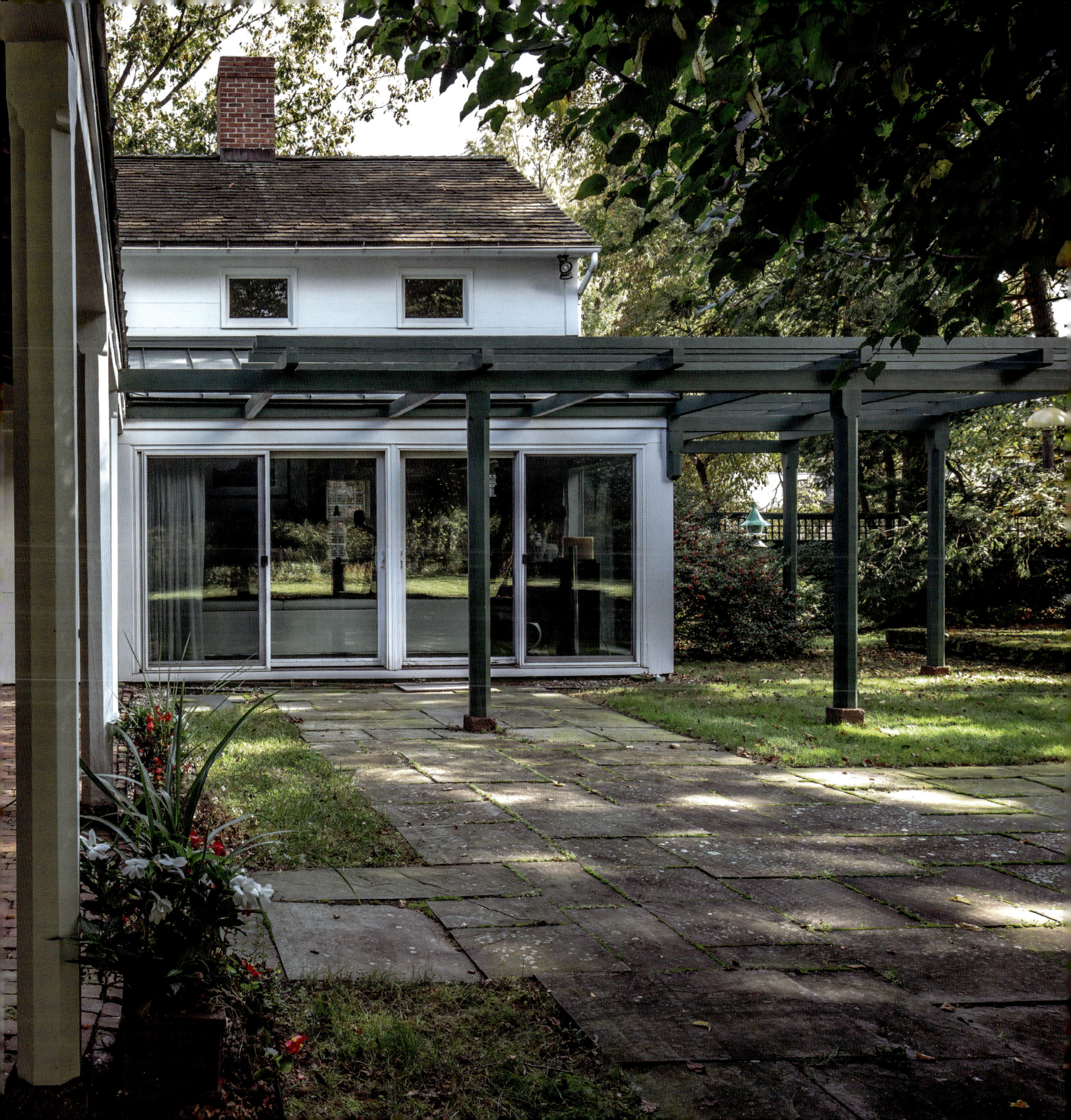

(preceding spread)
The rear of the house with both additions — the windows hanging on the 1983 addition's porch on the left, which are now backed by mirrors, were from the nineteenth century rooftop belvedere removed in the early twentieth century.

The floorboards and nearly half of the paneled wall are original.

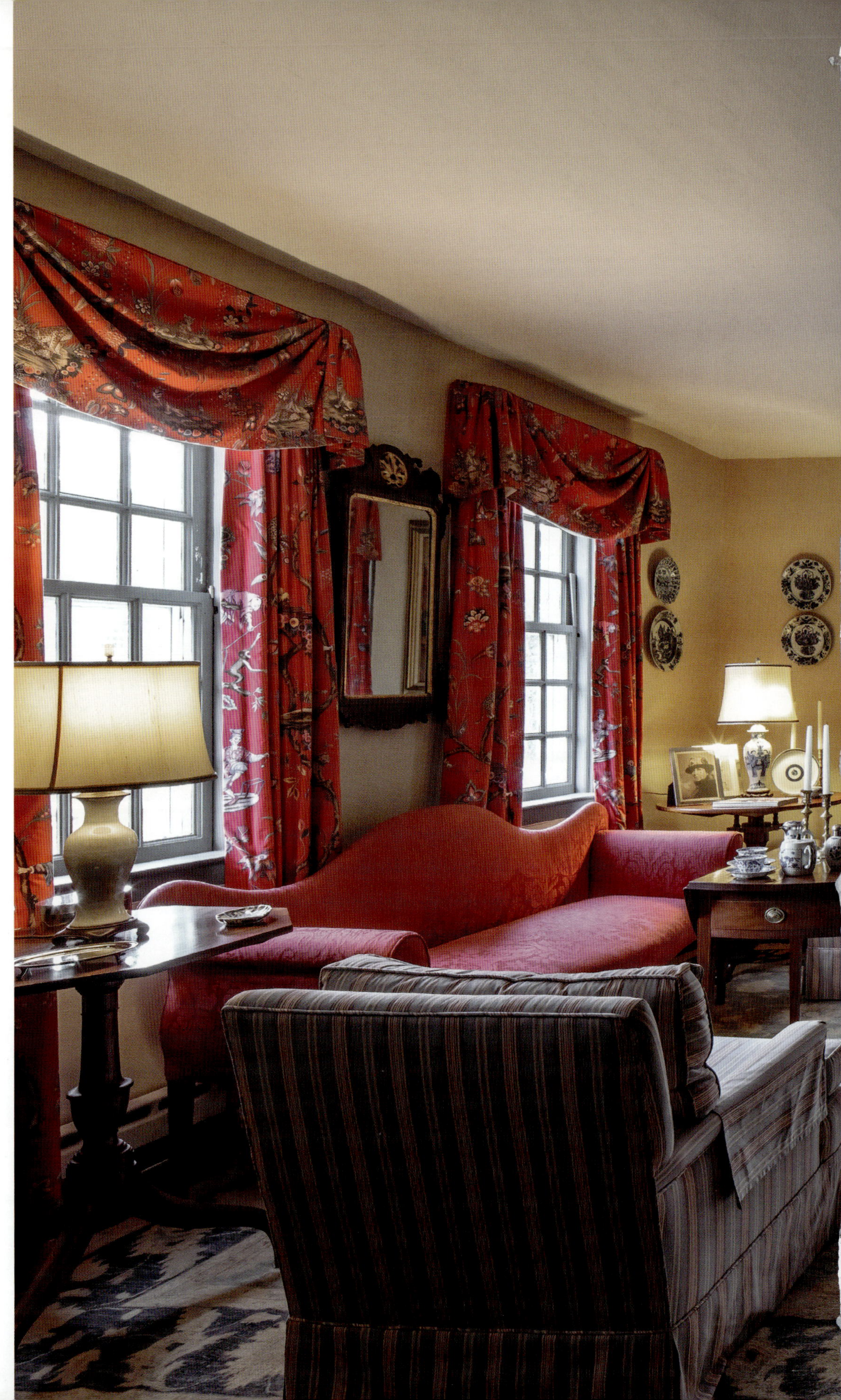

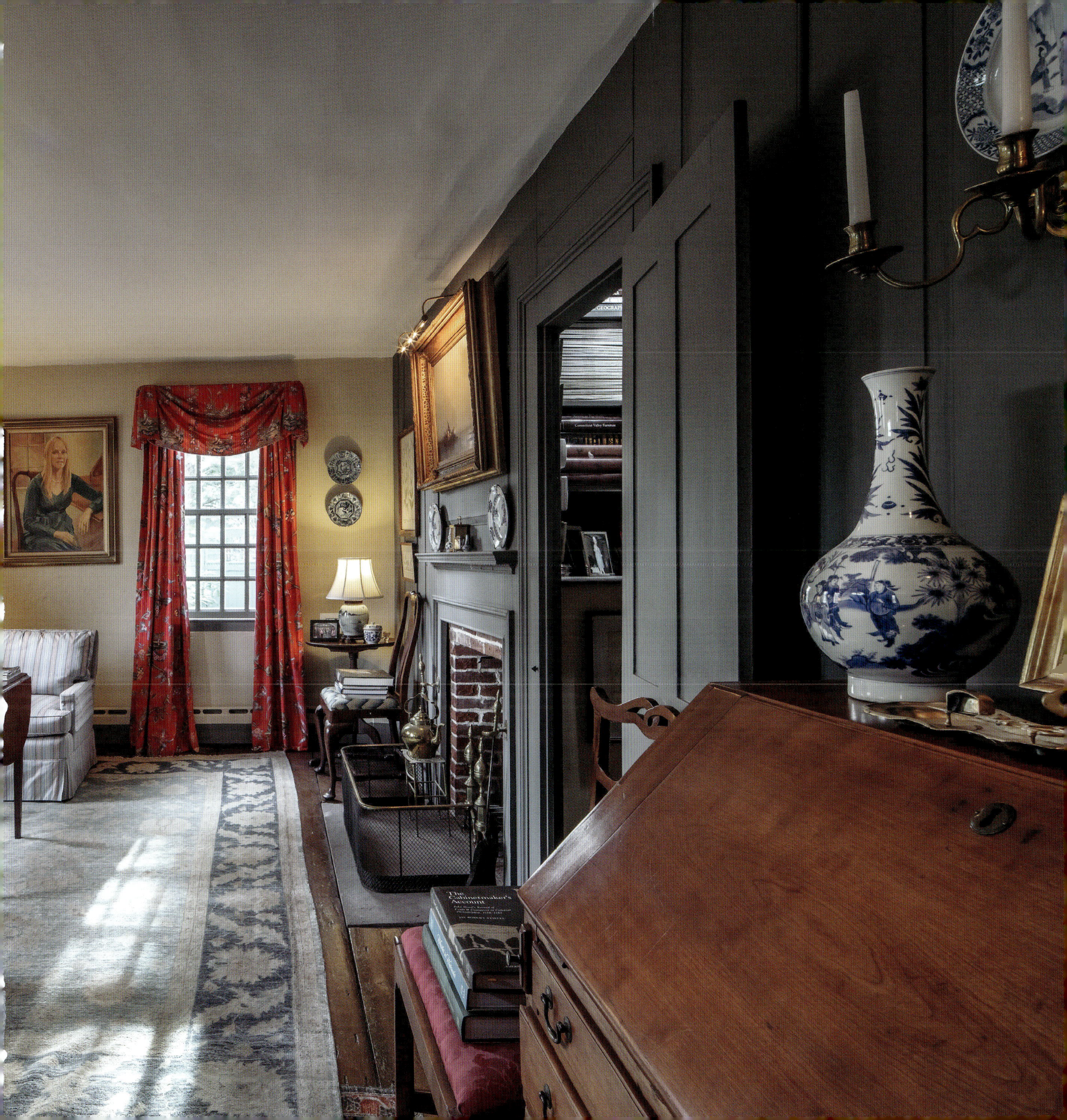
Connecticut Valley Furniture
The Cabinetmaker's Account

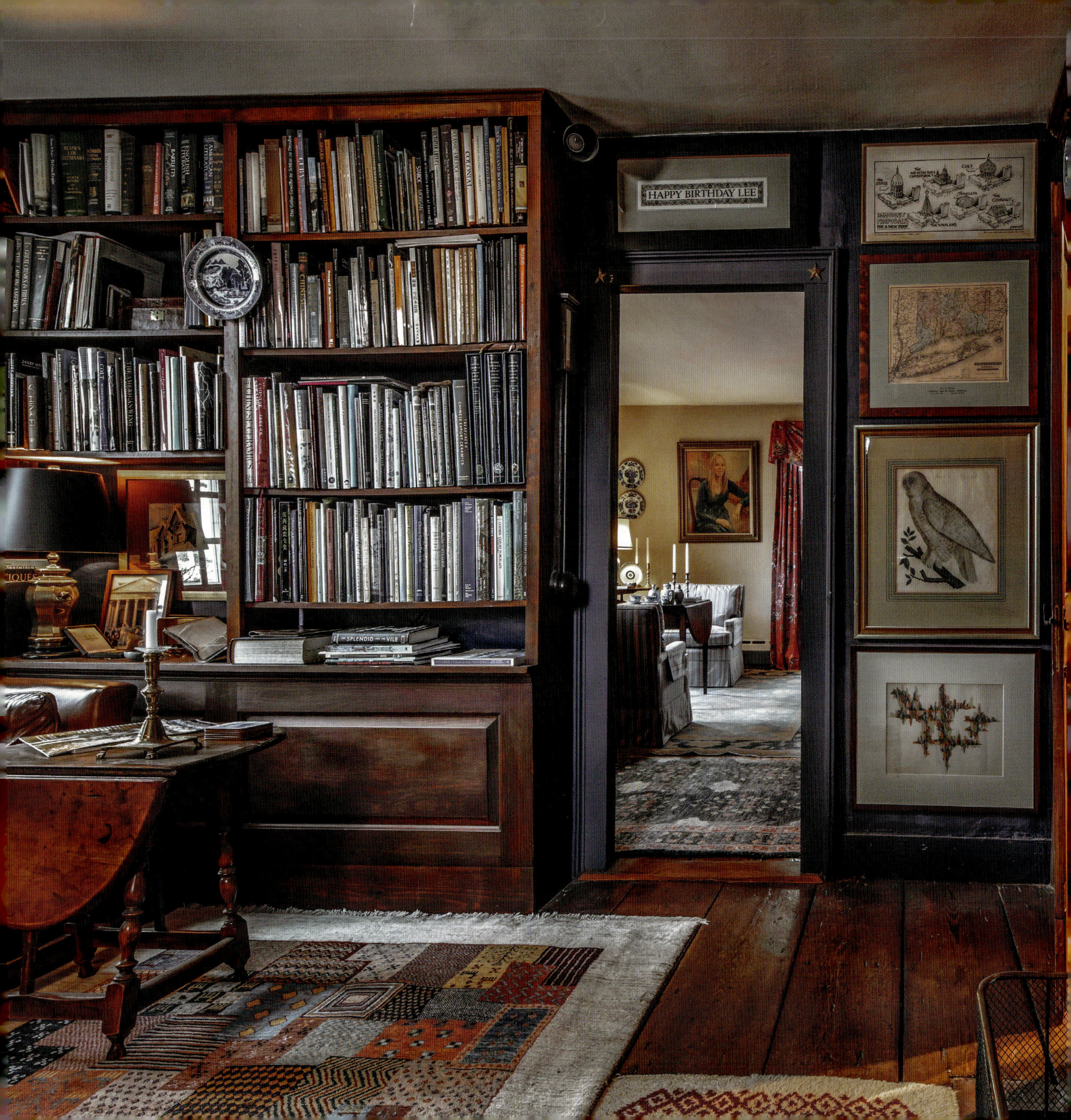
HAPPY BIRTHDAY LEE

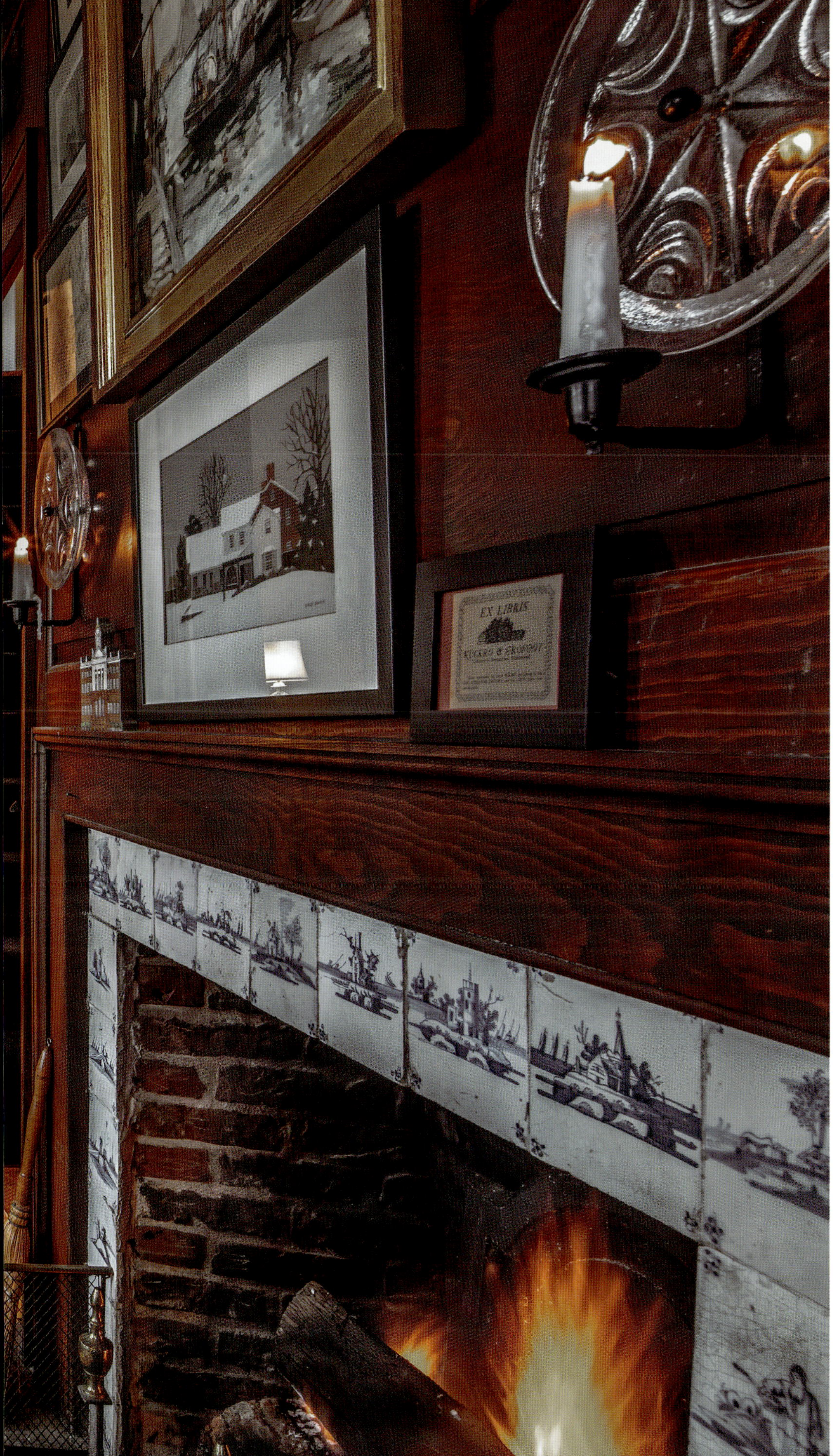

The library fireplace was rebuilt using the original bricks. The antique Delft tiles were added in the restoration. Although there was no evidence that Delft tiles were installed by Hooker, they were sold and used in Wethersfield during the colonial period.

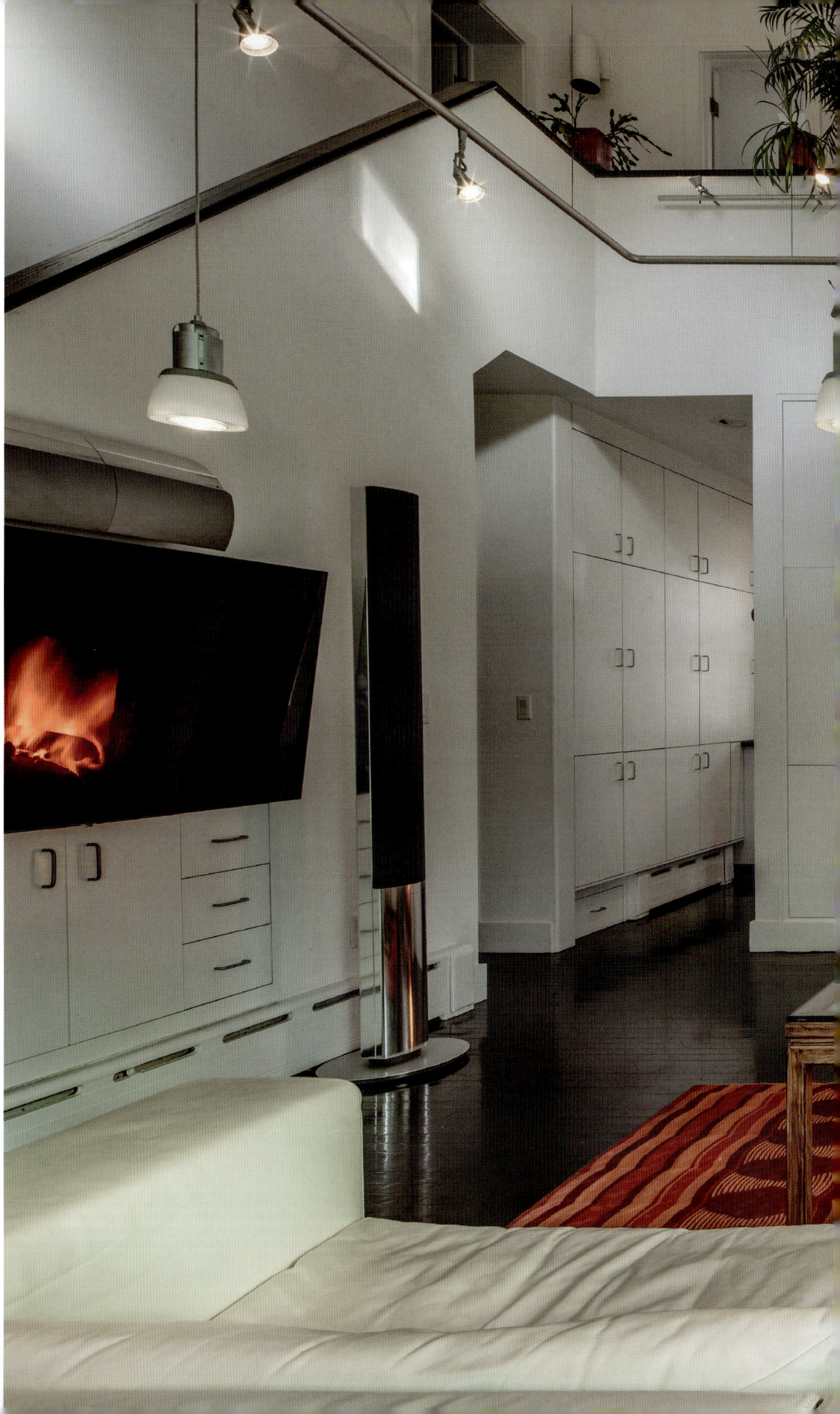

Showing the interior of the 1976–1977 addition.

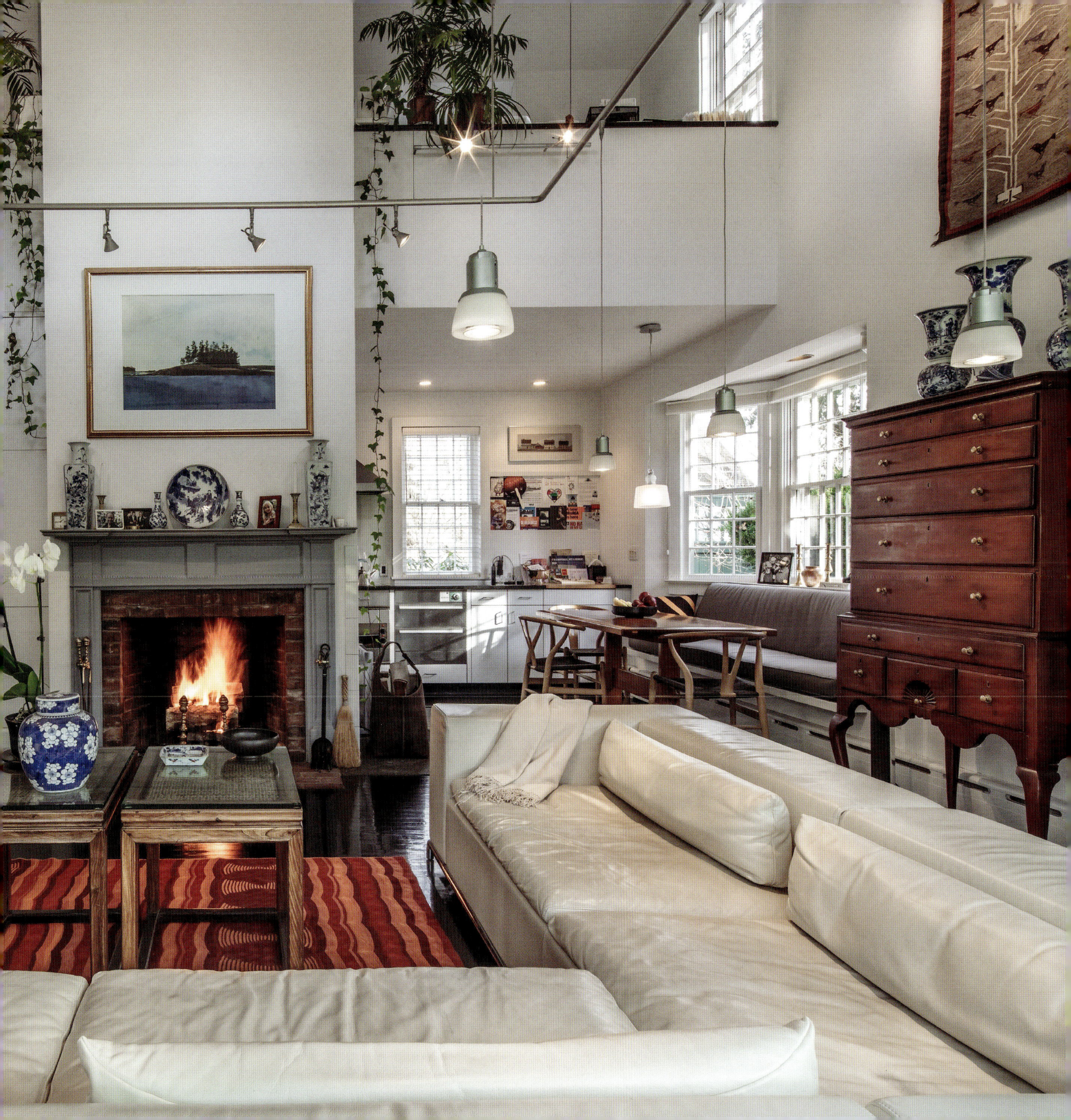

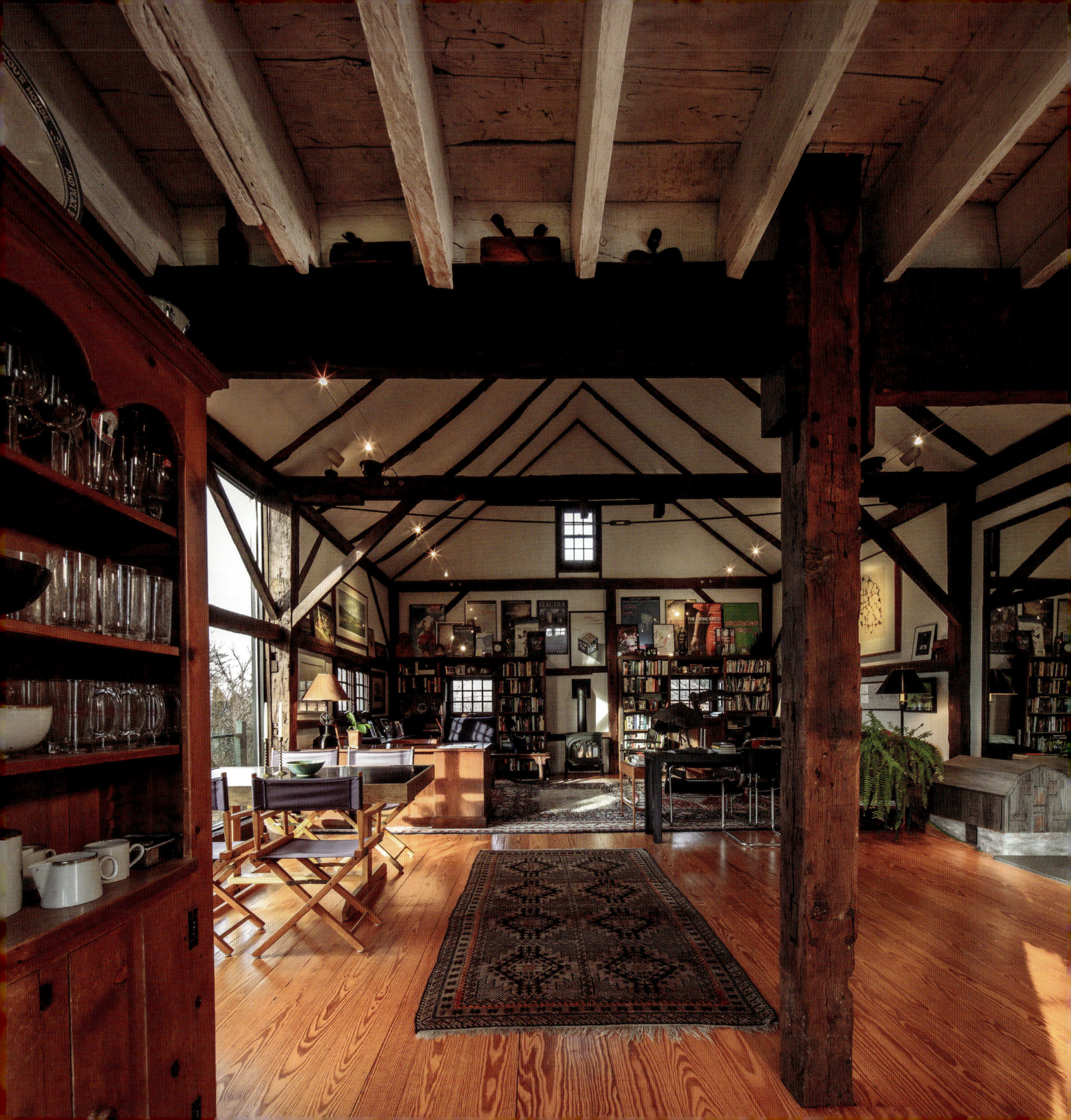

Narrow oak flooring in the interior was removed to expose the original, wide hard pine floors, three fireplaces were rebuilt, two walls of paneling were restored based on surviving sections, and one paneled fireplace wall was rebuilt based on examples from the period. The corner cupboard in the dining room, once the original kitchen, was reproduced by Jonathan Steucek. He based the cupboard on one in the Samuel Hanmer Sr. house (1765), two doors away at 493 Main Street.

The early eighteenth-century barn was converted to a studio in 1999.

In 1976, Lee and Anne hired builder Samuel DiMauro to construct an addition, designed by Anne's older brother, architect David Crofoot. The addition was centered on an 1811 fireplace mantle, made by master builder James Francis for the north front parlor of the Zachariah Bunce house at 340 Main Street, that was removed to restore the parlor to its mid-eighteenth-century appearance. The Kuckros continued to enlarge their circa 1725 house with the addition of an ell and garage designed by James Vance & Associates Architects in 1983.

In 1984, they repaired the frame of the early eighteenth-century barn, replacing parts as necessary, and in 1999, they converted the barn into a studio, designed by James Vance and skillfully executed by John Armstrong.

OUR OLDEST HOUSE, RESCUED FROM MODERNITY

George Hubbard House

— 481 Main Street —

Paul and Donna Courchaine, collectors and students of early American culture, were looking for a home to accommodate their collection of late seventeenth and early eighteenth-century American furniture. The steep roof and upper-story overhang of the house at 481 Main Street caught their attention. They suspected they would find evidence of an early eighteenth or possibly late seventeenth-century dwelling behind the twentieth-century siding and paneled post and beams. They purchased the home in 1980.

The George Hubbard House — the two-story addition on the right, which encloses the chimney, is a twentieth-century addition to and remodeling of a one-story sunroom. The addition on the left is a seventeenth-century house from Ipswich, Massachusetts.

Within days of the closing, they took down a part of a beaverboard ceiling and pried off some of the paneled casings in the southeast room. As they suspected, the second-floor joists were beaded, the corner posts were chamfered, and the summer beam chamfers ended in decorative lambs-tongue stops. Customarily during the seventeenth century, these framing members were originally exposed and meant to be seen. The evidence confirmed the Courchaines' belief that their house was built during the seventeenth century, beginning life as a single ground-floor room, a single second-floor chamber, and an open attic under a steeply pitched gable roof, its ridge parallel to the street.

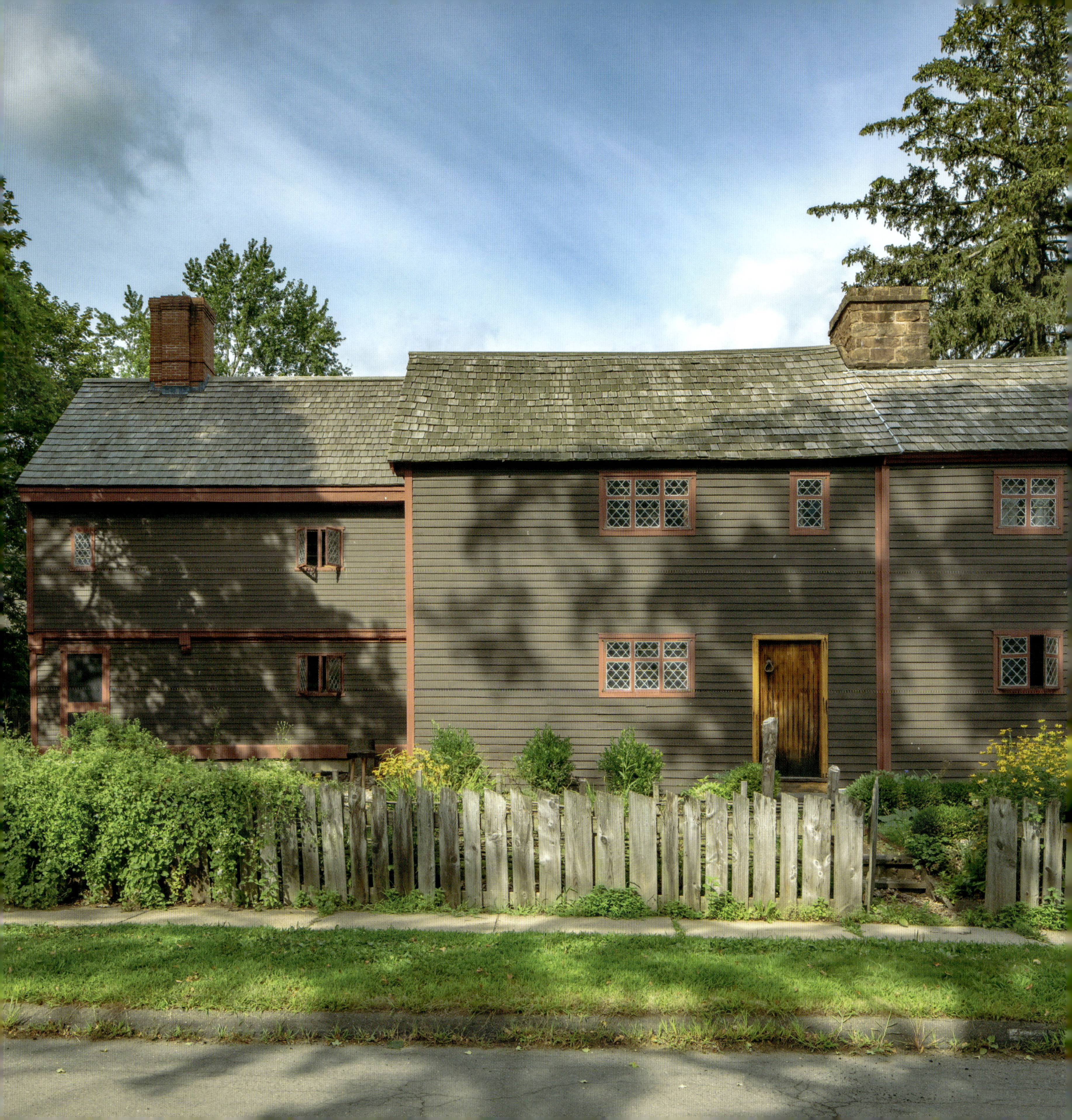

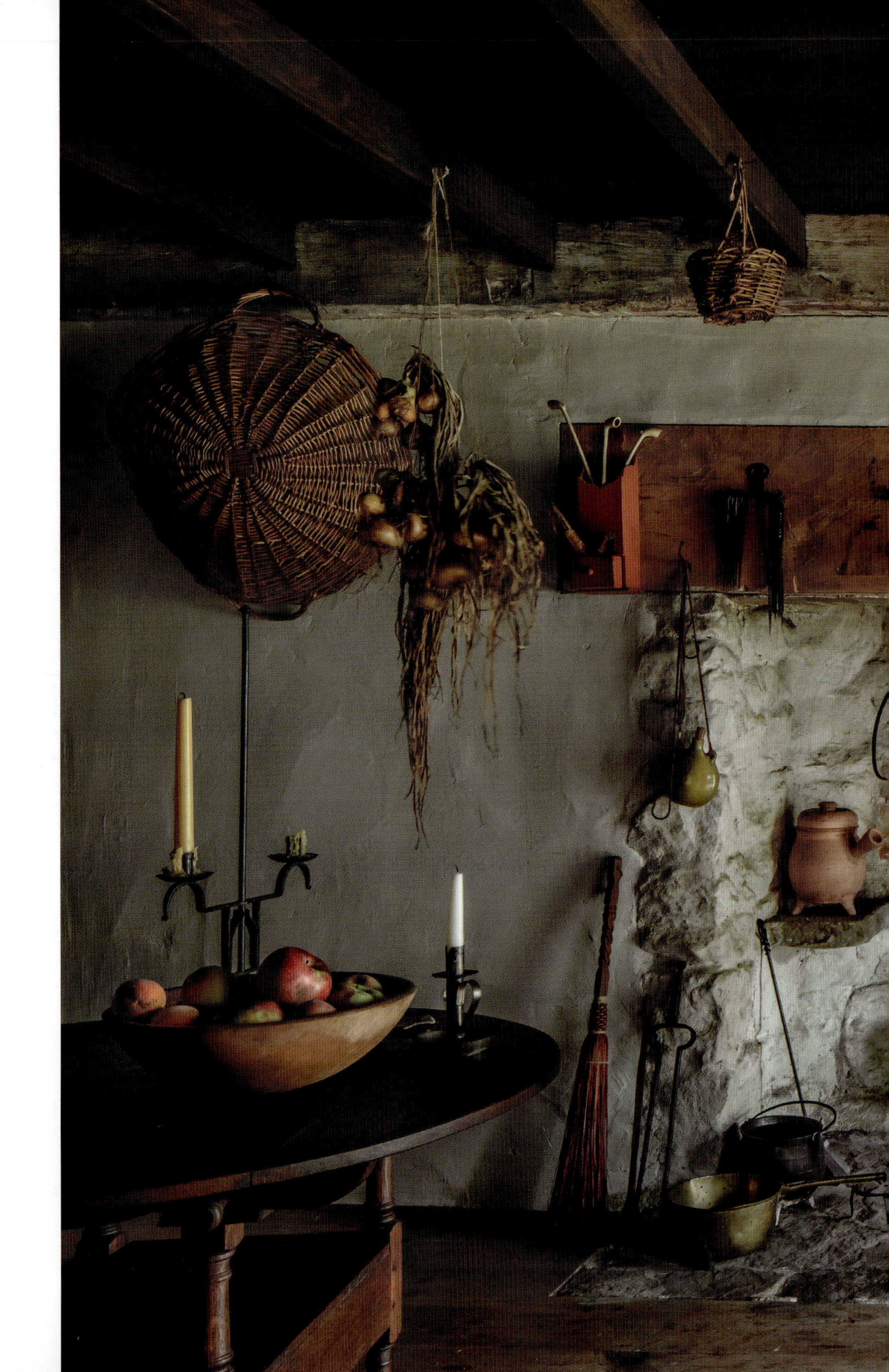

The hall of the Hubbard House with its great fireplace.

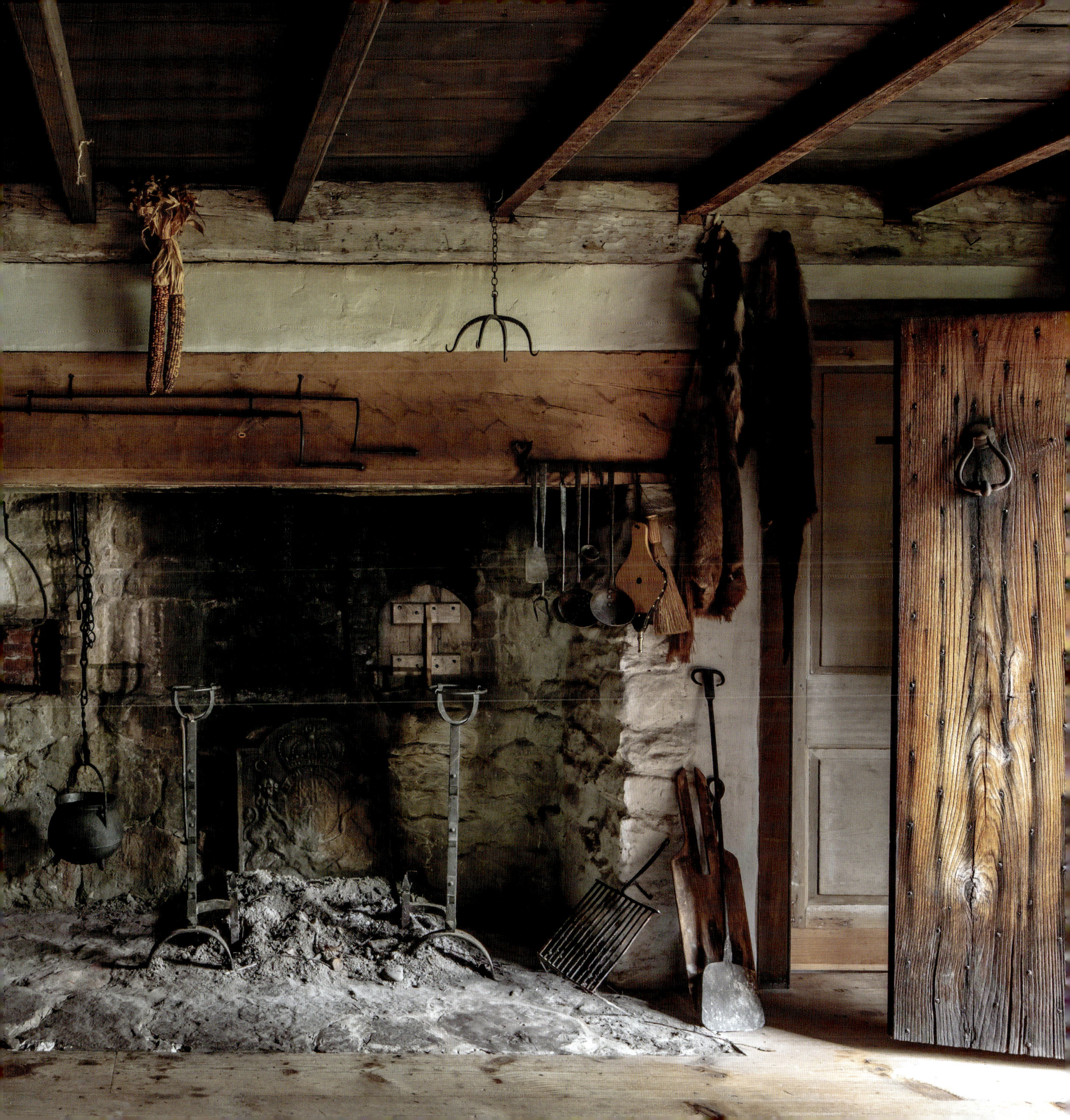

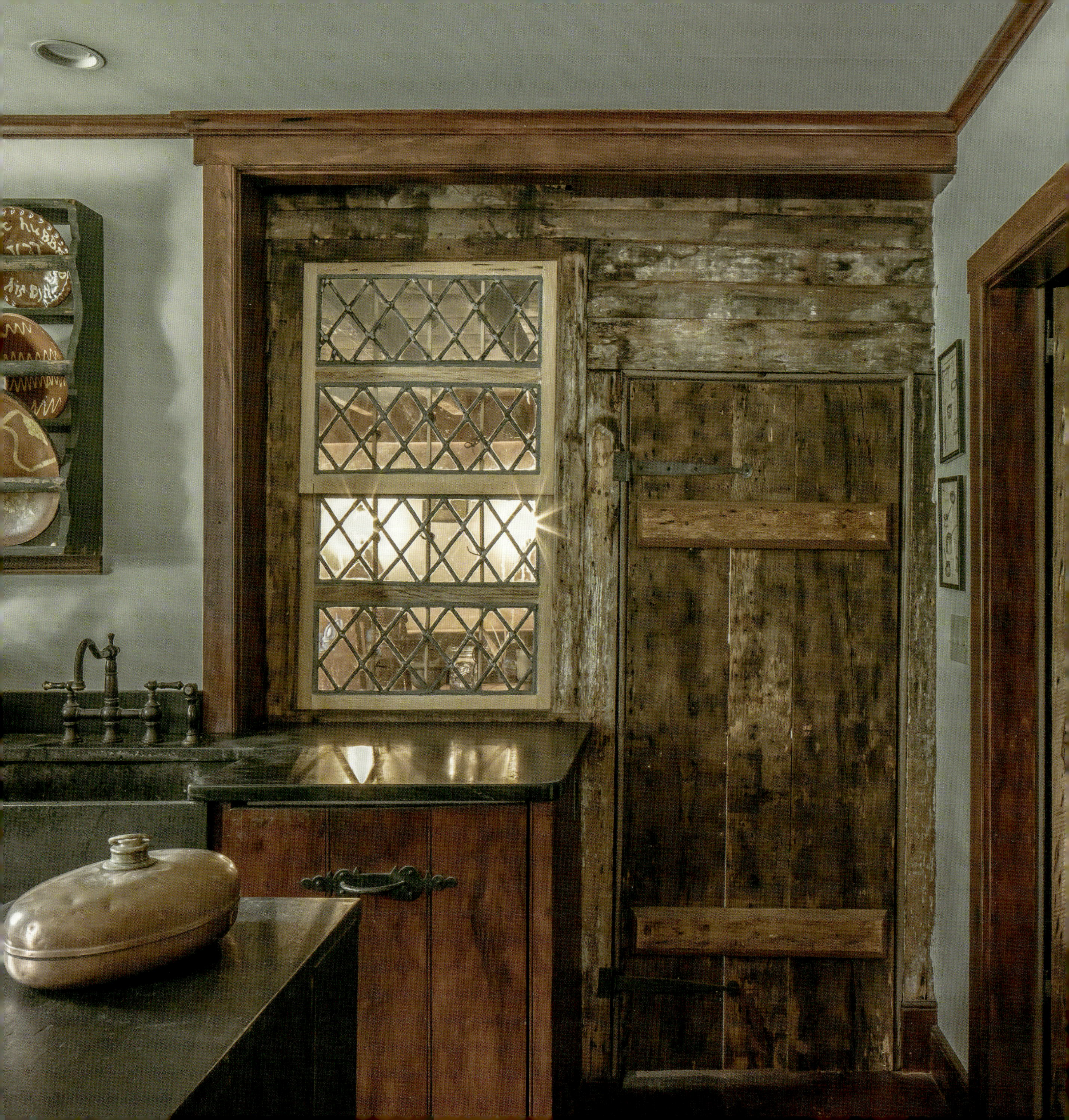

Eager to find evidence of the original exterior, the Courchaines moved into a motel so a restoration contractor could proceed. Once the wall framing was completely exposed, the location, size, and shape of the original window and door openings were apparent. They even found nail holes where the hinges of the original casement windows had been secured. The most significant find was along the north girt where a number of contiguous mortises were empty. These mortises originally held the ends of rafters, which were removed when a masonry chimney was built inside the frame. This meant the frame was assembled during the earliest days of the settlement when houses were heated by temporary wattle and daub (stick and mud) chimneys built outside the end wall.

The kitchen was added in 2005.

It could be that this house frame was made in Massachusetts, transported by ship, and assembled here, as was done with the house erected by the Plymouth Colony in Windsor in 1633. Or it could be that this frame was made in Wethersfield by a Massachusetts carpenter. In any case, the fact that the frame was erected without an interior chimney indicated the Hubbard House dated from the earliest days of Wethersfield's settlement.

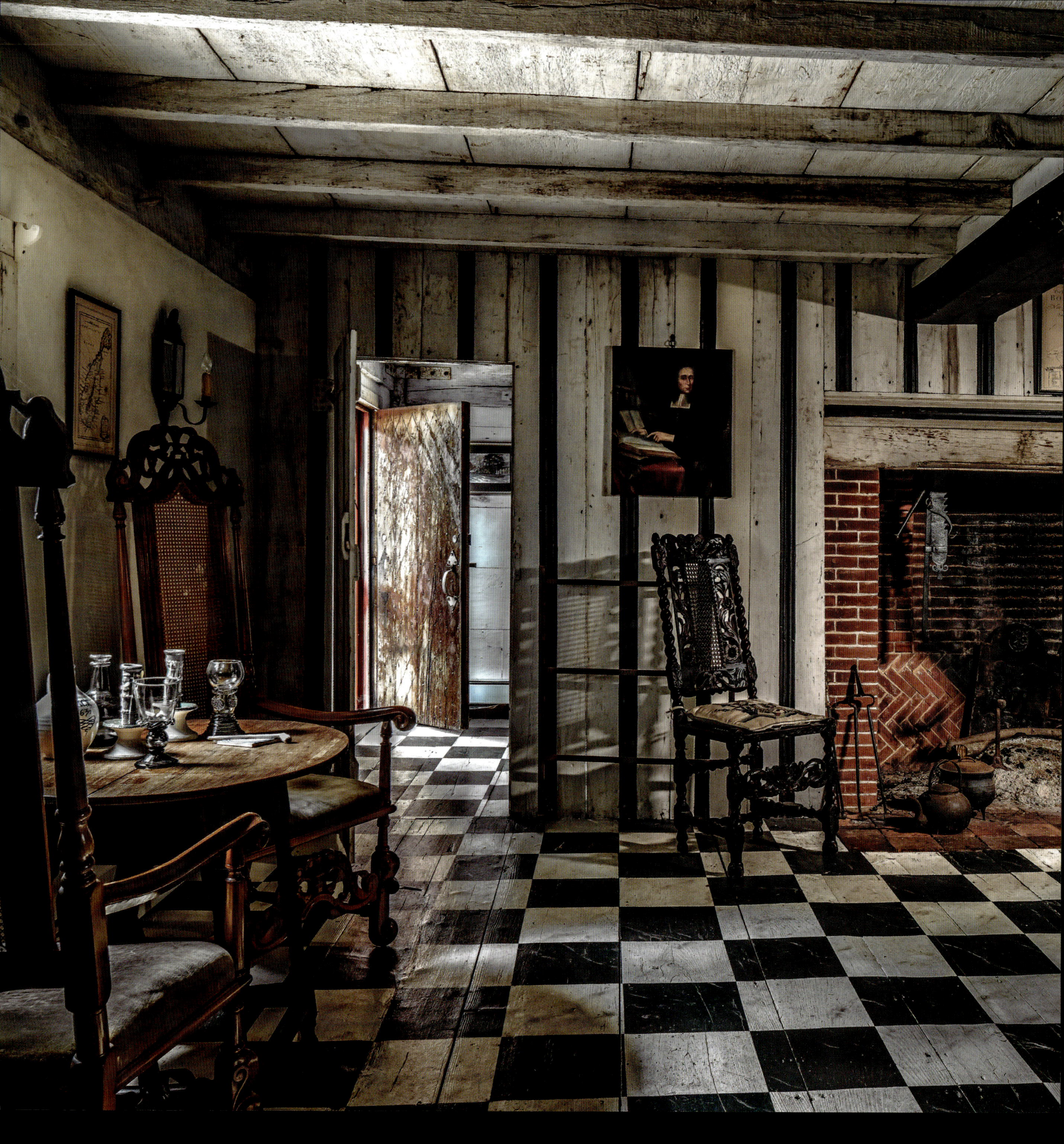

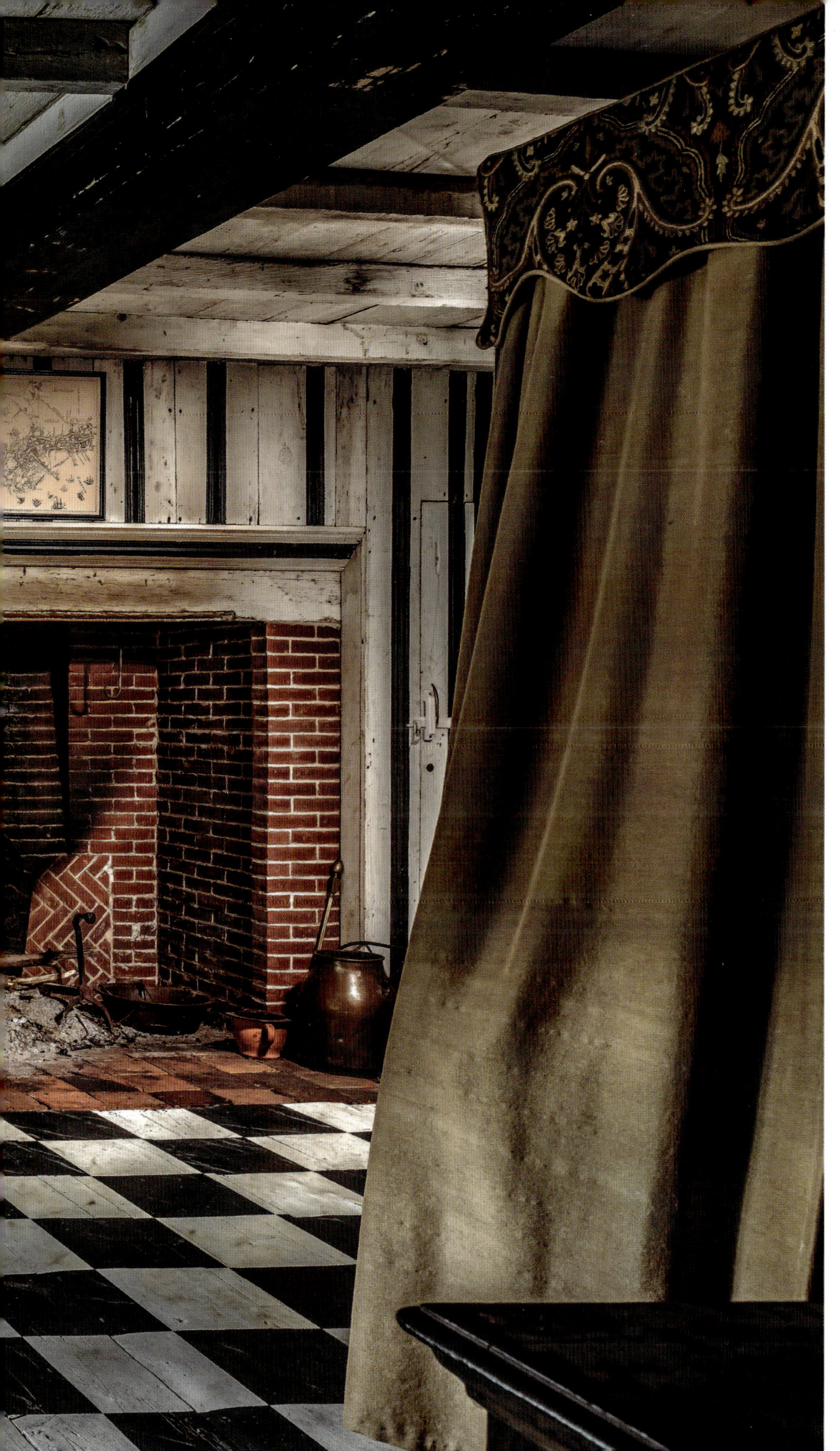

The hall of the 1685 Ipswich house with its restored fireplace.

According to the Wethersfield Land Records, the house stood on the northern part of a three-acre home lot belonging to George Hubbard in 1640, the first year town land records were kept. Hubbard, sufficiently conversant in the local Algonkian tongue, was designated as the negotiator for the purchase of corn from the Wangunks. He served as the translator when the proprietors purchased land from the tribe in 1636, and he was also appointed to collect the tax on beaver skins.

The massively framed summer beam in the hall of the Hubbard House.

Not many years after initial construction, Hubbard extended the rear slope of the original roof to cover an additional room against the rear wall of the house. This new room included a stairway that began close to the new back wall and ascended at an angle parallel to the slope of the extended roof until it reached a door in the rear wall of the front chamber. When a masonry chimney was finally built inside the frame, it included a fireplace for both ground-floor rooms.

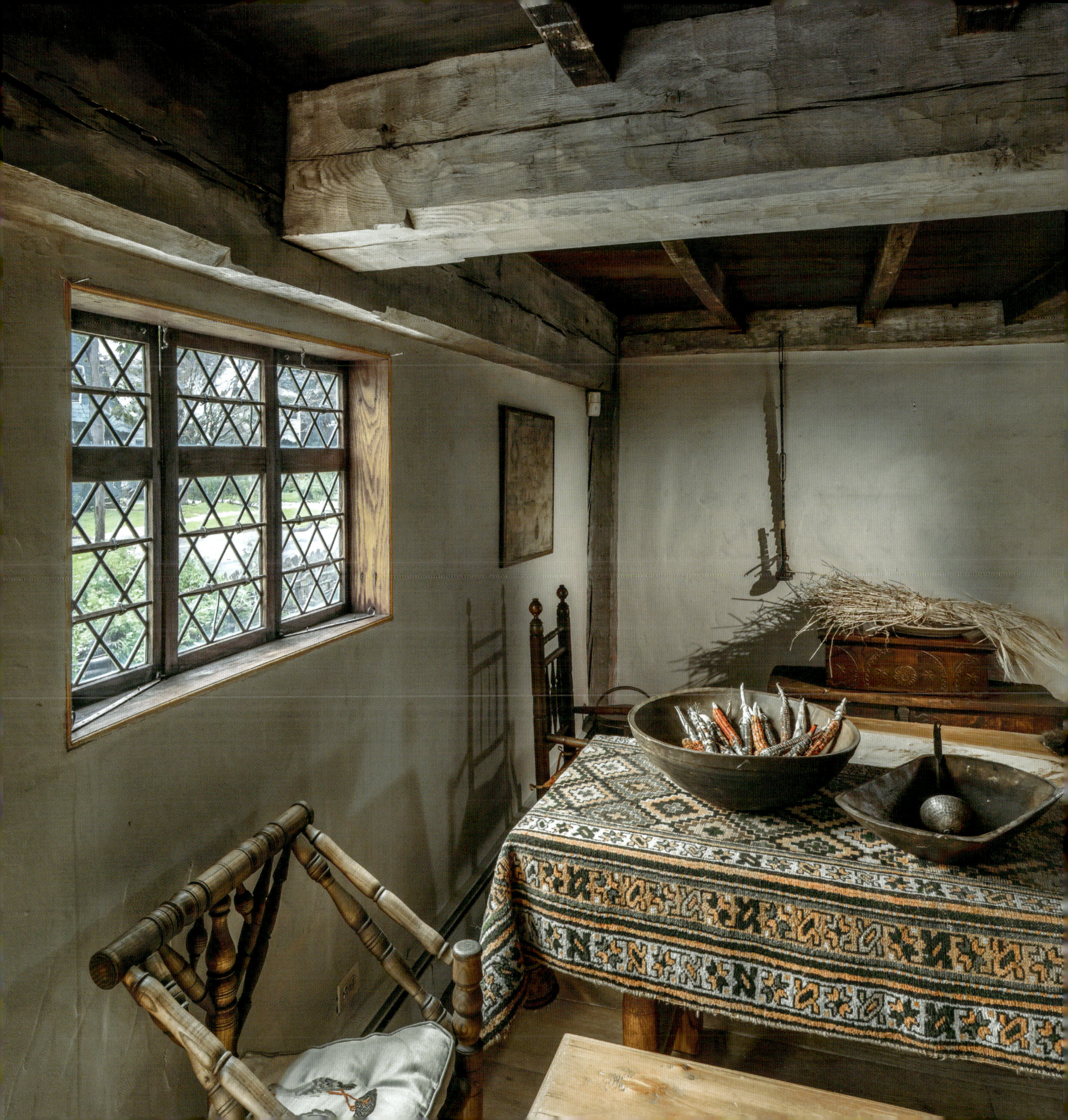

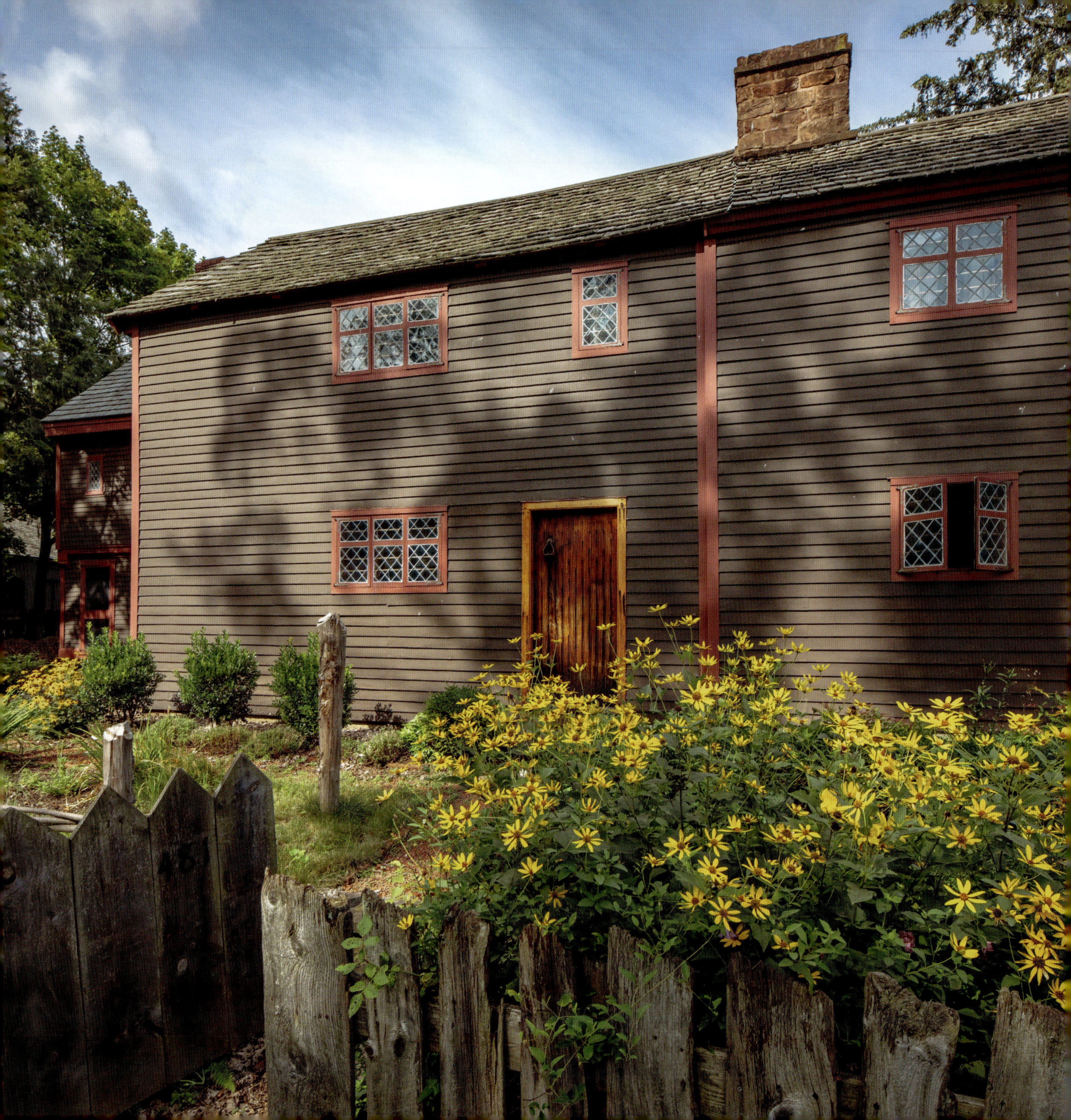

Although Hubbard eventually moved to another town, his house remained in the family for several generations. In 1662, his son sold the three-acre property (now 481 and 471 Main Street) with "a dwelling house thereon standing" and a "new house frame" to John Blackleach. (WLR 1/221) When the Blackleach house burned down, it was replaced by the brick house at 471 Main Street.

The Hubbard House is a restored seventeenth century treasure.

The restoration of the Hubbard House required the installation of footings, a foundation, and new sills. The crew restored the exterior with oak clapboards, a board and batten door, and casement windows. The end wall had a single casement in the attic and double casements on the first and second floors. The front wall had triple casements on both floors and a single, off-center casement window over the board and batten door. In the interior, the exposed sections of the original frame were cleaned and varnished. Modern electrical, plumbing, and insulation were concealed beneath new lath and plaster walls.

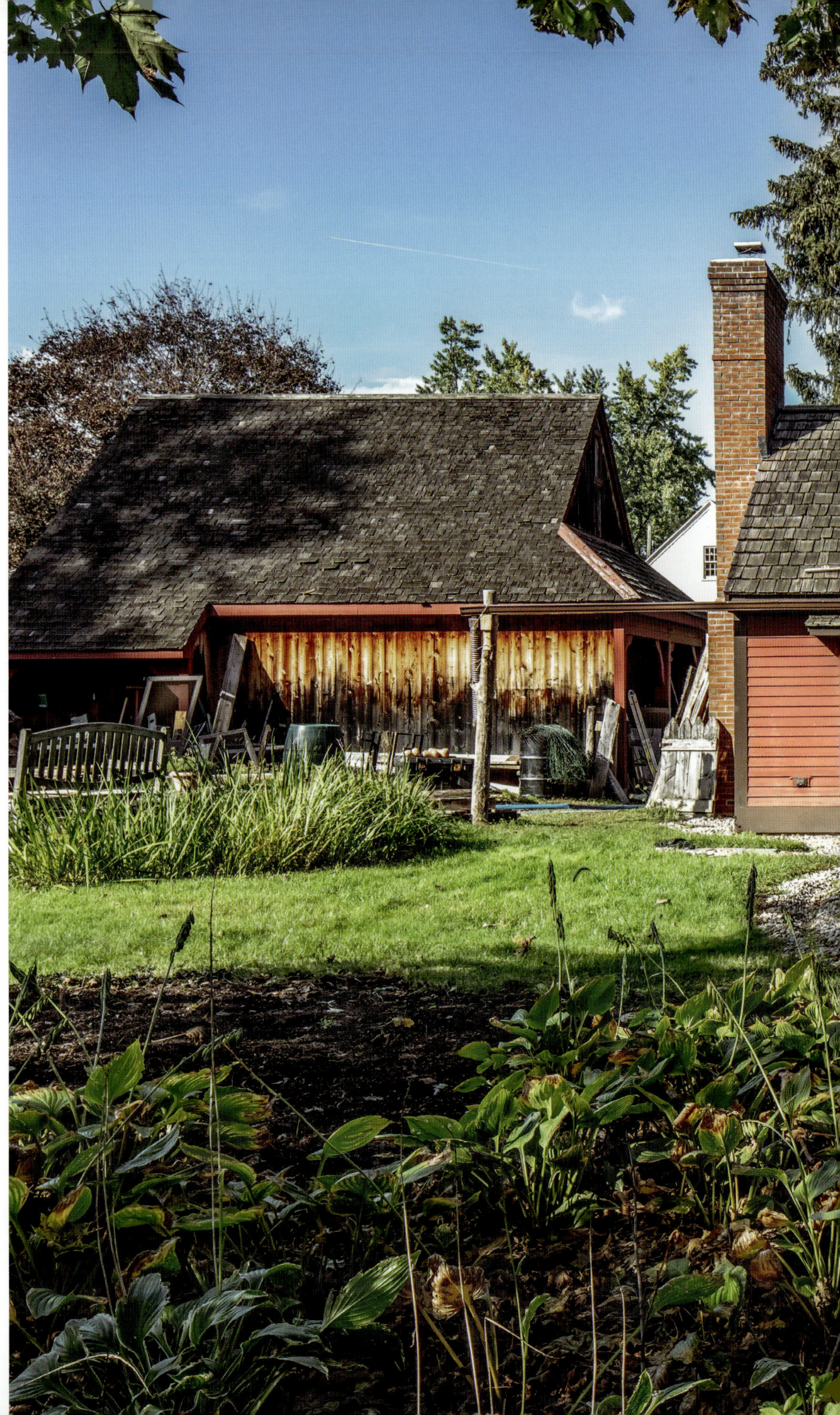

The rear of the house showing the door into the 2005 kitchen and sitting room addition.

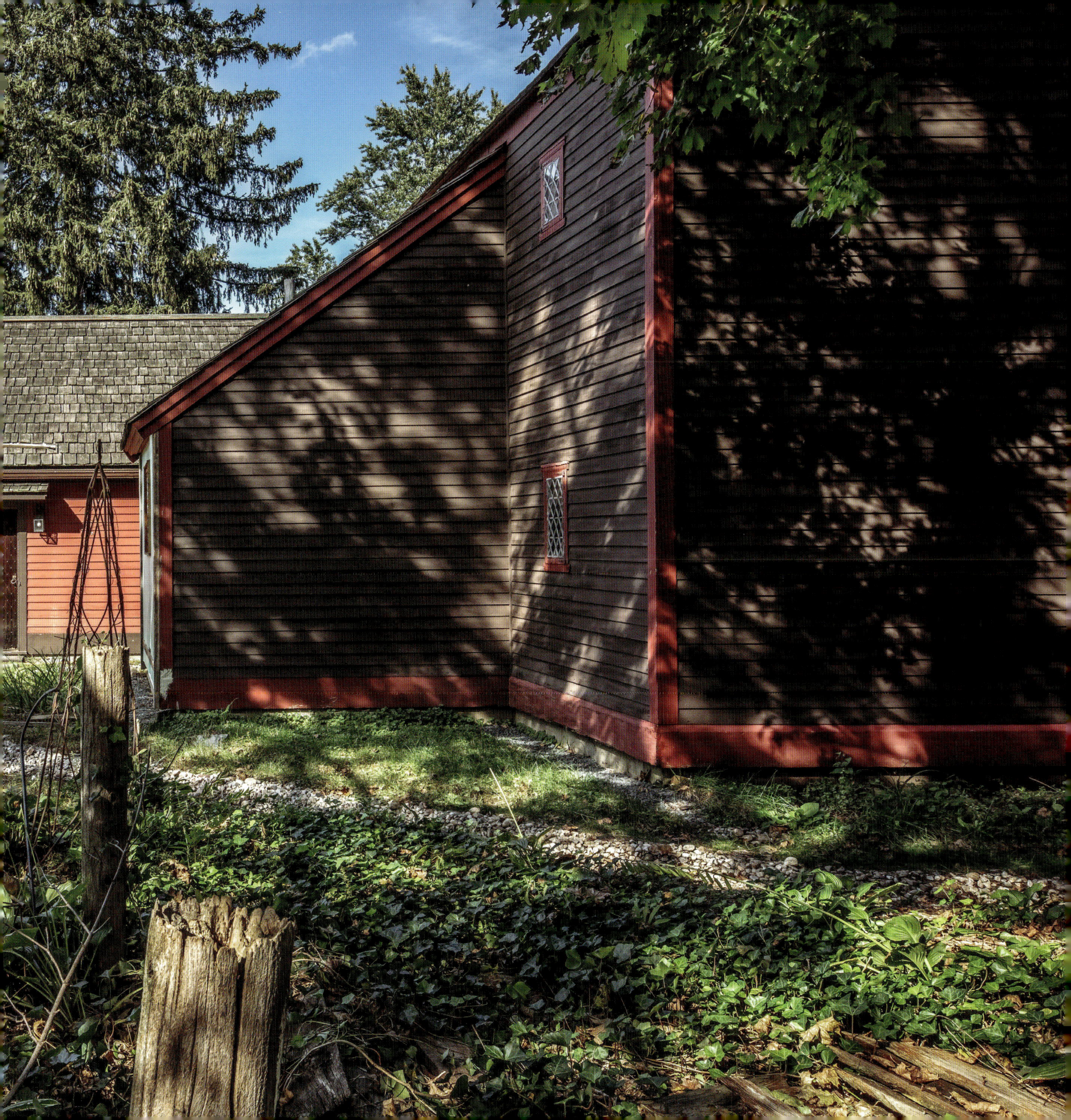

During the 1980s, the Courchaines replaced the one-story bedroom addition, constructed on the south side of the house during the 1950s, with a seventeenth-century two-story house from Ipswich, Massachusetts, which they had purchased in pieces from a dealer in Concord. The reassembled house looks right at home next to its Wethersfield counterpart.

The Courchaines questioned how to treat the sunroom and bedroom, which had been added to the north side of the house during the 1920s. They proposed, and the Historic District Commission agreed, that this early twentieth-century section should be remodeled in the same Jacobean style as the seventeenth-century part of the house.

The chamber of the Hubbard house — the great beam and joists are chamfered.

The Courchaines' professional restoration and sensitive remodeling of the George Hubbard House was a labor of love, undertaken in stages over a span of almost thirty-five years. They restored the identity and character of the town's oldest dwelling and also incorporated its aesthetic in the design of the additions made to accommodate modern living. ♛

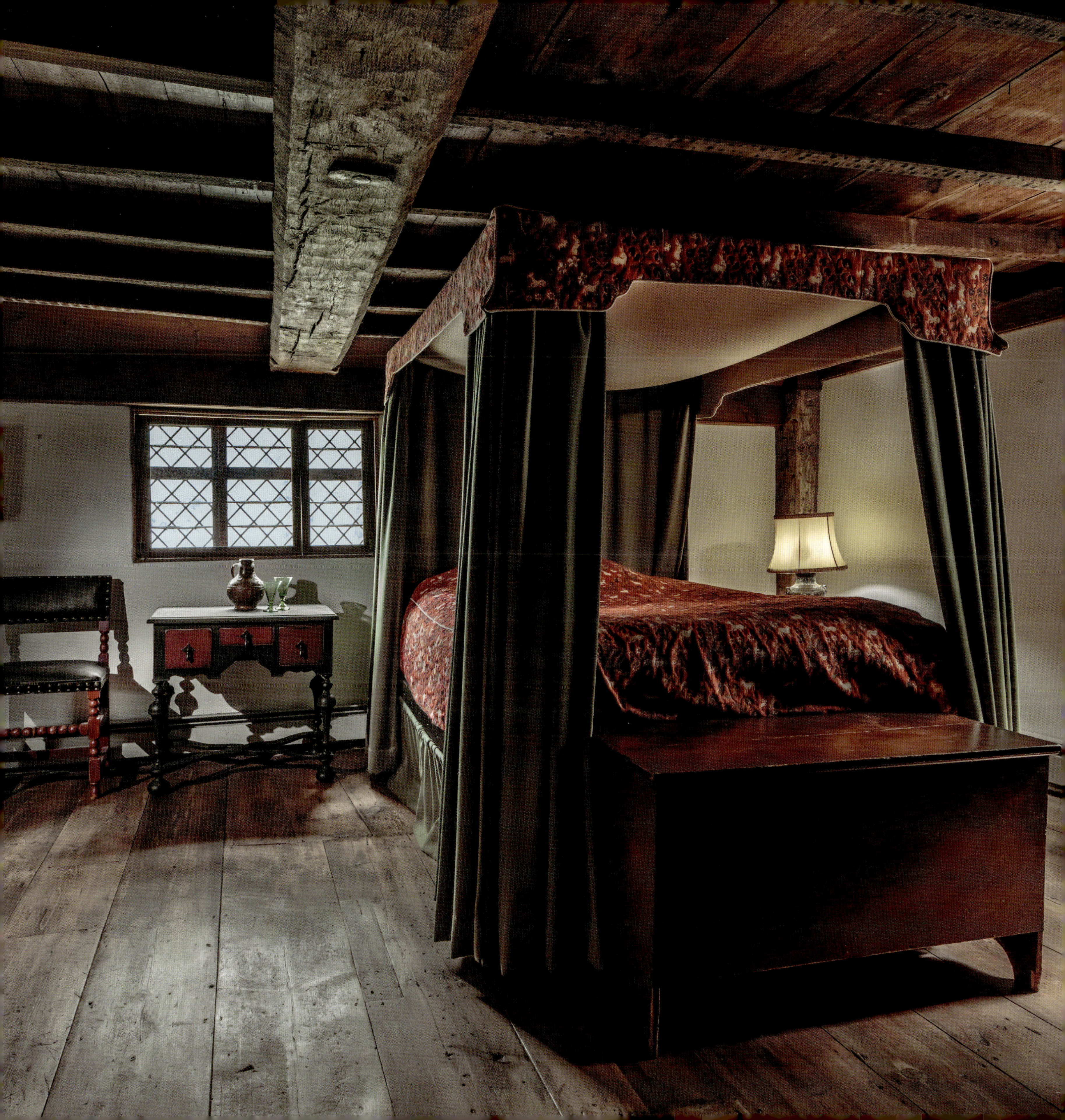

AN ENDURING CENTER OF CIVIC LIFE

Wethersfield High School (Keeney Memorial Cultural Center)

— 200 Main Street —

In 1893, the town of Wethersfield purchased two and a half acres from William G. Comstock of Comstock, Ferre & Co. to erect a brick and brownstone building as the new high school. It was designed by Hartford architect Brooks M. Lincoln, who designed the impressive Venetian Gothic-detailed Masonic Temple on Ann Street in Hartford. In 1916, the town added a wing on either side. A new high school was built on the Silas Deane Highway in 1929, and this structure became Center School, an elementary school. It was renamed for Governor Thomas Welles in 1933. In addition to its operation as a school, the building was used for town and public meetings and for the town court. It later housed the Historical Society's first museum, the draft and rationing boards during World War II, the public library, board of education offices, and, until 1958, served as Town Hall.

Wethersfield's junior and senior high school — the gracious curving entrance stairs and fountain were added in 2000.

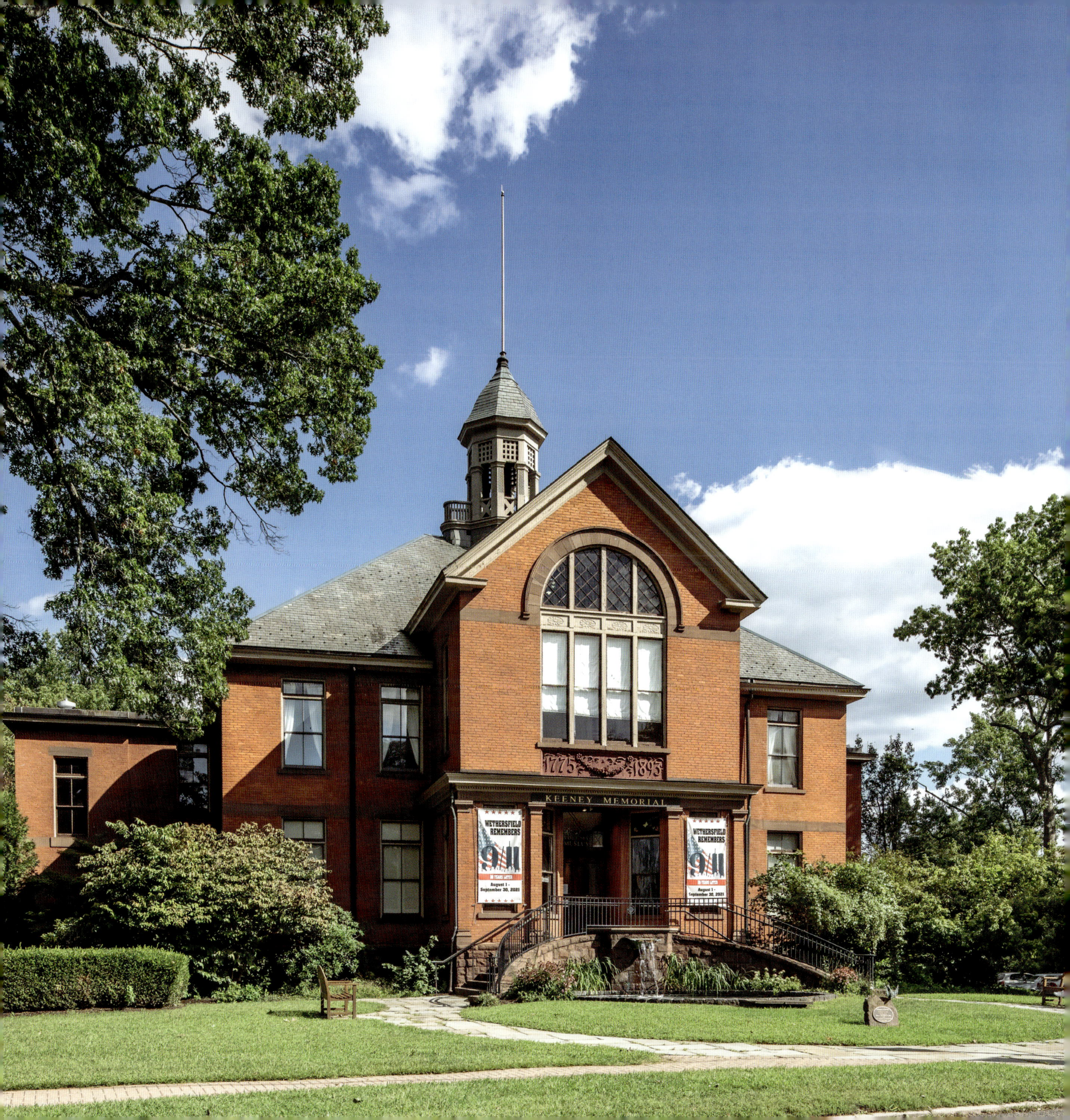
1775
1893
KEENEY MEMORIAL
WETHERSFIELD REMEMBERS
9/11
20 YEARS LATER
August 1 - September 30, 2021
WETHERSFIELD REMEMBERS
9/11
20 YEARS LATER
August 1 - September 30, 2021

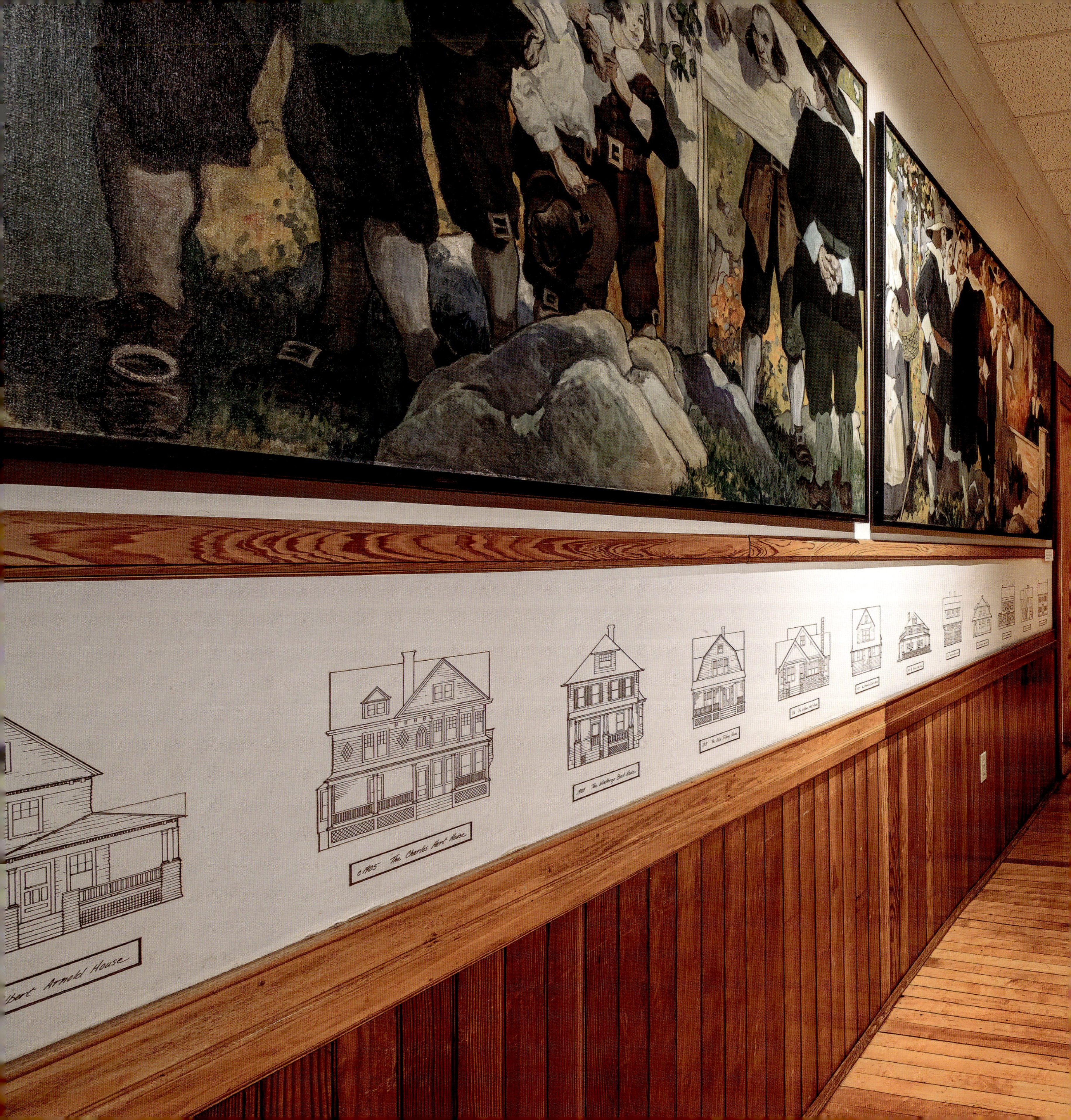
Arnold House
c1905 The Charles Hart House

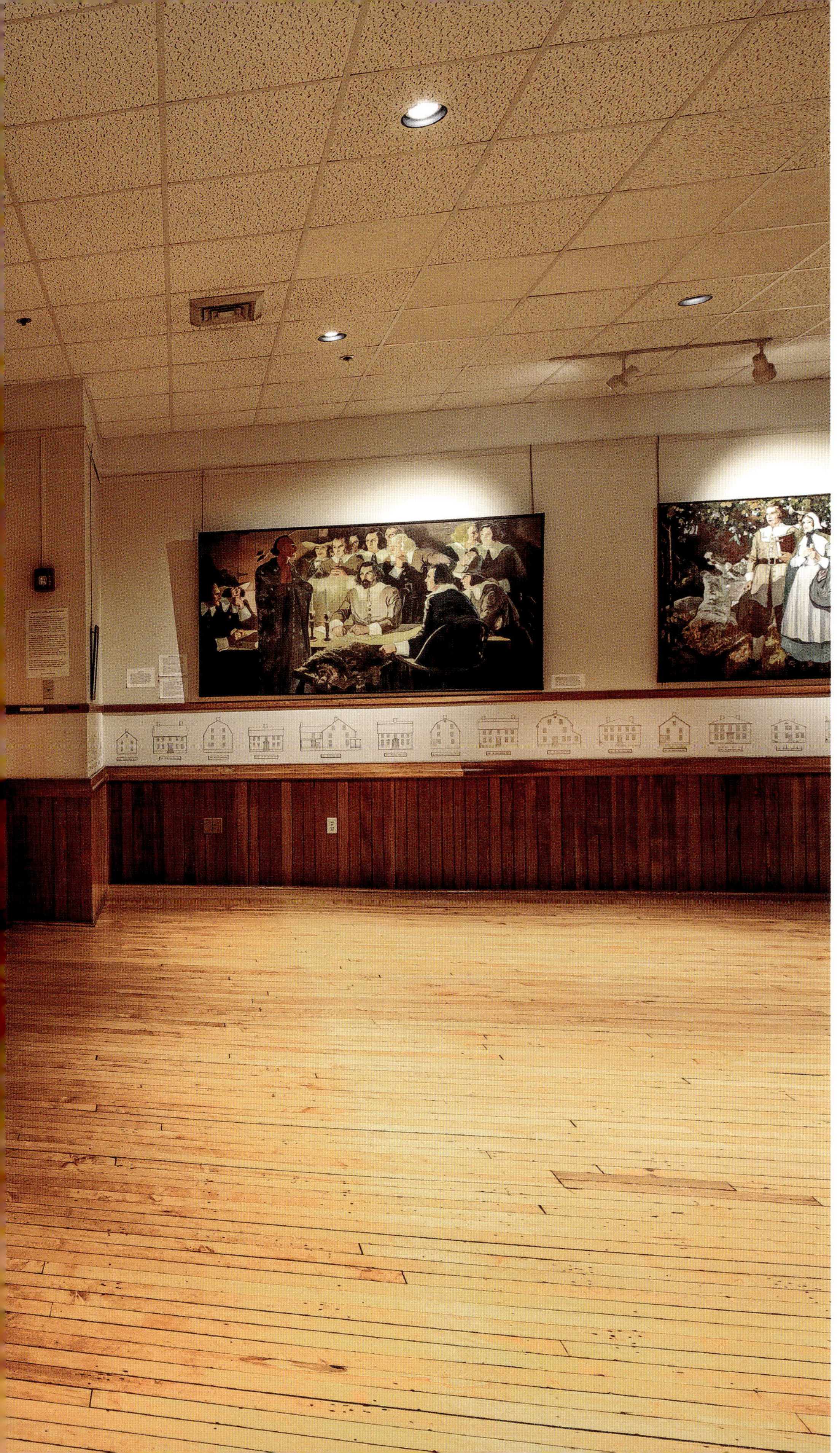

The Rotary Room houses five WPA paintings by Ralph Lewis Nelson and Anne Crofoot Kuckro's elevations of the façades, titled 300 Years of Domestic Architecture.

The Board of Education moved its offices out of both this building and the Henry Deming House at 222 Main Street in 1983, leaving two vacant, surplus town buildings in the center of the Historic District. The Historical Society board saw an opportunity to provide a needed museum and meeting space in the high school and a restaurant in the Deming House to serve the town and visitors. Both would also bring foot traffic and activity back to the town center.

The Society's ambitious and comprehensive redevelopment proposal to the town for the two properties was accepted, and its investment and commitment spurred the revitalization of the once moribund center, generating decades of increasing property values and tax revenues, new businesses and restaurants, an untold number of building permits, new construction activity, and increased visitation.

The Society's permanent exhibit on Wethersfield History.

The redevelopment of the Keeney was conceived in 1983 as a 350th anniversary gift to the town. However, the building didn't open until 1990 after renovations, which included extensive interior changes, a new elevator, all new mechanicals, three gallery spaces, an education classroom, function space, and a hall for cultural concerts and events. The building was named the Keeney Memorial Cultural Center in honor of Ensign Robert Allan Keeney, one of the town's last casualties of World War II. Keeney perished in the sinking of the cruiser Indianapolis, which resulted in the greatest loss of life at sea from a single ship in US Naval history.

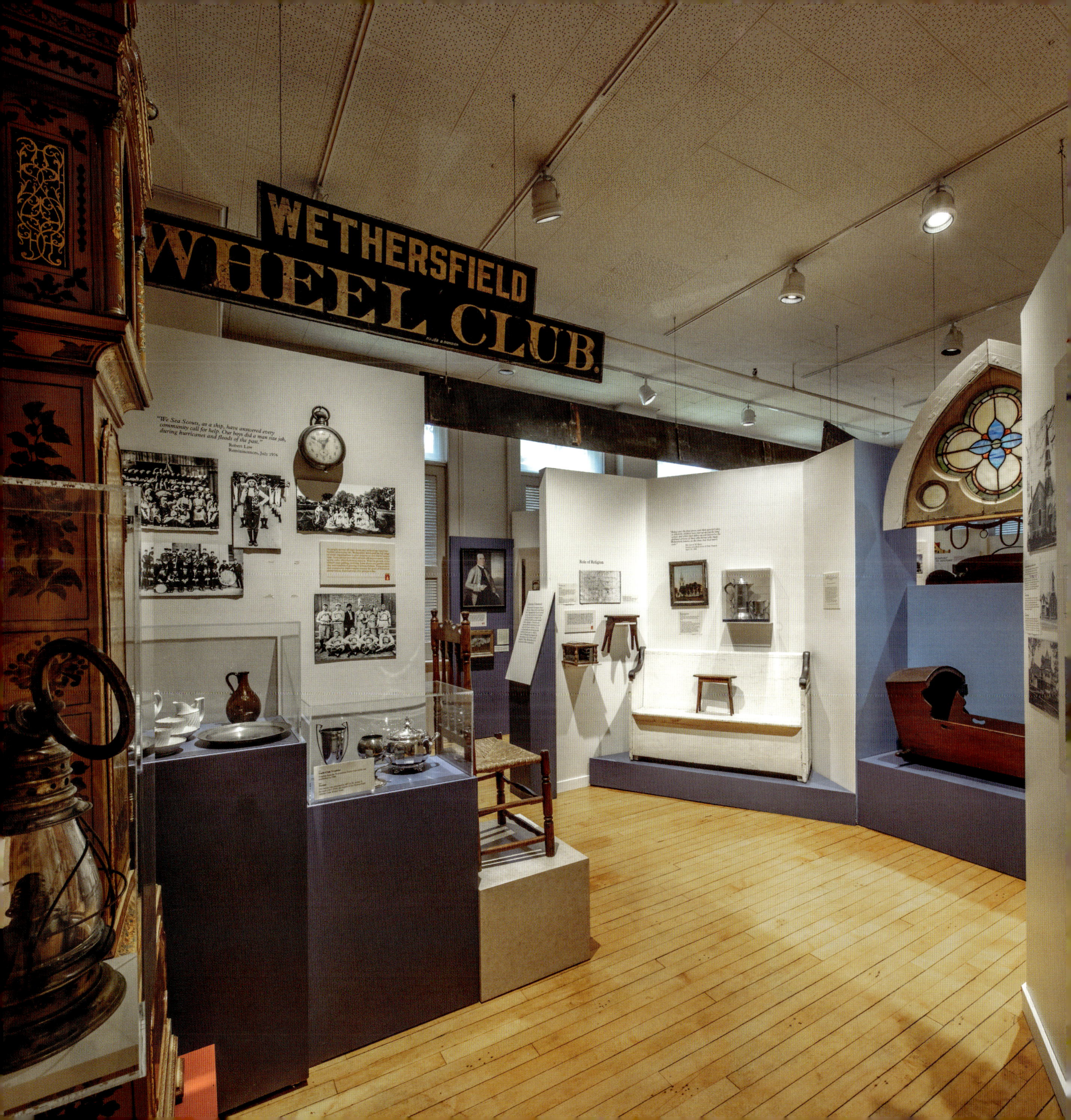
WETHERSFIELD
WHEEL CLUB.
"We Sea Scouts, as a ship, have answered every community call for help. Our boys did a man size job, during hurricanes and floods of the past."
Robert Low
Reminiscences, July 1976
Role of Religion

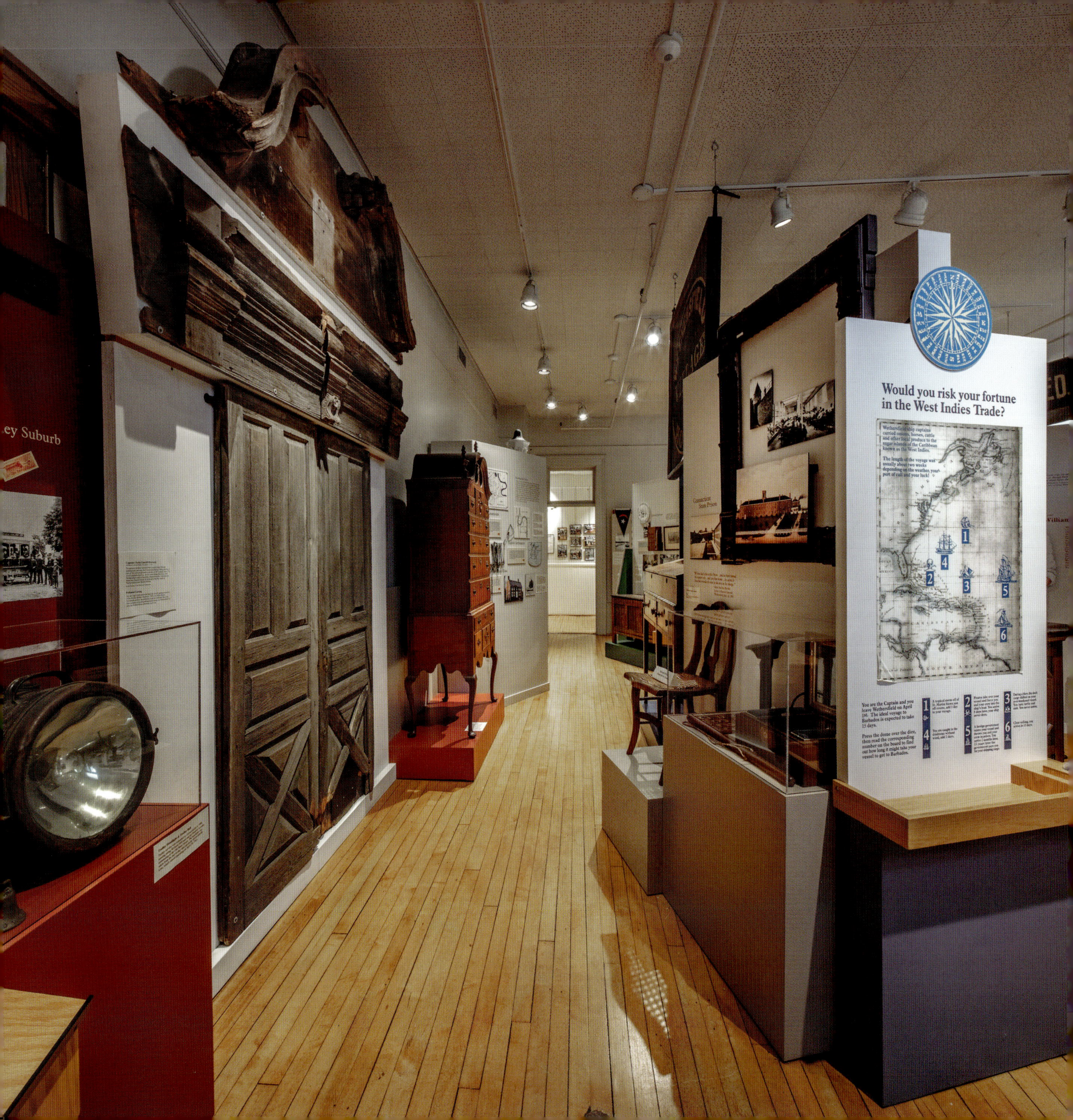
Would you risk your fortune
in the West Indies Trade?

The Historical Society continued to enhance the building. In 1999, the original 1894 narrow recessed brownstone stairs designed for the high school were replaced with a welcoming front entrance, fountain, and garden designed by landscape architects CR3 as more appropriate for the Museum and Cultural Center. In 2017, the Society enhanced the rear entrance with a sheltering canopy, brick pavers, and seating area.

The exhibit includes, mounted on the left, the surviving iconic scroll and pedimented doorway of the Captain Charles Churchill House.

The Keeney is home to the Wethersfield Museum and showcases the Historical Society's permanent exhibit about the town's history: *Wethersfield: Legendary People, Ordinary Lives* and the award-winning exhibit *Castle on the Cove: The Connecticut State Prison and Wethersfield*, as well as changing exhibits.

The Keeney also houses five Works Progress Administration, Federal Arts Project paintings by Ralph Lewis Nelson (1885–1967). They were created in 1936, only two years after the town's tercentenary celebration, which expressed civic pride as Connecticut's "most Auncient Towne." (Adams and Stiles 1904) The paintings, depicting Wethersfield's settlement and early town life, are colorful, romantic, Colonial Revival visions of history and were originally hung in the town's elementary schools. One, "The Public Mart," was hung in the Keeney when it was the Governor Thomas Welles School.

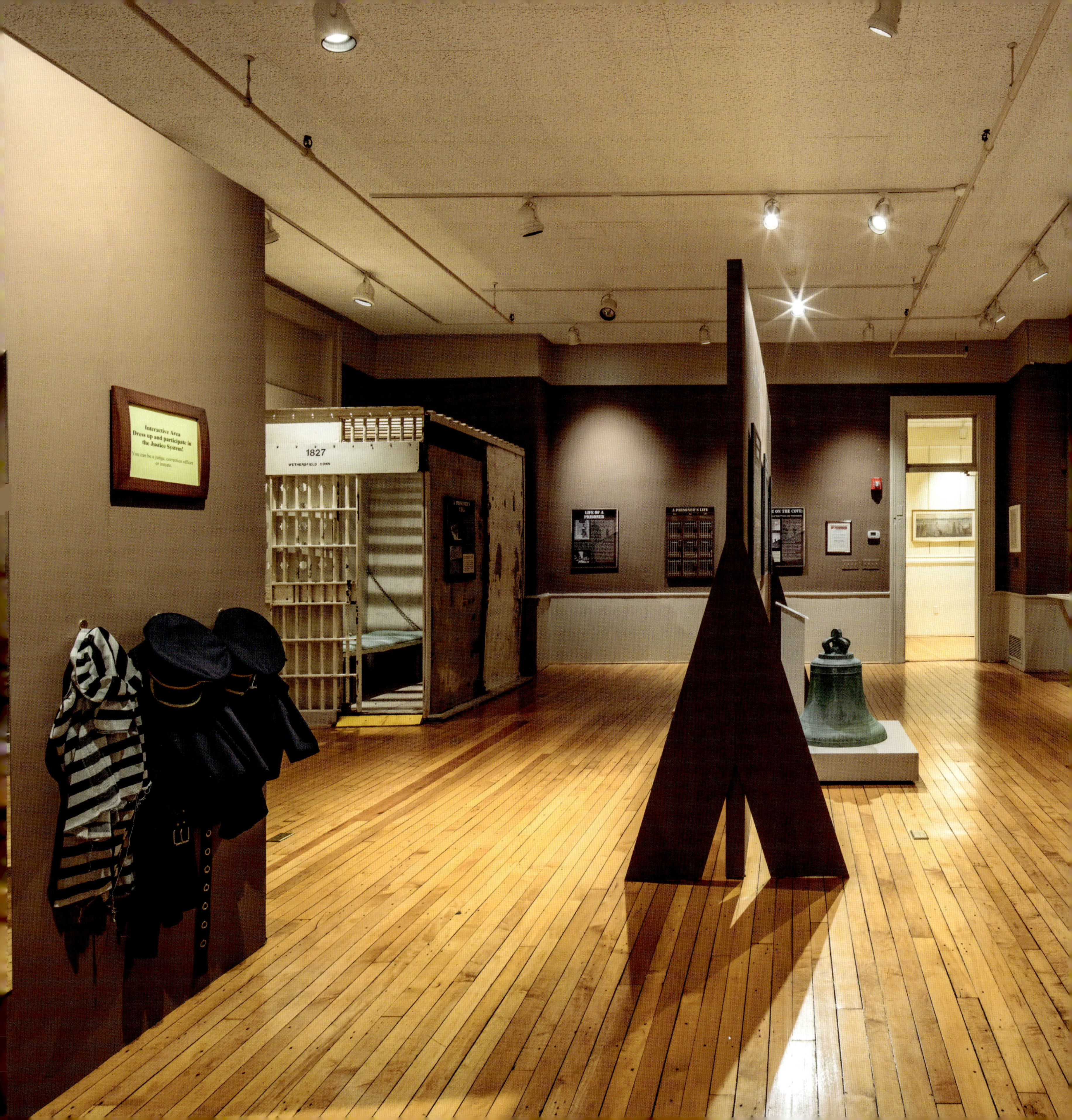
Interactive Area
Dress up and participate in
the Justice System!
1827
WETHERSFIELD CONN
LIFE OF A PRISONER
A PRISONER'S LIFE

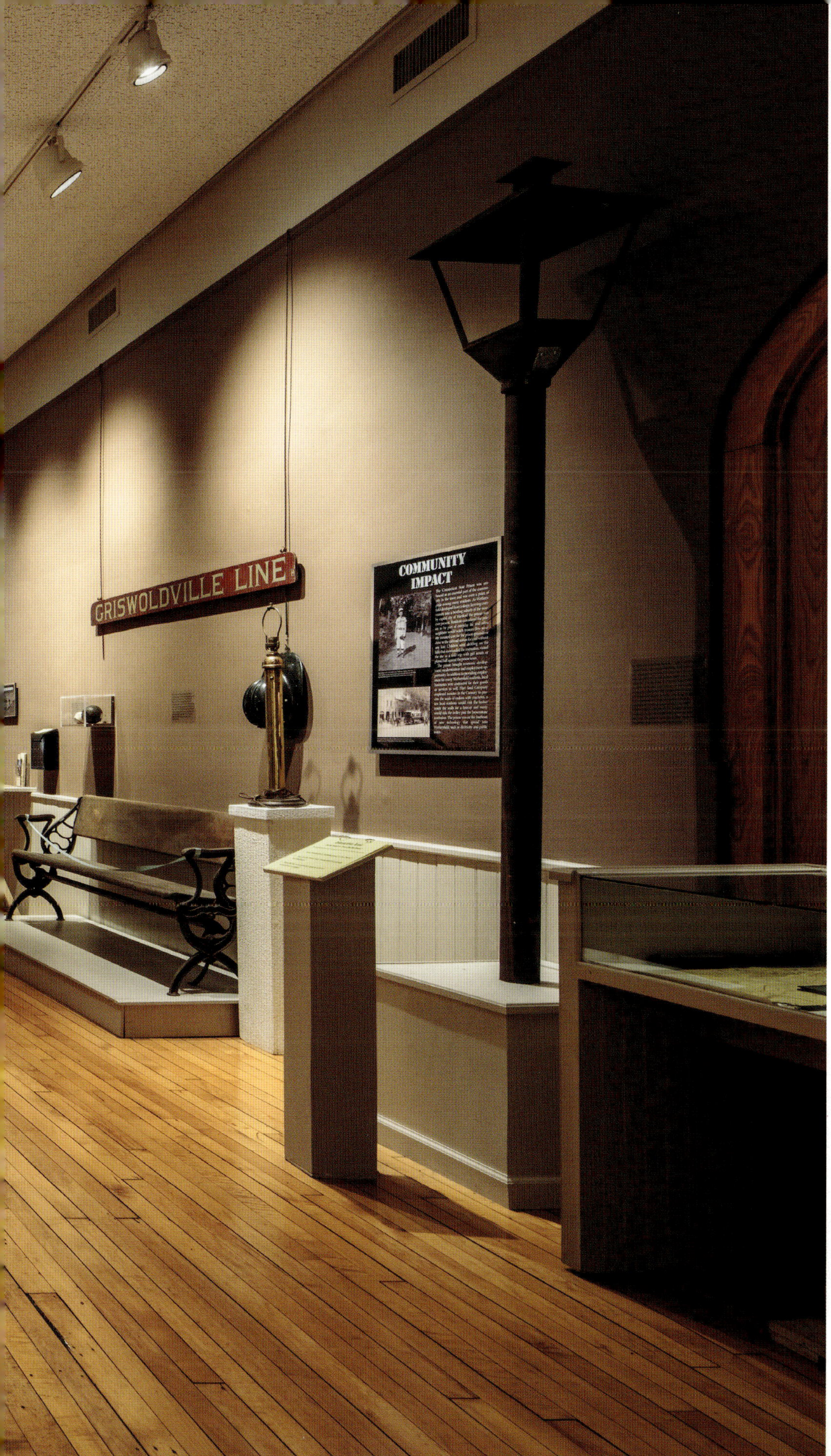

The exhibit Castle on the Cove — The Connecticut State Prison and Wethersfield.

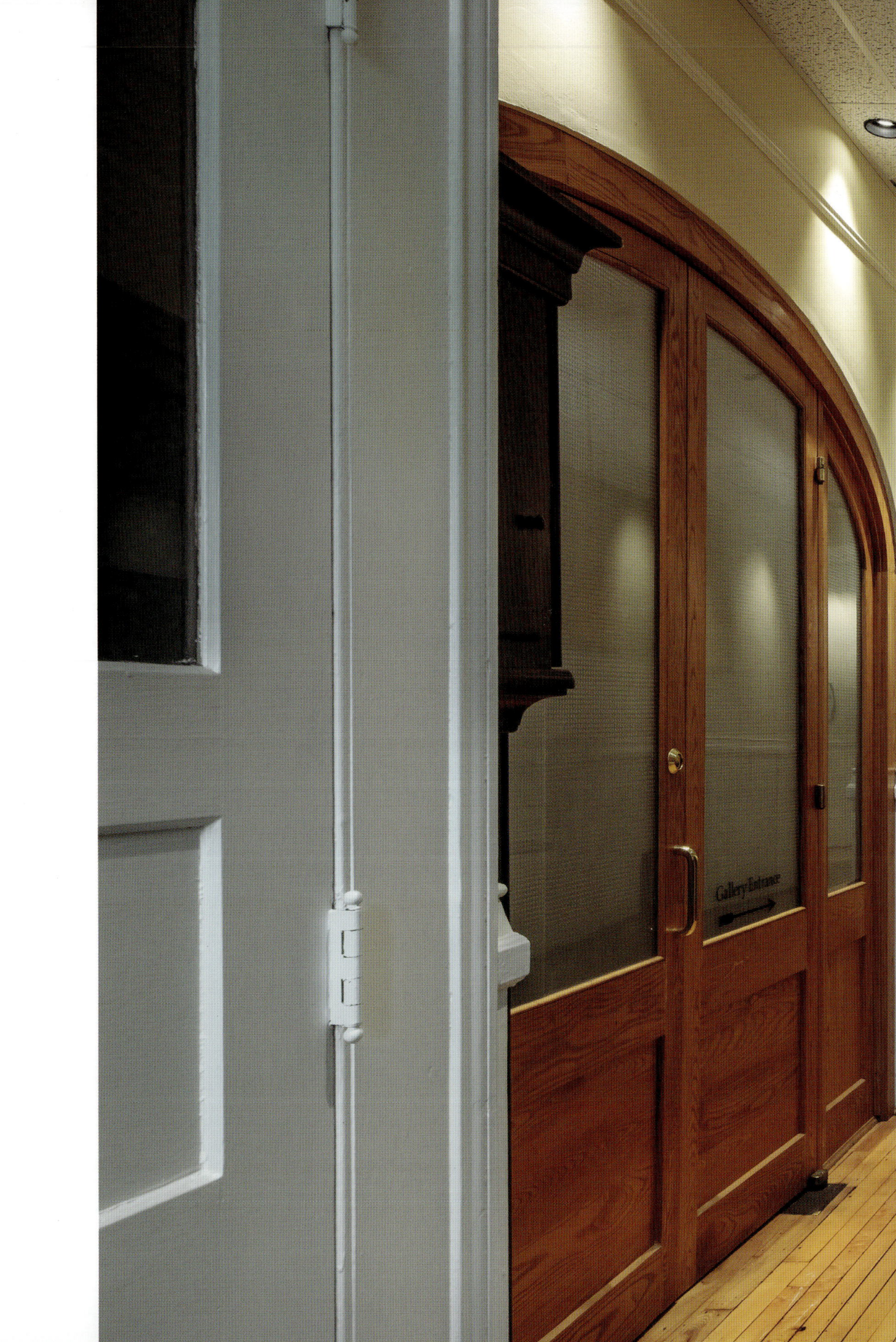

A view of the entrance hallway of the Keeney Memorial Cultural Center.

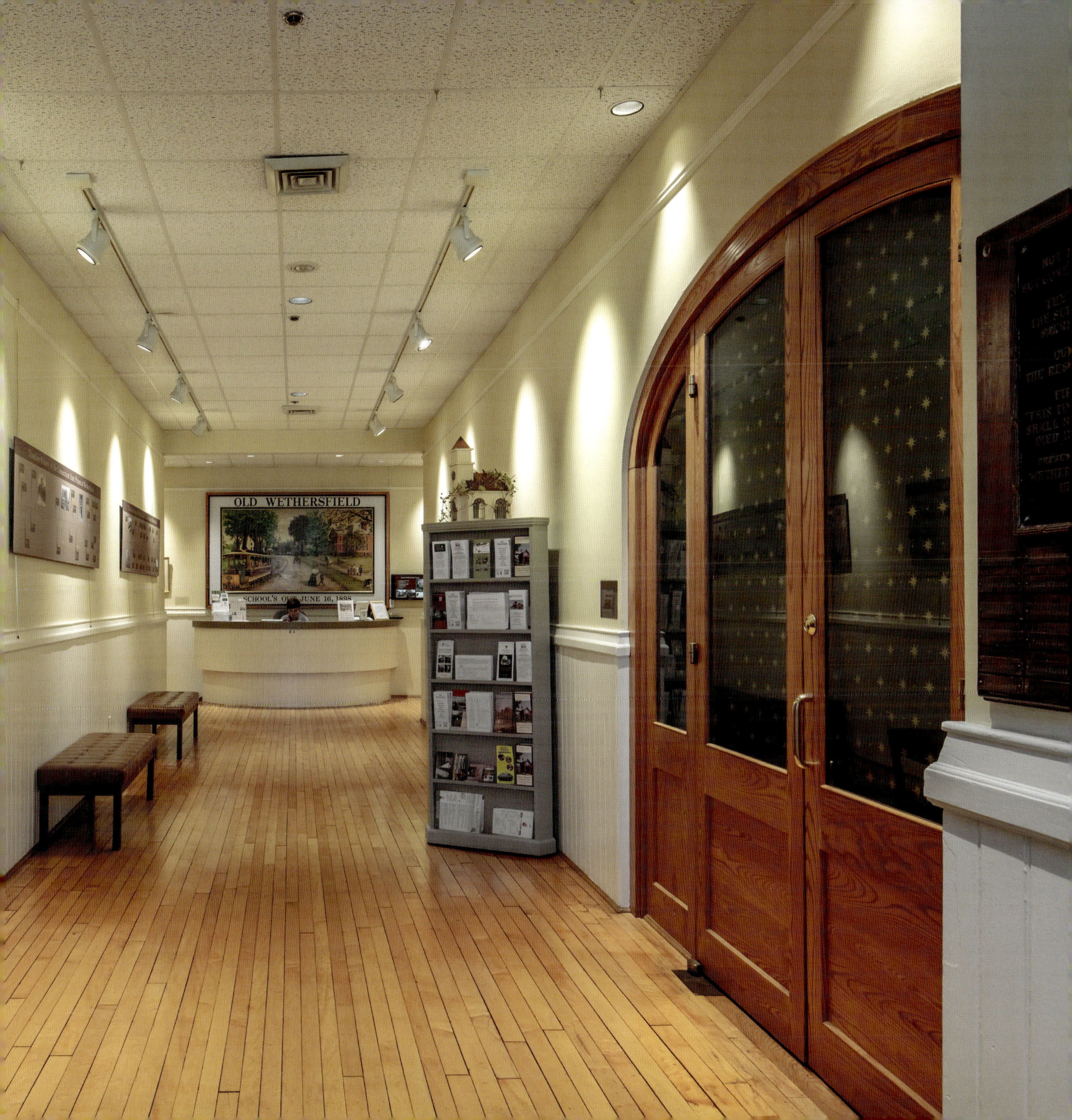
OLD WETHERSFIELD
SCHOOL'S OUT JUNE 16, 1898

The ballroom was originally an assembly room and auditorium.

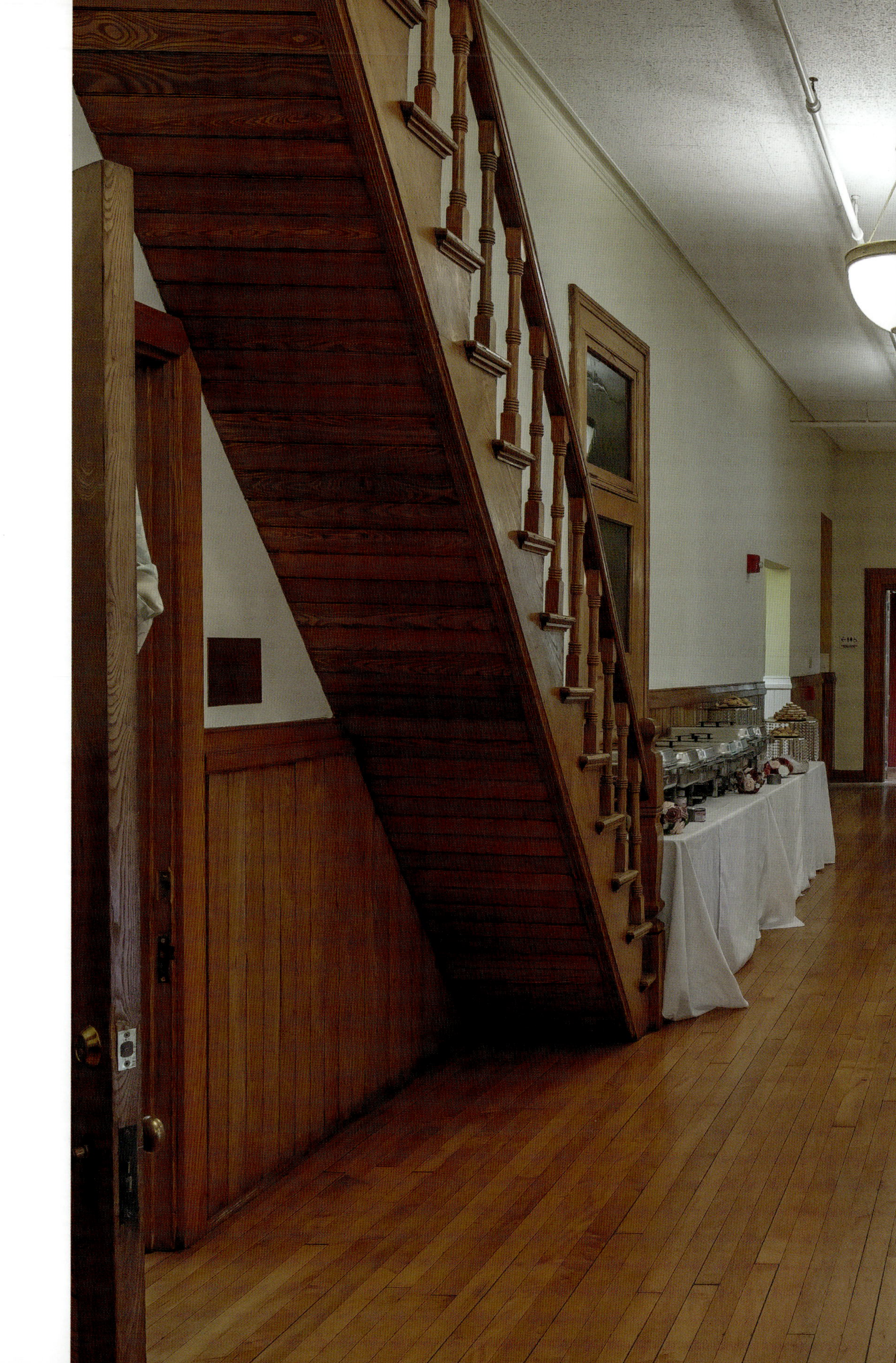

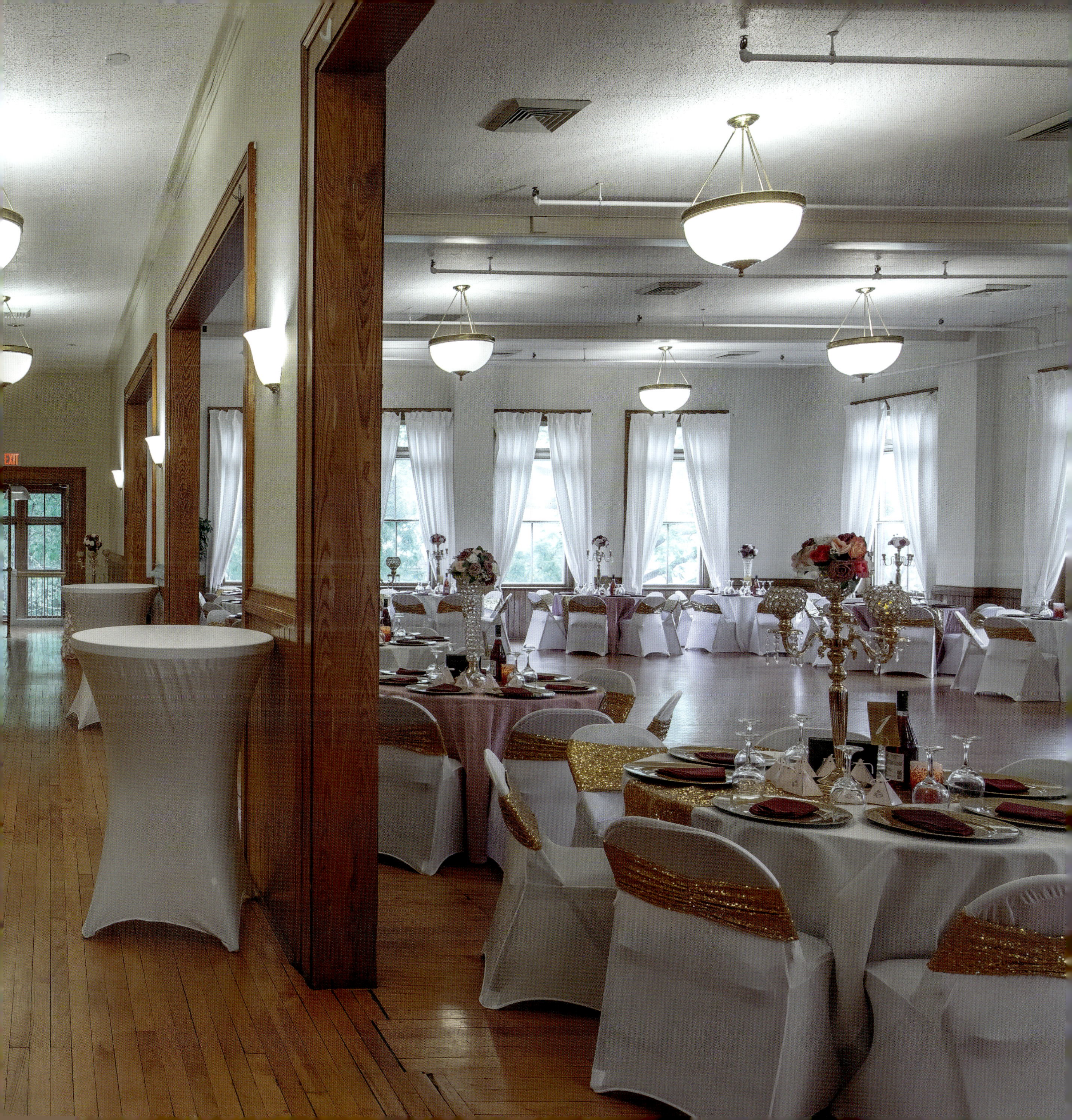
EXIT

The Board of Education placed four of the paintings on permanent loan to the Wethersfield Historical Society in 1996 for display at the Keeney. A missing fifth painting was sent to the Society in 2022 and was restored and reunited with the other Nelson paintings.

In the same gallery as the Nelson paintings is an architectural frieze, *300 Years of Domestic Architecture 1637–1937*, with Anne Crofoot Kuckro's (1945–2010) elevations of houses from each decade.

The south stairway is in one of the wings that was added in 1916.

The Keeney Memorial Cultural Center welcomes business, community, and social groups to use its meeting spaces and facilities in the heart of the state's largest historic district. ♛

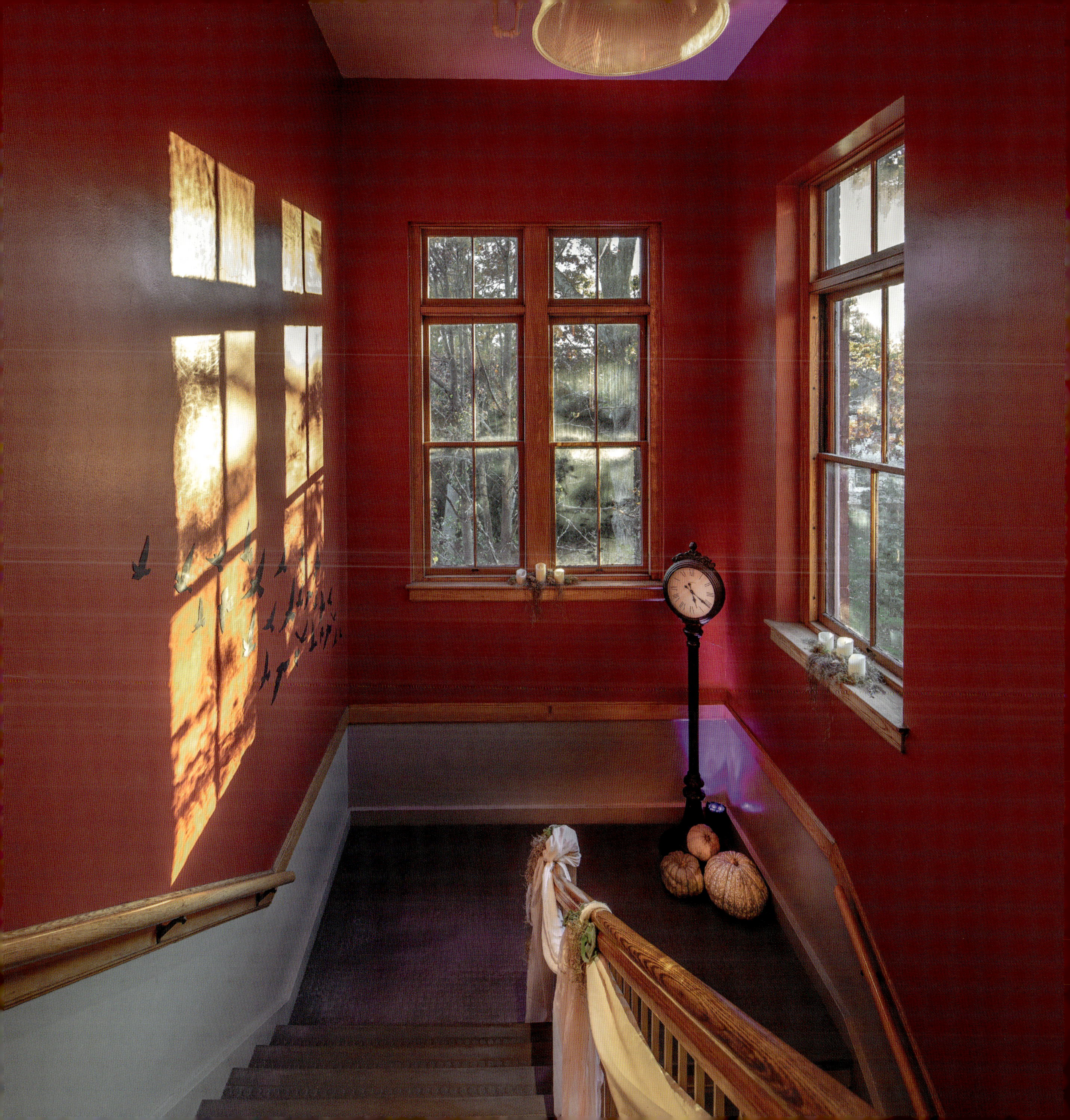

NINETEENTH-CENTURY SPLENDOR, BREAKFAST INCLUDED

Silas W. Robbins House

— 185 Broad Street —

Silas W. Robbins (1822–1910) operated a general store with his brother, Richard, and served as treasurer and then director of the Wethersfield Novelty Company. Robbins was one of the incorporators of the Willimantic Linen Company along with Elisha Johnson, who was the first manufacturer of linen thread in the United States. They later worked to incorporate the Merrick Thread Company in Holyoke, Massachusetts.

The triumphantly restored Silas W. Robbins House — the porte cochere is on the right.

Robbins married Johnson's daughter, Sophia Jane, in 1854. The next year, the father-in-law formed the Johnson, Robbins & Co. seed business with Robbins and his two brothers. Robbins started breeding Jersey cattle in 1859 and was one of the most successful breeders of fine stock in the country; he was one of the founders of the American Jersey Cattle Club. He also raised pheasants. A Wethersfield postmaster for many years, he was elected state senator in 1889, was a director of American National Bank, and was a trustee of Mechanics Savings Bank, both in Hartford.

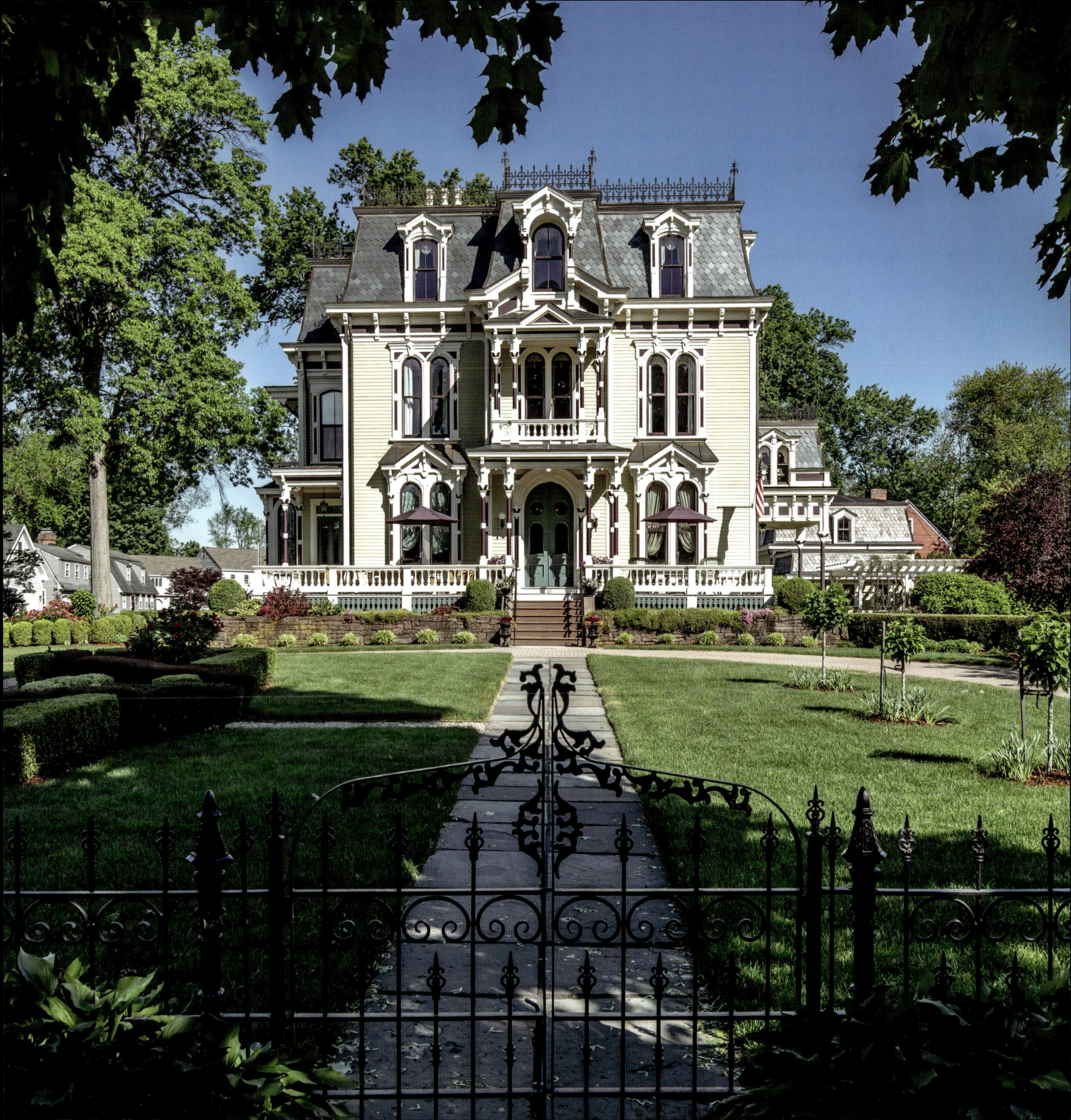

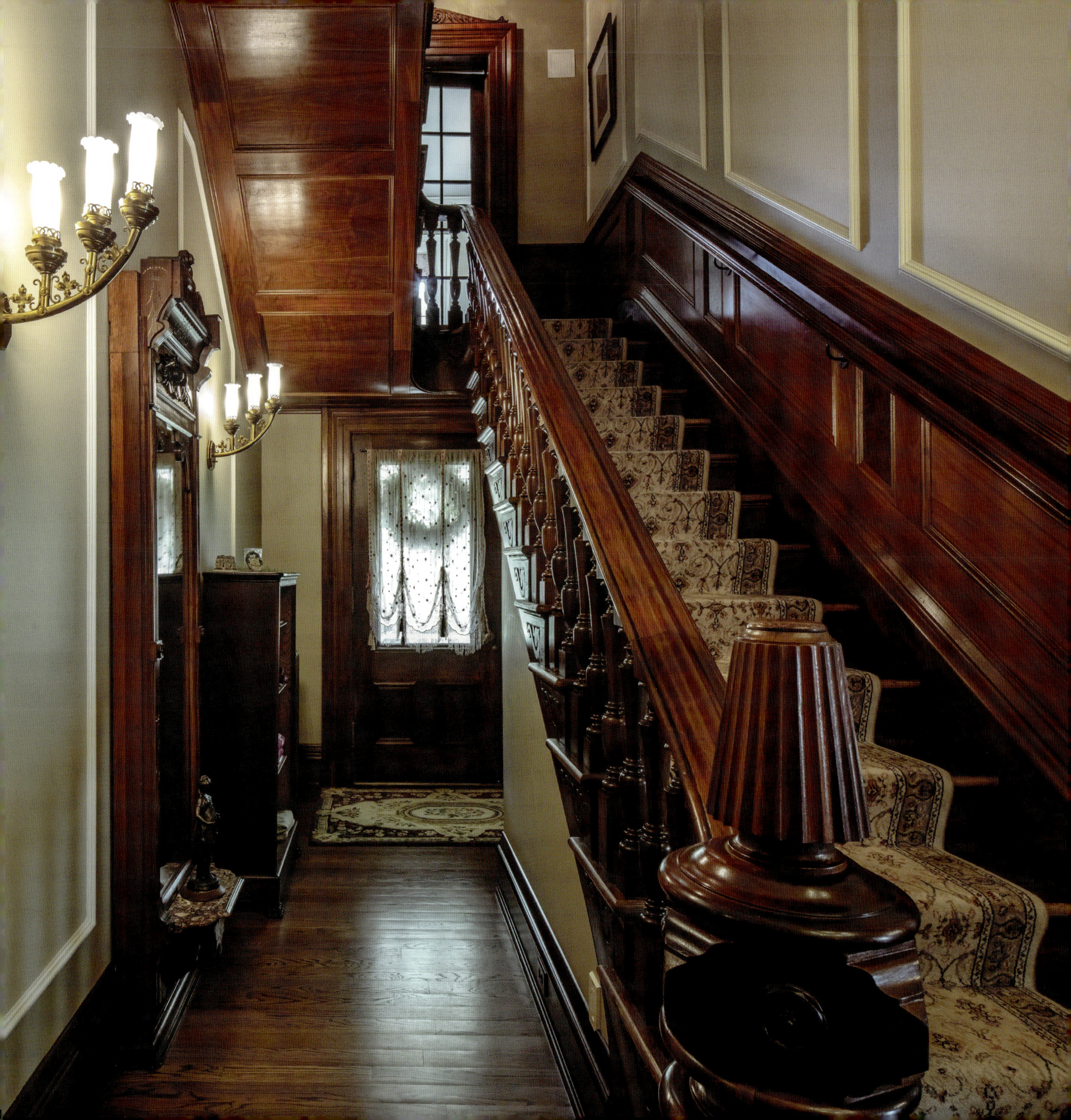

The main staircase, salvaged from the fire, has a walnut railing with turned walnut balusters and panels of walnut and walnut burl on the staircase wall.

According to Tilden's Atlas of Hartford County (1869), Elisha Johnson owned a home lot that extended from 185 Broad Street to 174 Main Street, which Sophia Jane evidently inherited. By 1870, the Robbins had four children. Like the house his brother, Richard, had built eleven years earlier at 320 Main Street, Robbins' new house was French Second Empire in style. A comparison of the two houses leaves no doubt that Silas was the older brother. While the design was more conservative (its façade symmetrical in every detail), the architectural ornamentation is much more elaborate.

The front door, entrance portico, second-floor balcony, and central dormer form a pyramidal assemblage that project slightly from the body of the house, making it the obvious focal point of the design. The flanking windows are also graduated in height and width, with the largest on the ground floor and the smallest at the roof level. The strong cornice is supported by pairs of scrolled brackets The mansard roof terminates in a handsome cast-iron cresting rail.

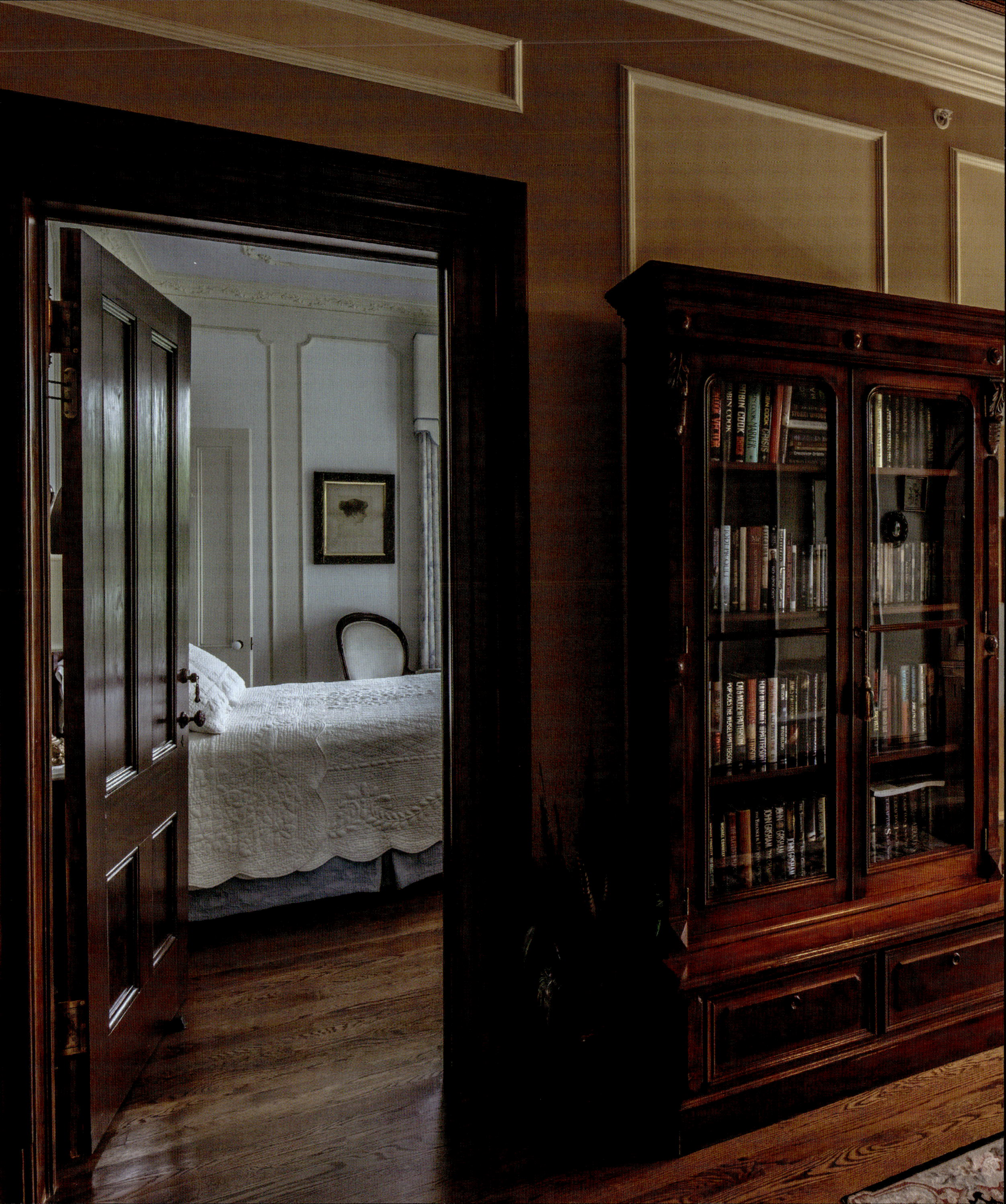
CRISIS
MARKER
JODI PICOULT
POP GOES THE WEASEL
PATTERSON
JOHN GRISHAM
GRISHAM

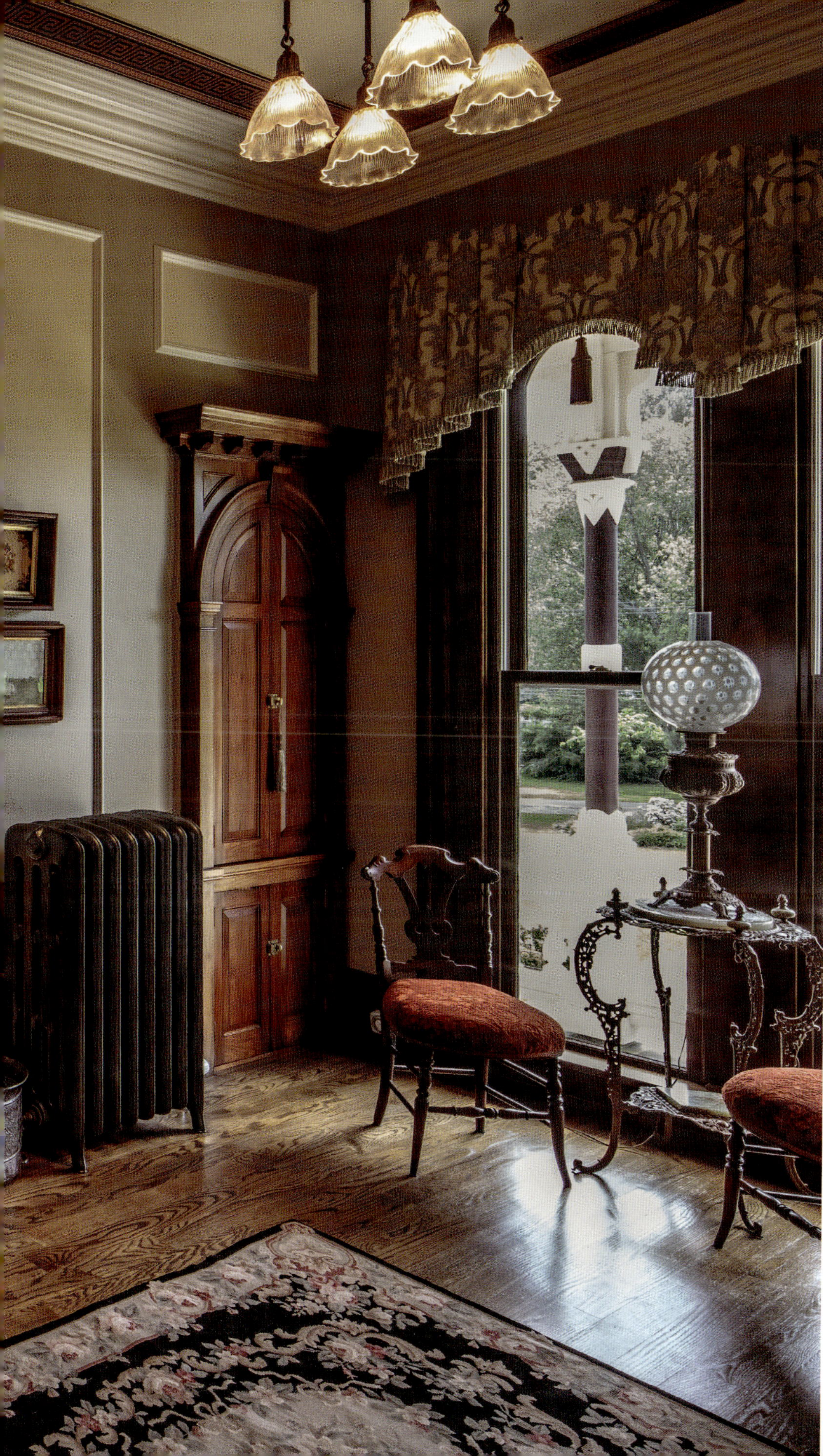

Because of fire and water damage, all the plasterwork had to be torn out and replaced. Powder-coated radiators throughout the house are original.

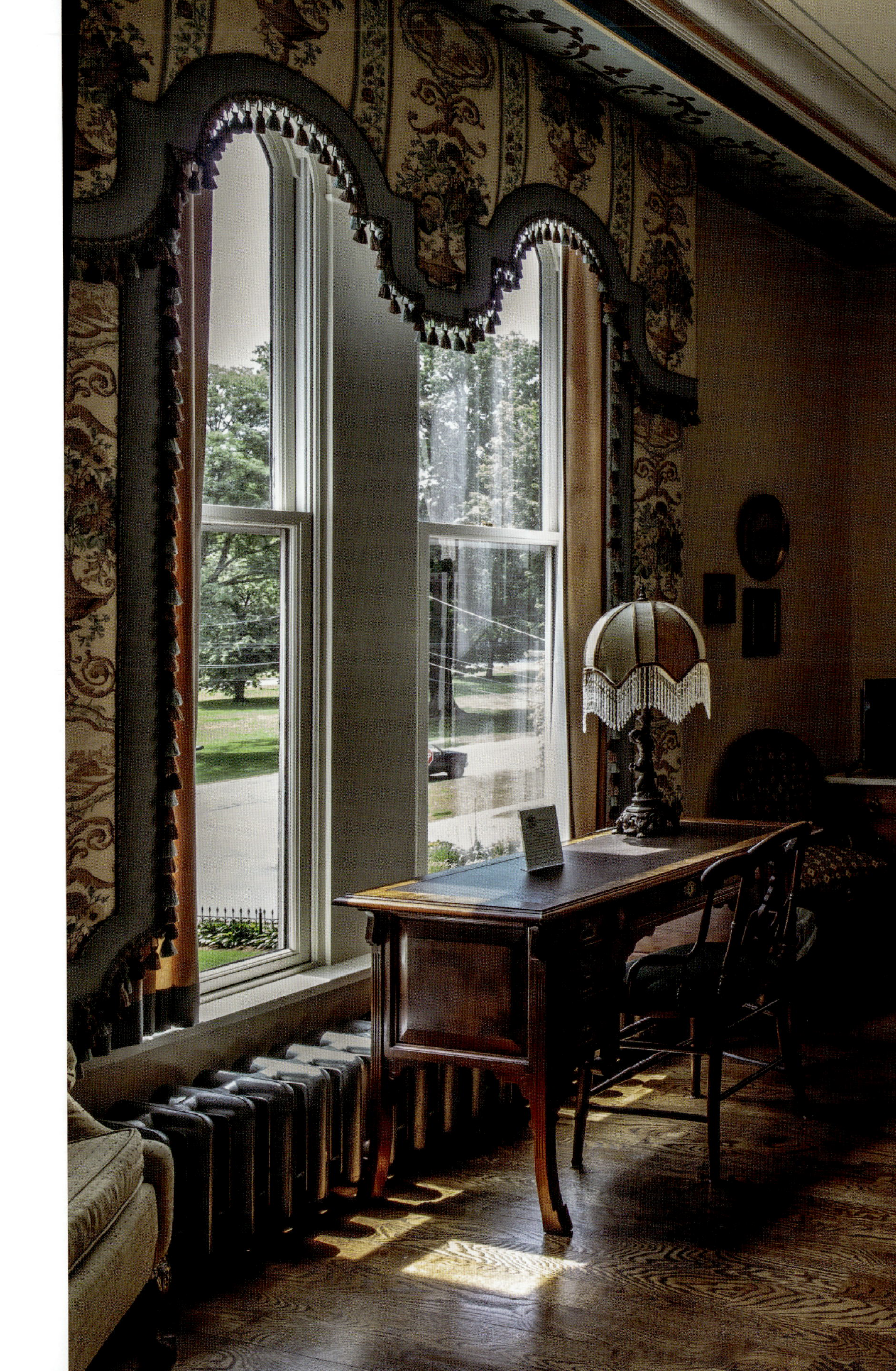

This front bedroom is called the Silas Robbins bedroom.

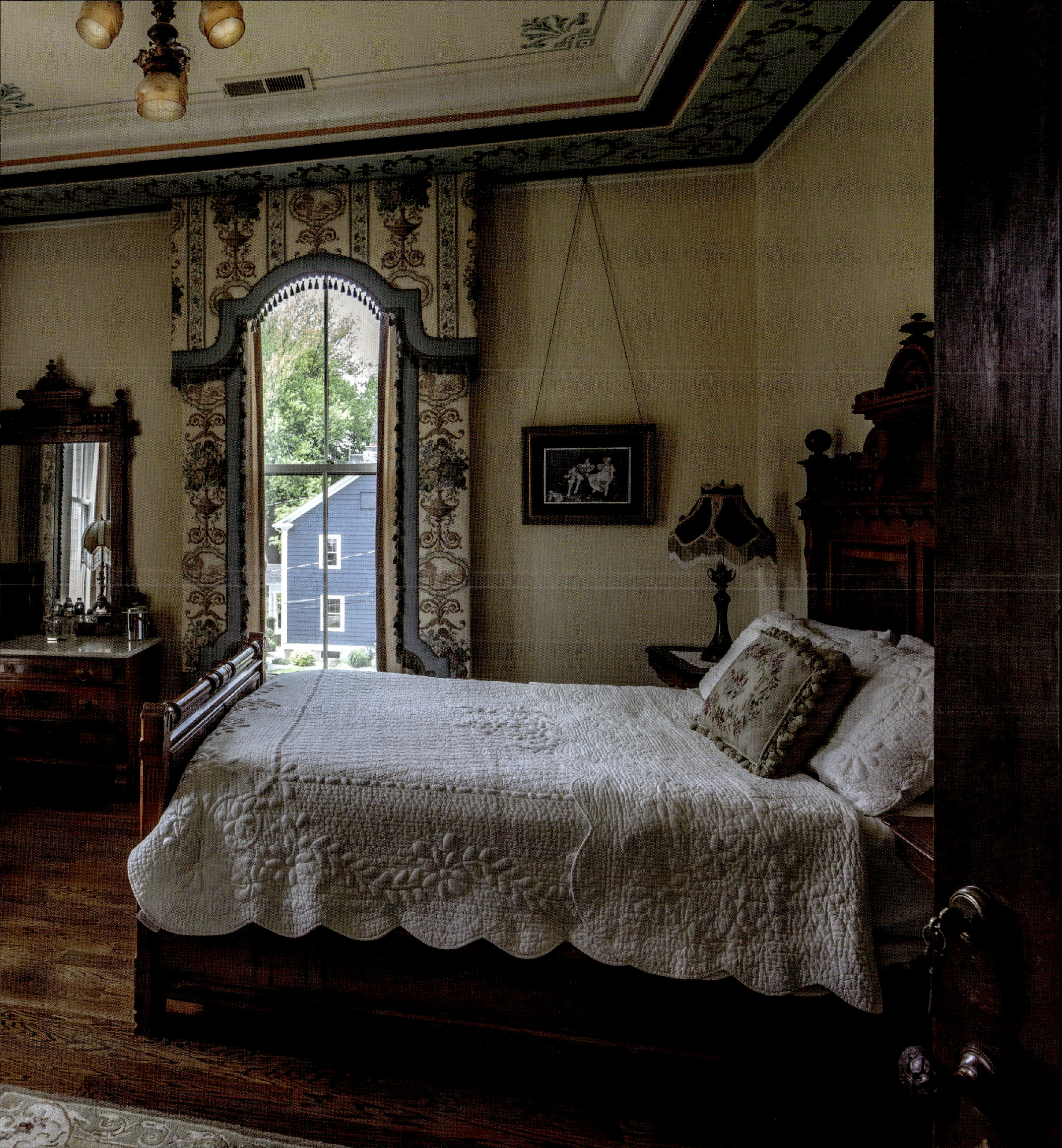

On the south side of the house, projecting bays and balconies are stacked three stories high. On the north side, there was a one-story porte cochere, now a porch, that provided shelter for those disembarking from their carriages.

In 1996, a fire spread through the house. There was serious damage to the south bay and the mansard roof. Inadequate protection from the elements caused additional damage. The owner applied to the Historic District Commission to demolish the structure. At the Commission's public hearing, local preservationists spoke passionately about the need to preserve this house, which in terms of sophistication and abundance of architectural detail is the most spectacular residence in Wethersfield's Historic District.

The tearoom with antique period tiles on the fireplace surround.

The Commissioners were urged to not accept the assessments marshaled by the owner from the health officer, building inspector, local engineer, and realtor without seeking second opinions from an architect, engineer, and/or restoration contractor. What might appear to be unsalvageable in the eyes of a person familiar with modern construction and building codes could well be preserved and restored to its former grandeur with the right contractor.

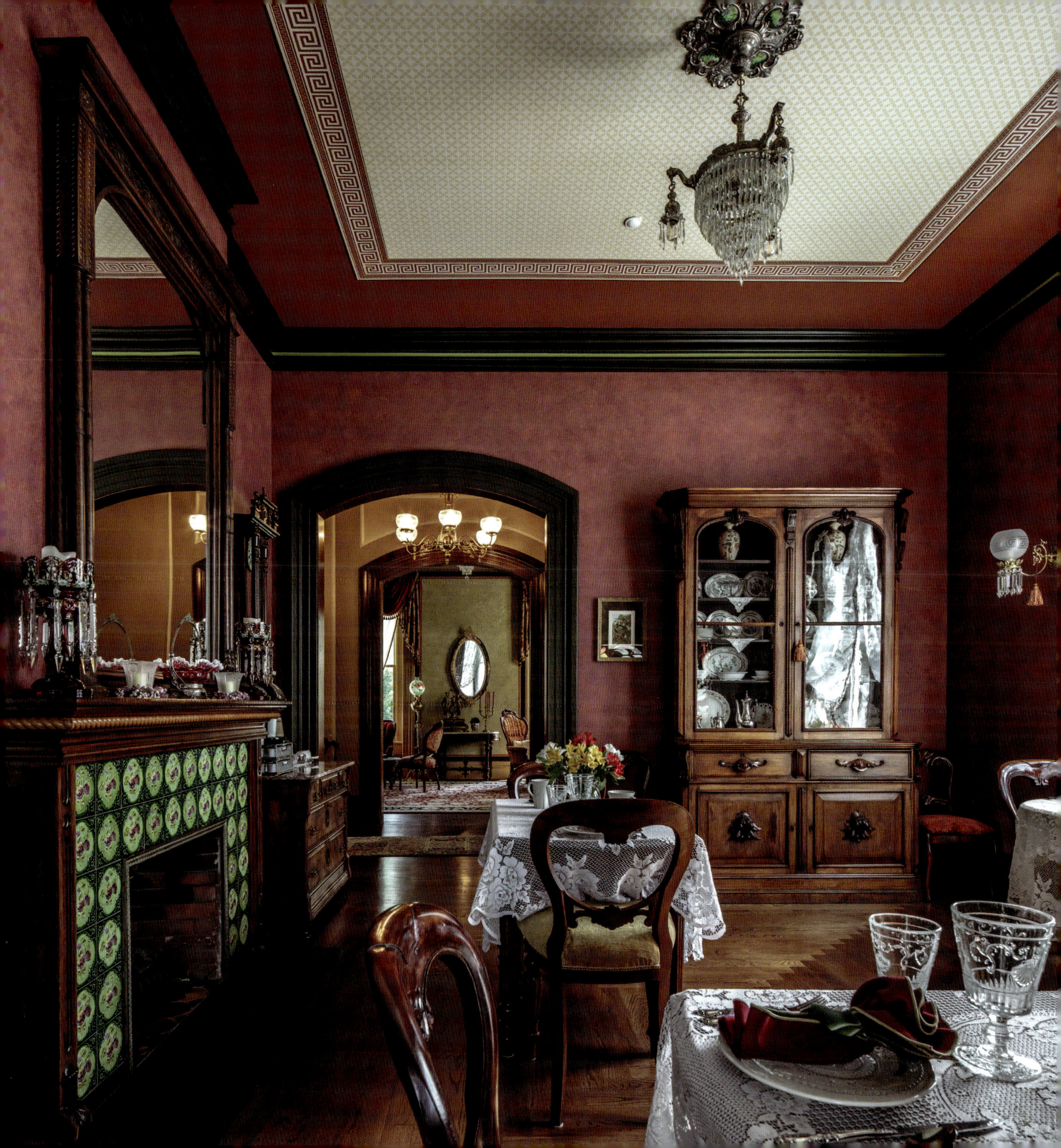

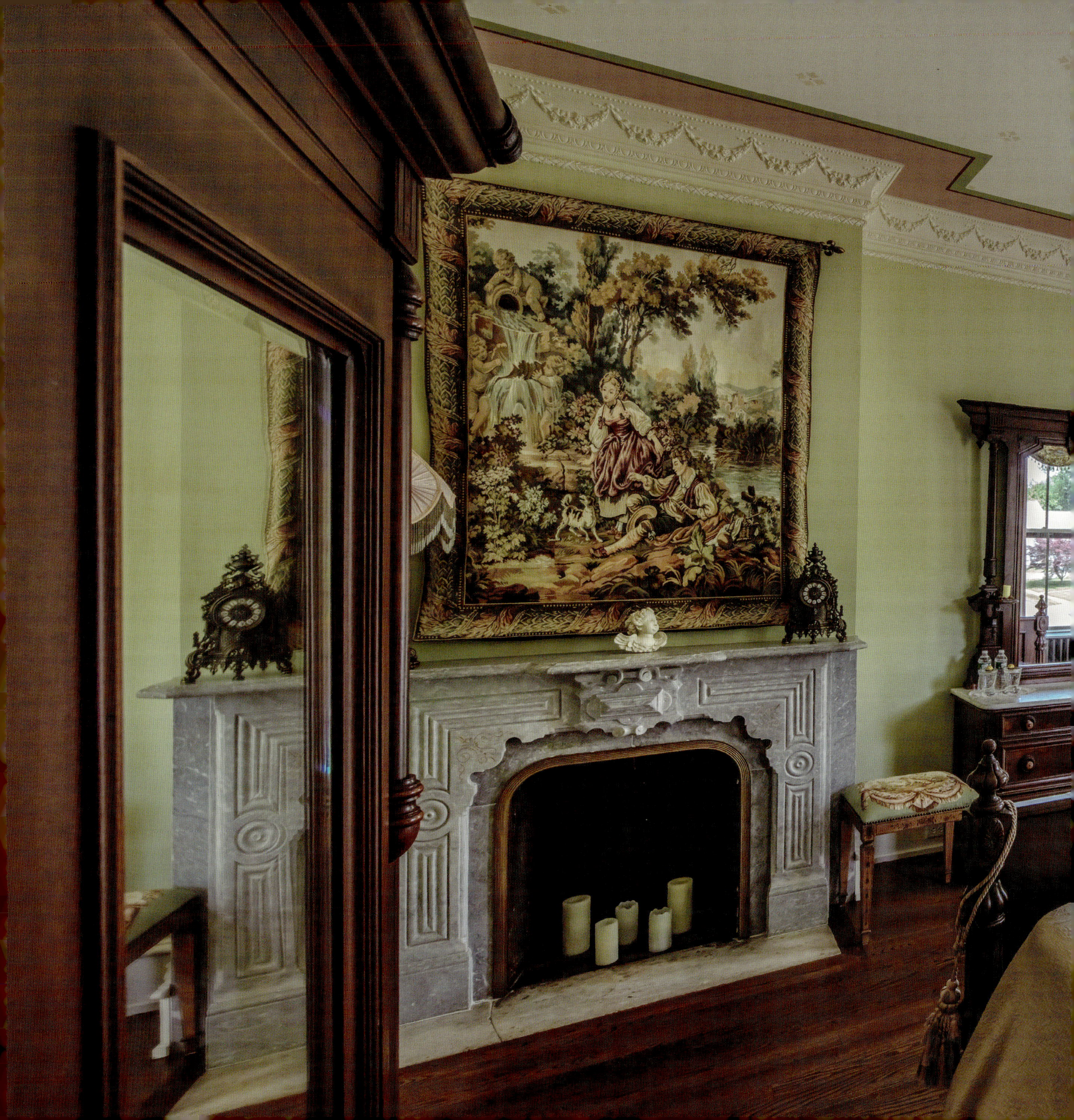

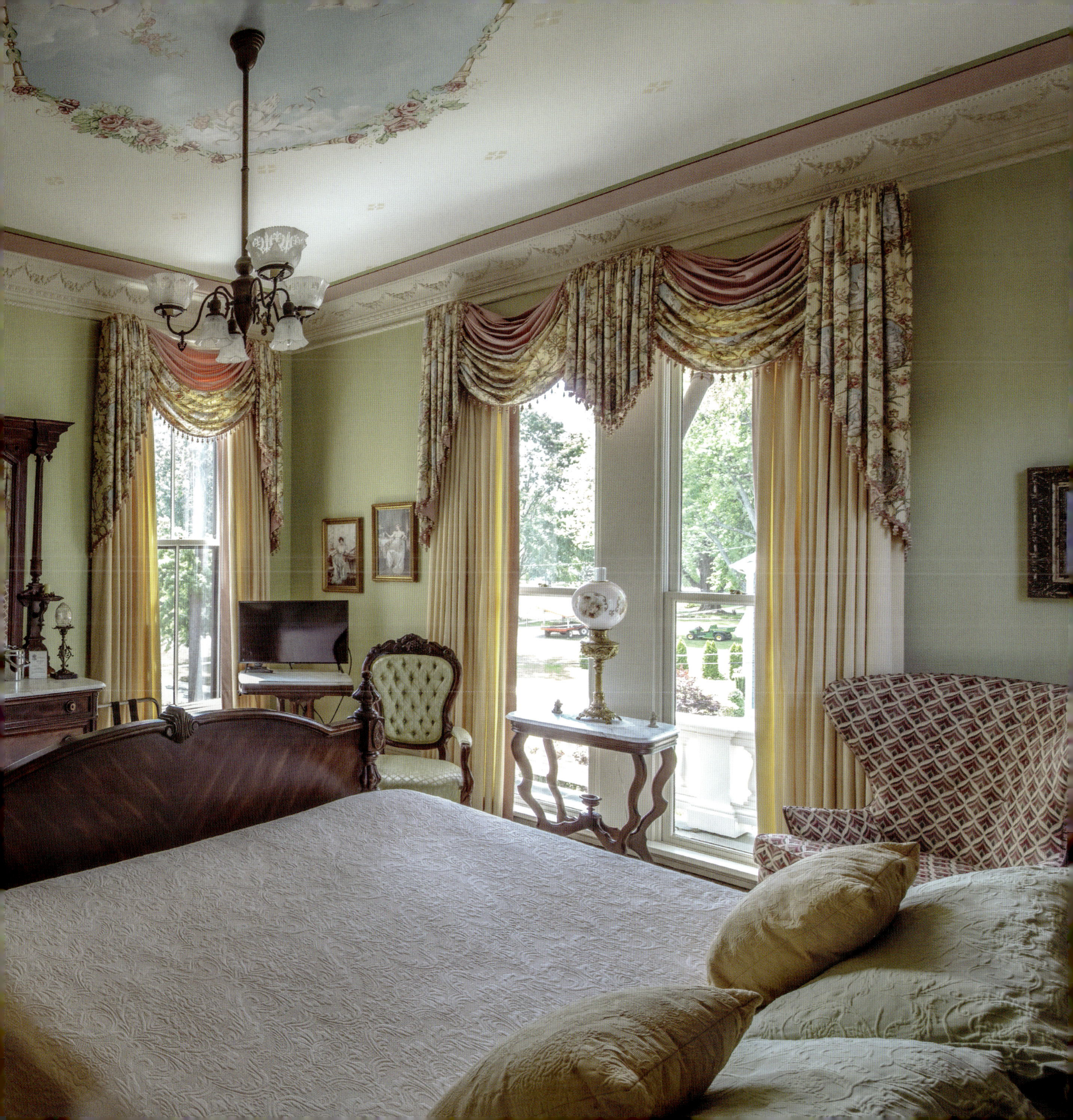

(preceeding spread)
A view of the cupid and roses bedroom.

The formal dining room handsomely restored.

(folowing spread)
(left) The parlor fireplace is original to the house.
(right) Beautifully restored with period antiques.

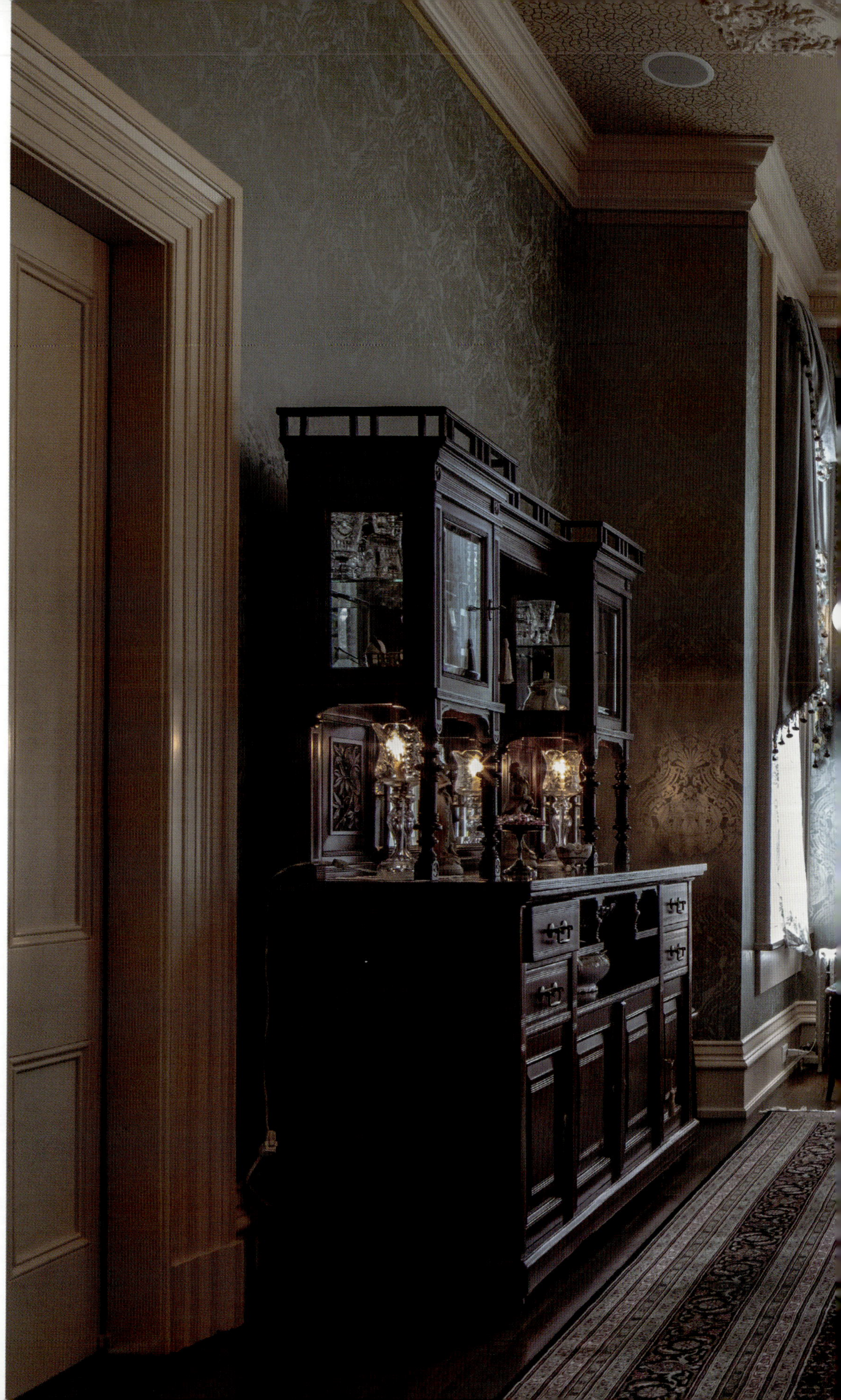

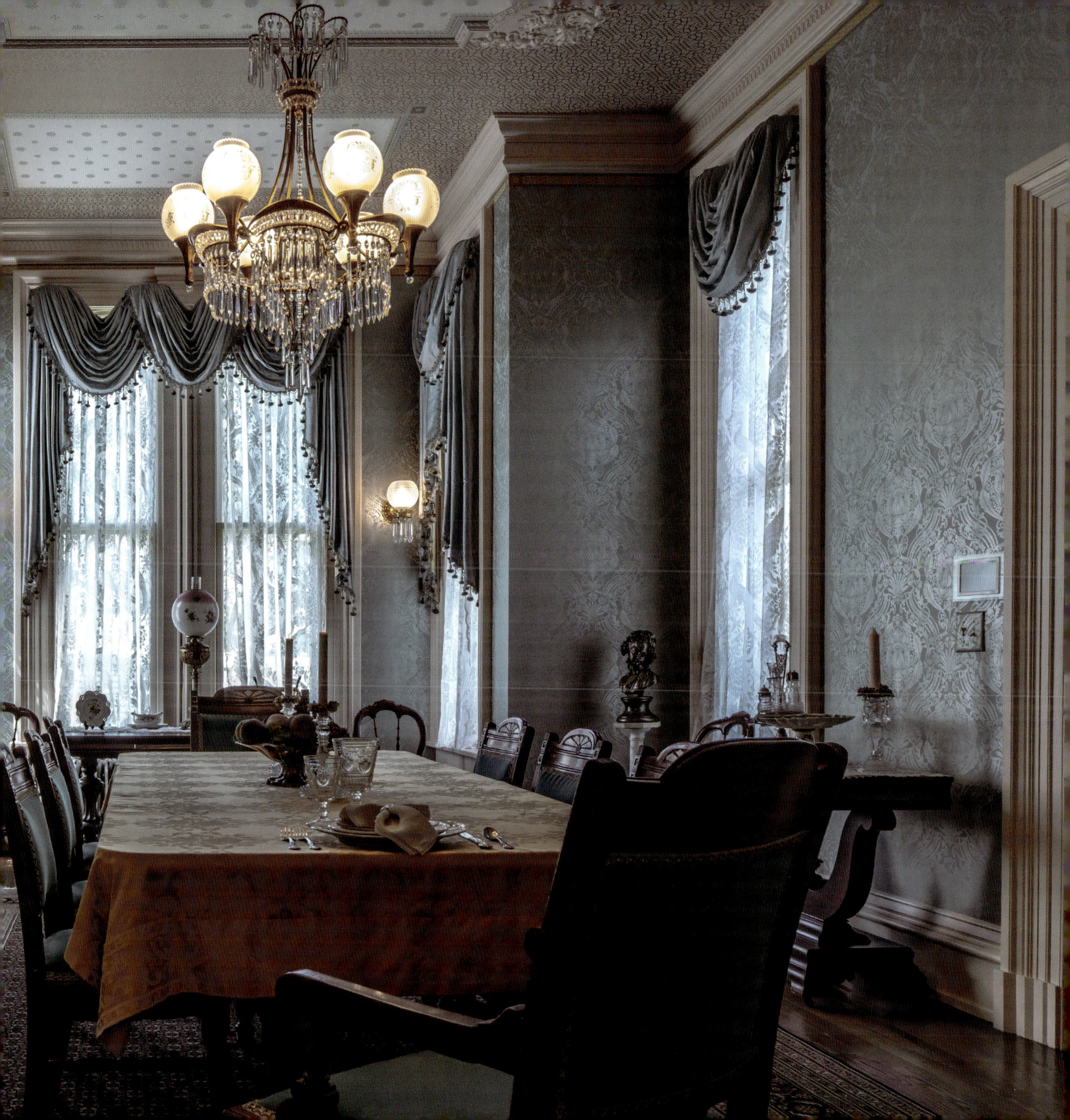

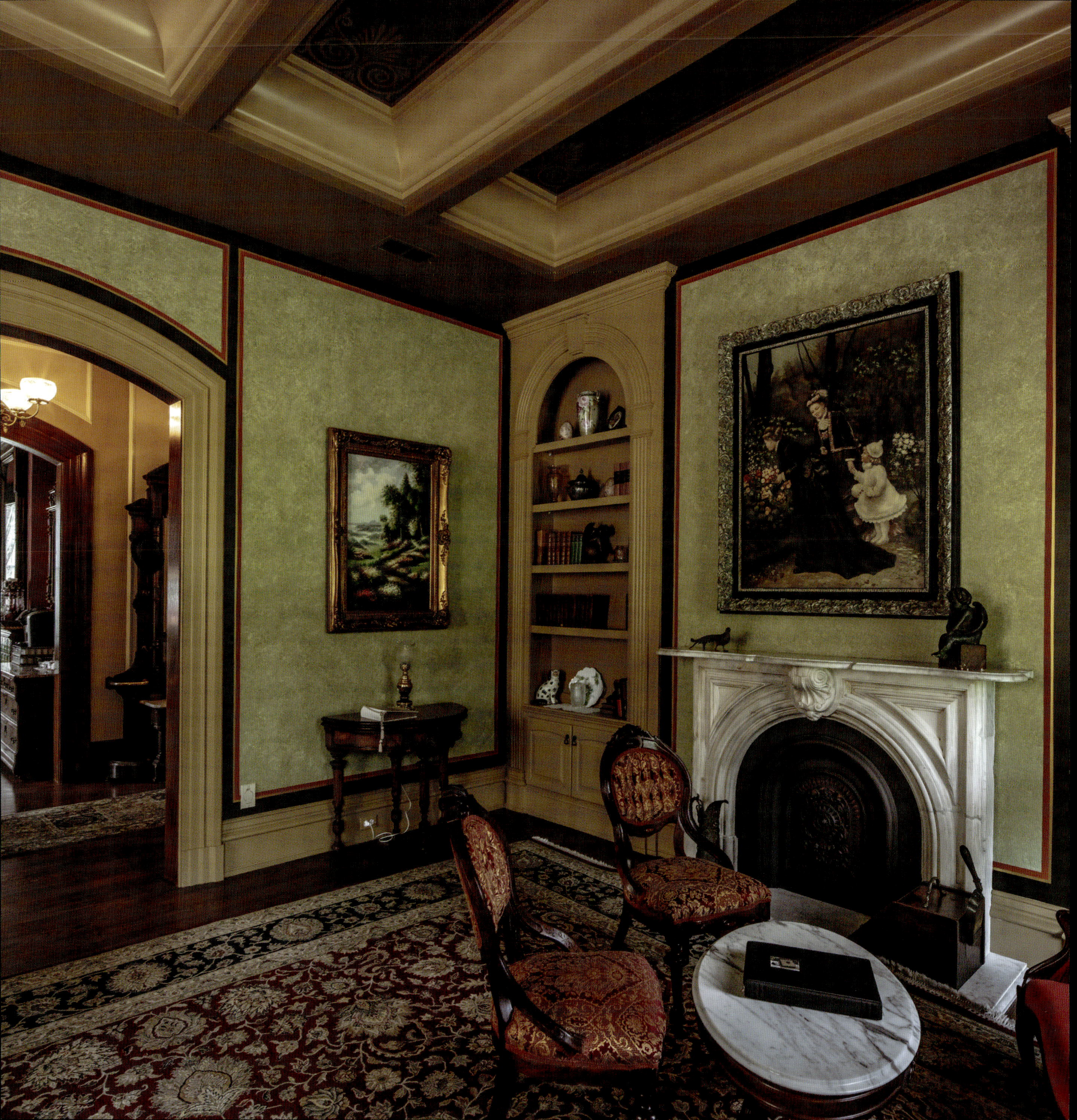

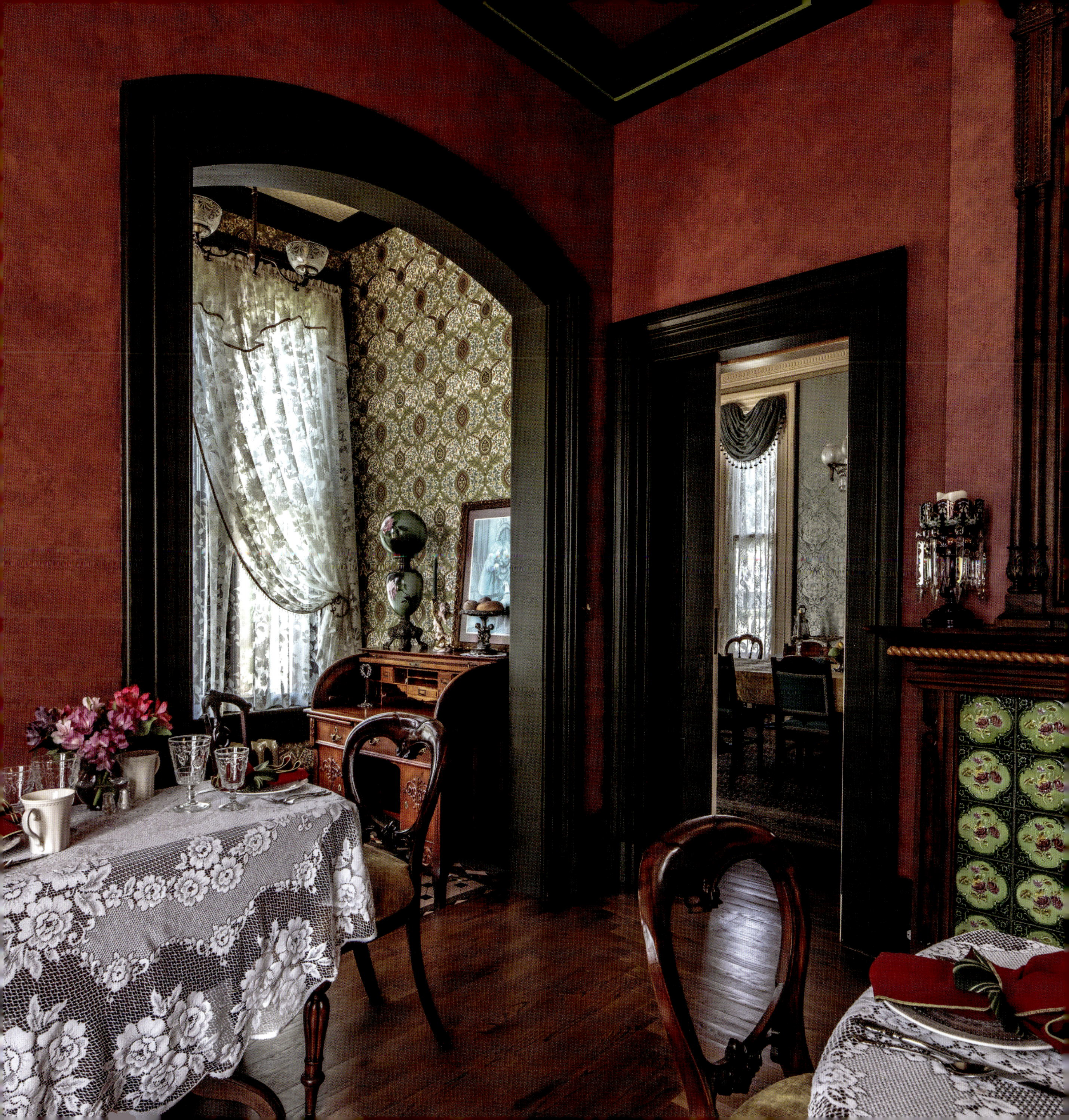

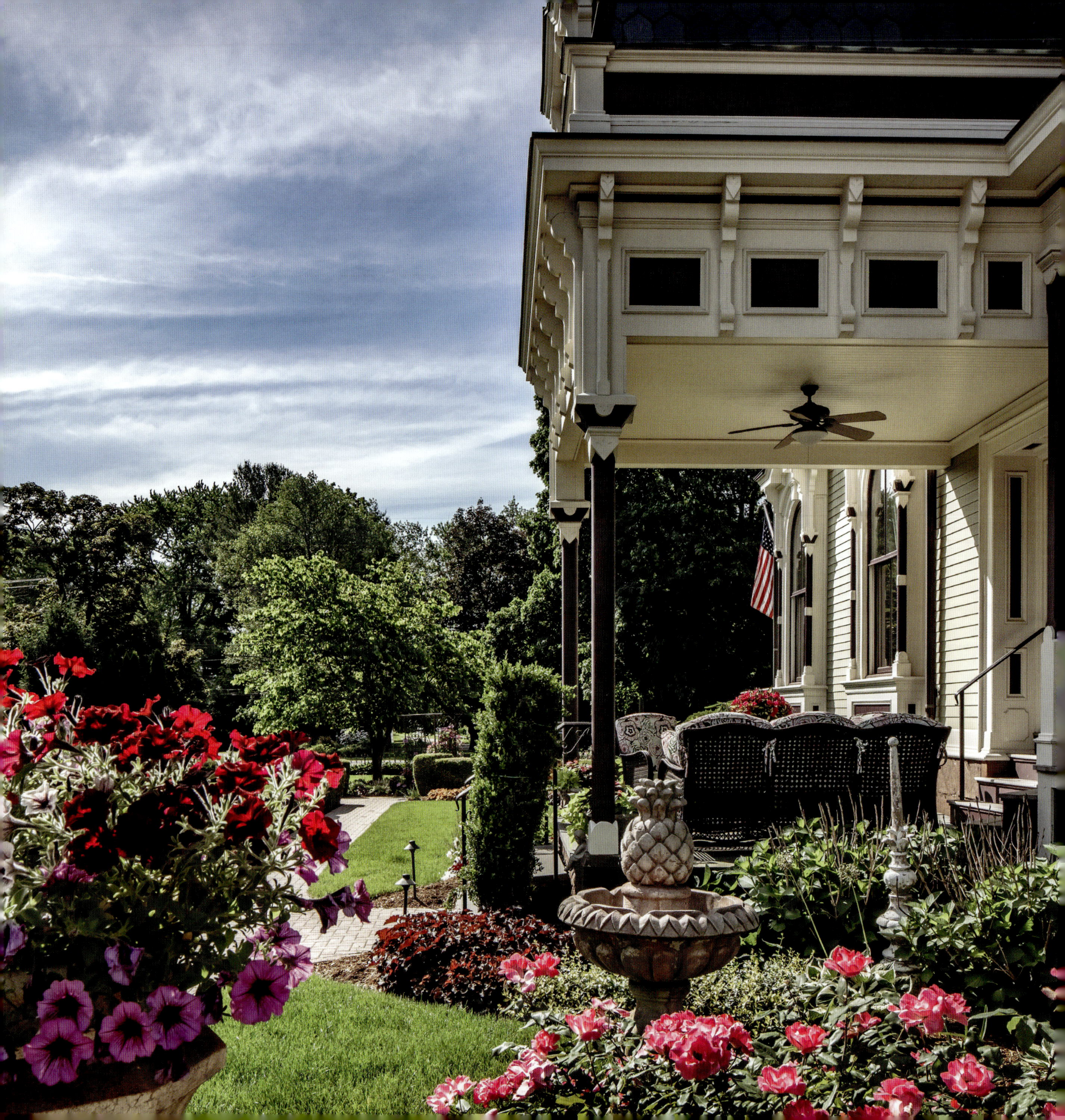

Public commenters asked the Commission to deny the applicant's request for permission to demolish this most important part of Wethersfield's heritage and requested the applicant to consider the neighbors and the community at large. Perhaps the owners could sell the Silas W. Robbins House to someone willing to preserve it. The Commission agreed with the preservationists.

The porte cochere is now a porch.

After a lengthy period of negotiation, John and Shireen Aforismo bought the house in 2001. It took six years of extensive restoration to the exterior, including a new slate roof, and the interior, stripped down to the studs because of moisture damage, until the house was restored to its original magnificence. The Aforismos inserted features like an elevator to adapt the interior to its new use as the Silas W. Robbins House Bed & Breakfast, opened in November 2007. ♛

A SEA CAPTAIN'S HOUSE LEARNS FRENCH

Daniel Francis House

— 357 Main Street —

Captain Daniel Francis (1770–1837) married Mehitabel Goodrich (1777–1845) in 1799. Their brick house at 357 Main Street was built about 1803 on land that she inherited from her father, Elizur Goodrich.

Captain Daniel was master of the sloop *Lucy*, which carried freight between Hartford, New York, and Philadelphia between 1810 and 1818. Daniel and Mehitabel had four daughters and five sons. Their son, Captain John Newton Francis (1817–1867) was master of the brig *Scotland*. He made over forty round trips between Hartford and Puerto Rico in that ship. Captain John then became master of the brig *Suwanee*, which was probably the last square-rigged vessel to come up the Connecticut River. He died from yellow fever on a trip to Panama and was buried in New Granada in 1867.

The 1803 Daniel Francis House after William Fay's 1869 remodeling.

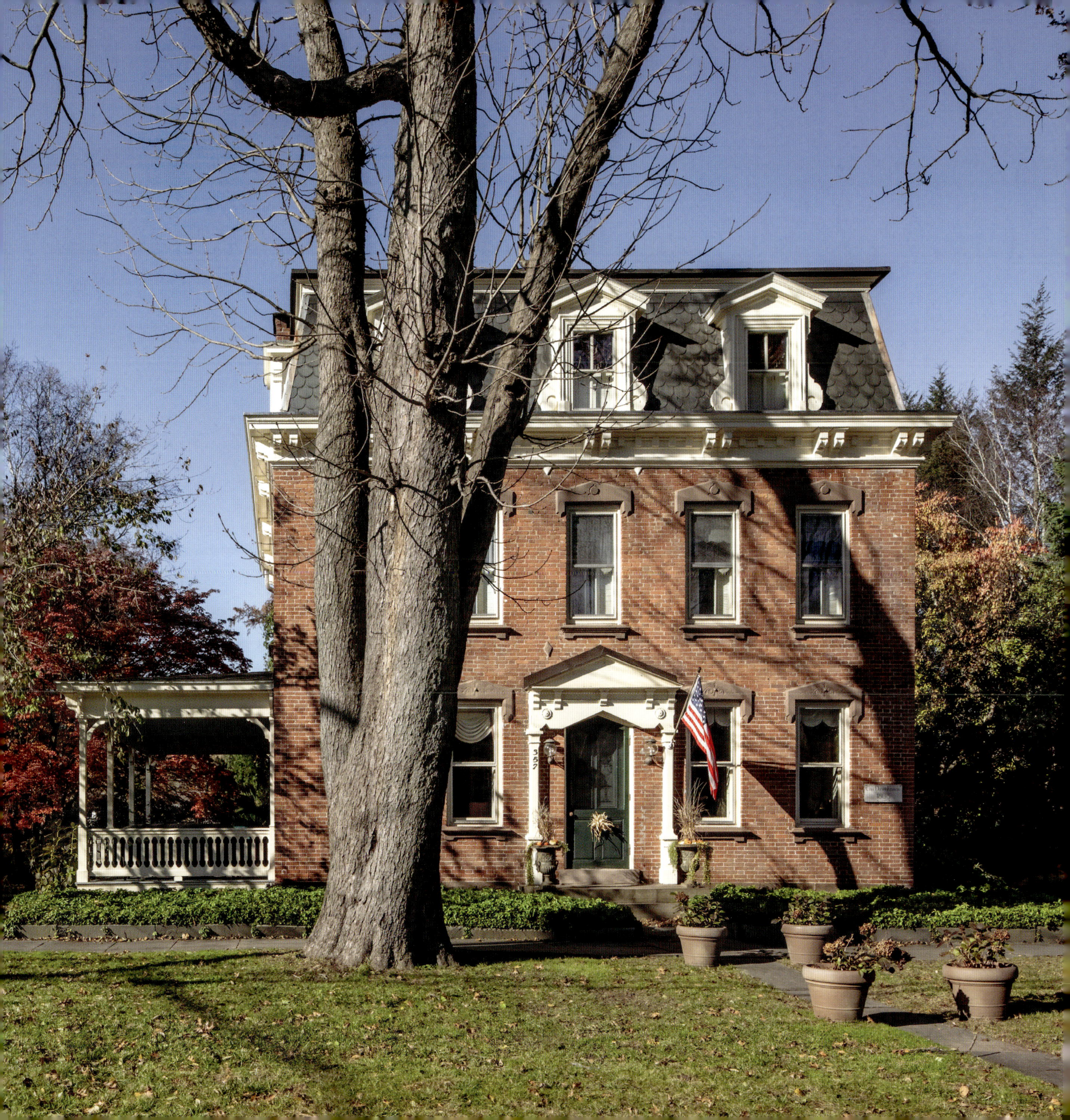
357

William P. Fay purchased the Francis House in 1869. Inspired by the Richard Robbins House at 320 Main Street, he decided to remodel his house in the French Second Empire style. This involved extensive alterations to the brickwork around the door and window openings. The front door opening was slightly narrowed and peaked, and the ground-floor windows were lengthened. Molded caps incised with Eastlake-style tracery were added above the windows on both floors. The height of the walls was increased by approximately eighteen inches and crowned with a bold bracketed cornice and mansard roof, punctuated by relatively simple dormer windows.

The window to the left of the fireplace in the parlor can be raised to provide access to the porch.

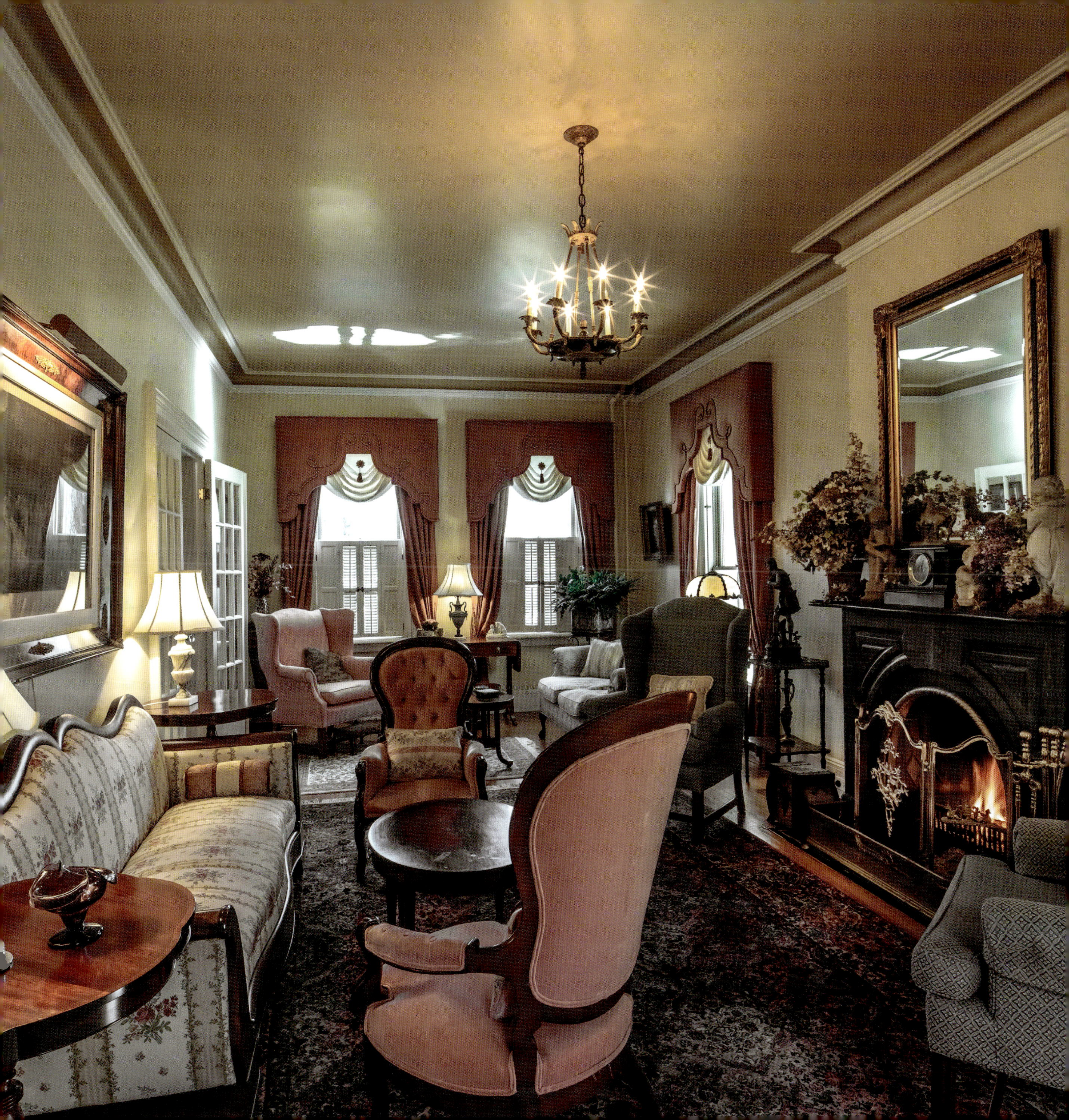

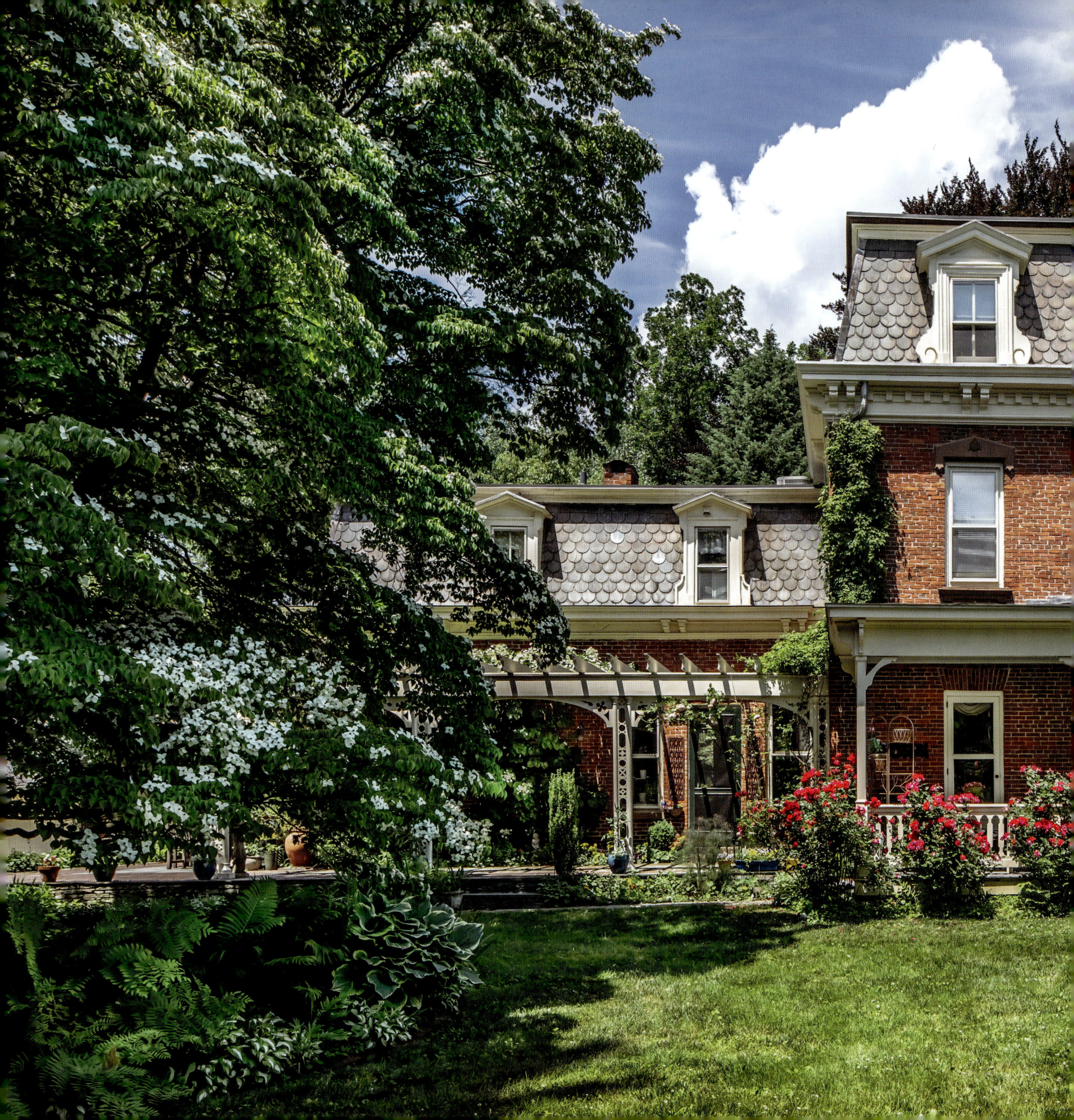

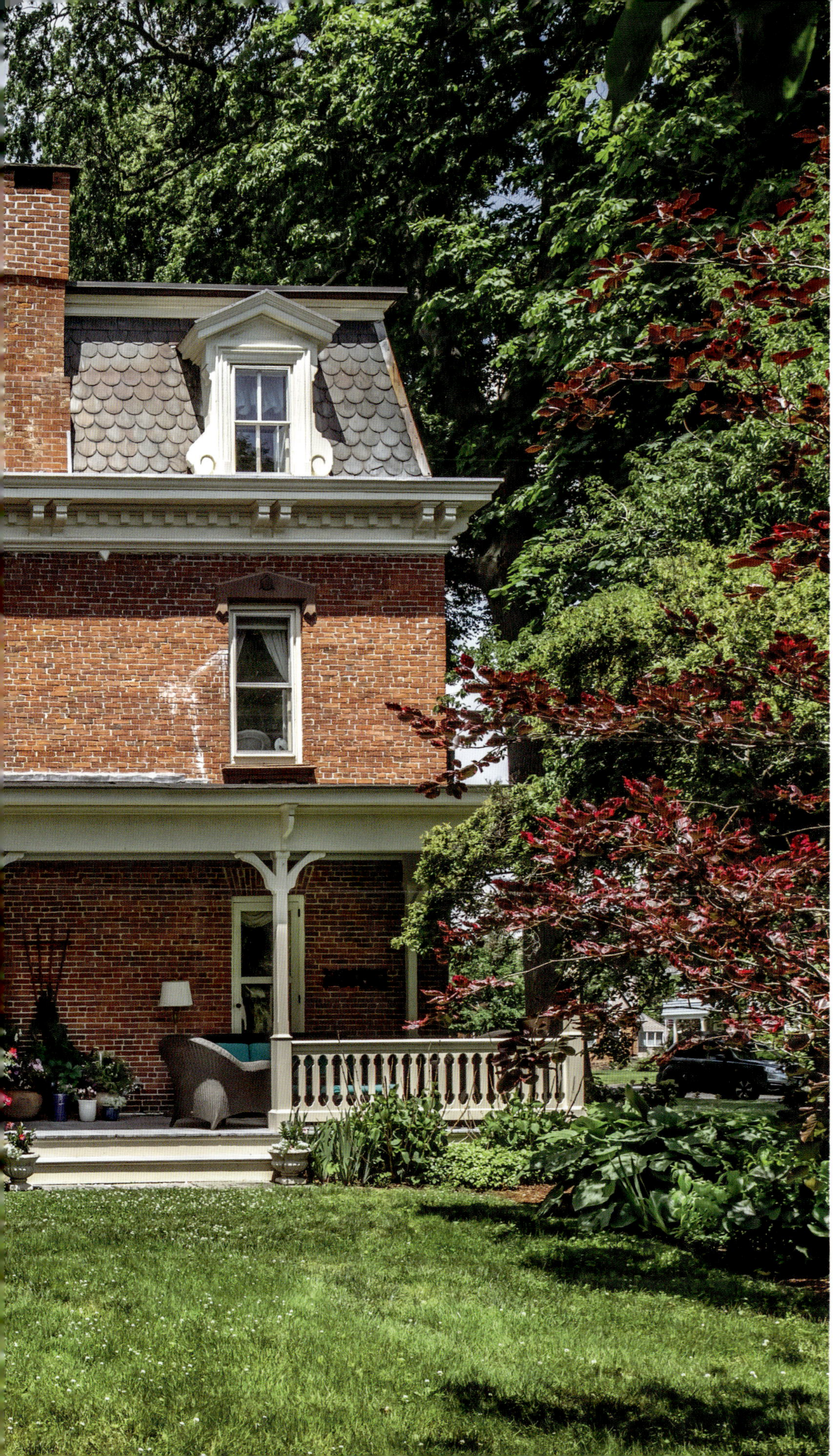

The south side showing the restored porch and pergola and the step-out windows from the parlor.

The dining room mural by Granby artist Carolann Dvorak depicts the Connecticut River on the left wall, the Wethersfield Cove on the right wall, and Francis's sloop Lucy *in the center between the windows.*

(following spread)
The view from the restored porch of the pergola, and south lawn and garden.

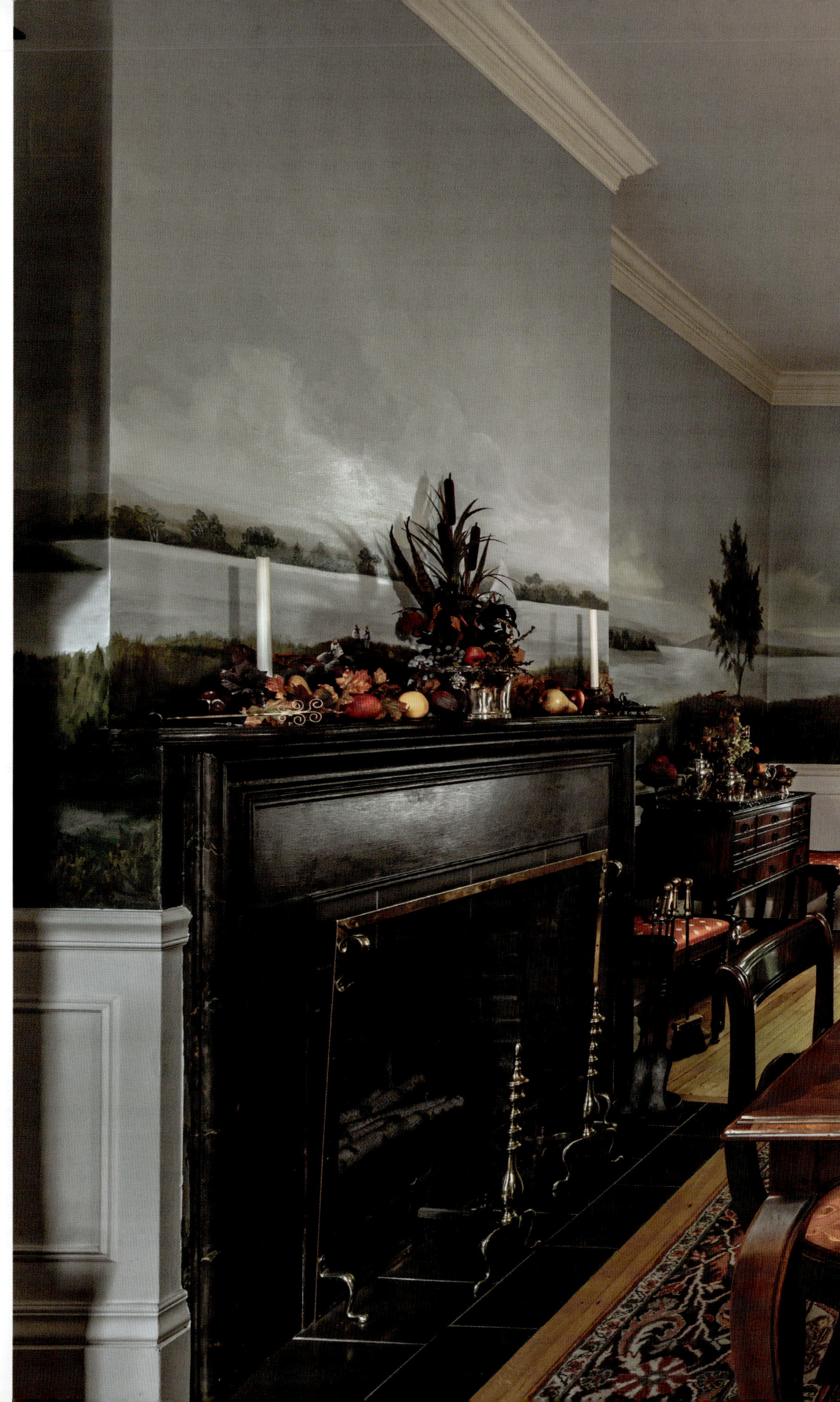

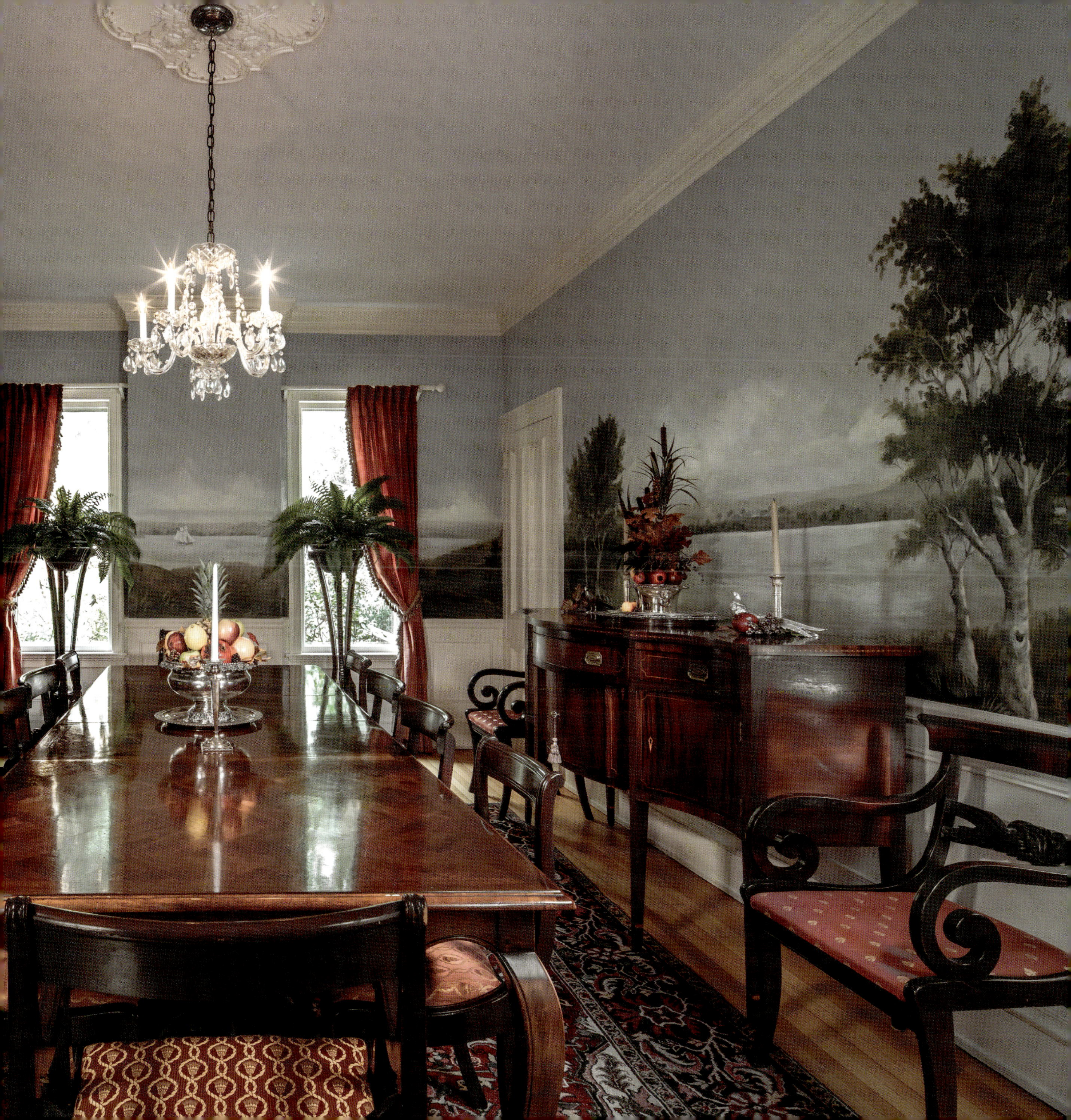

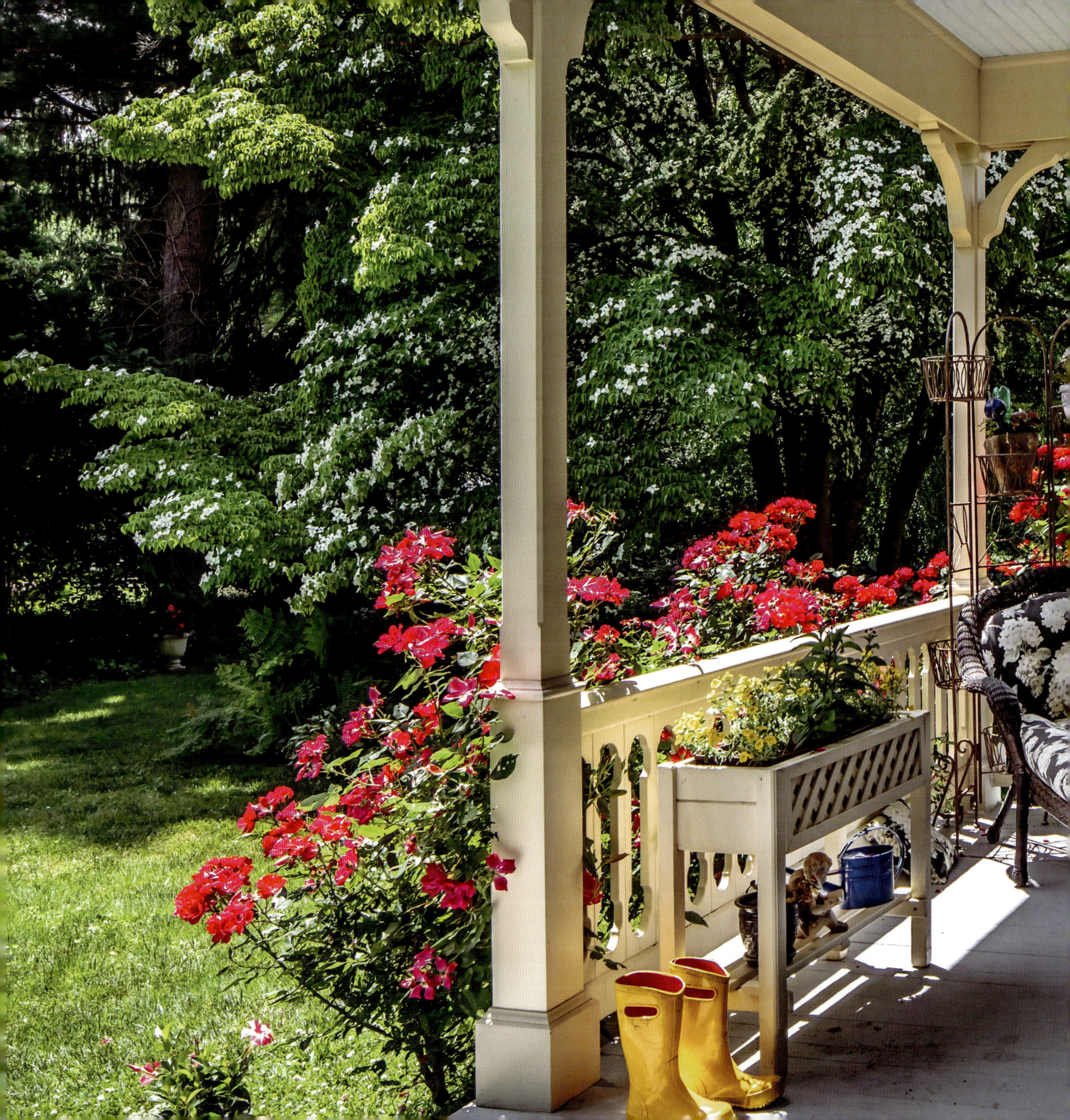

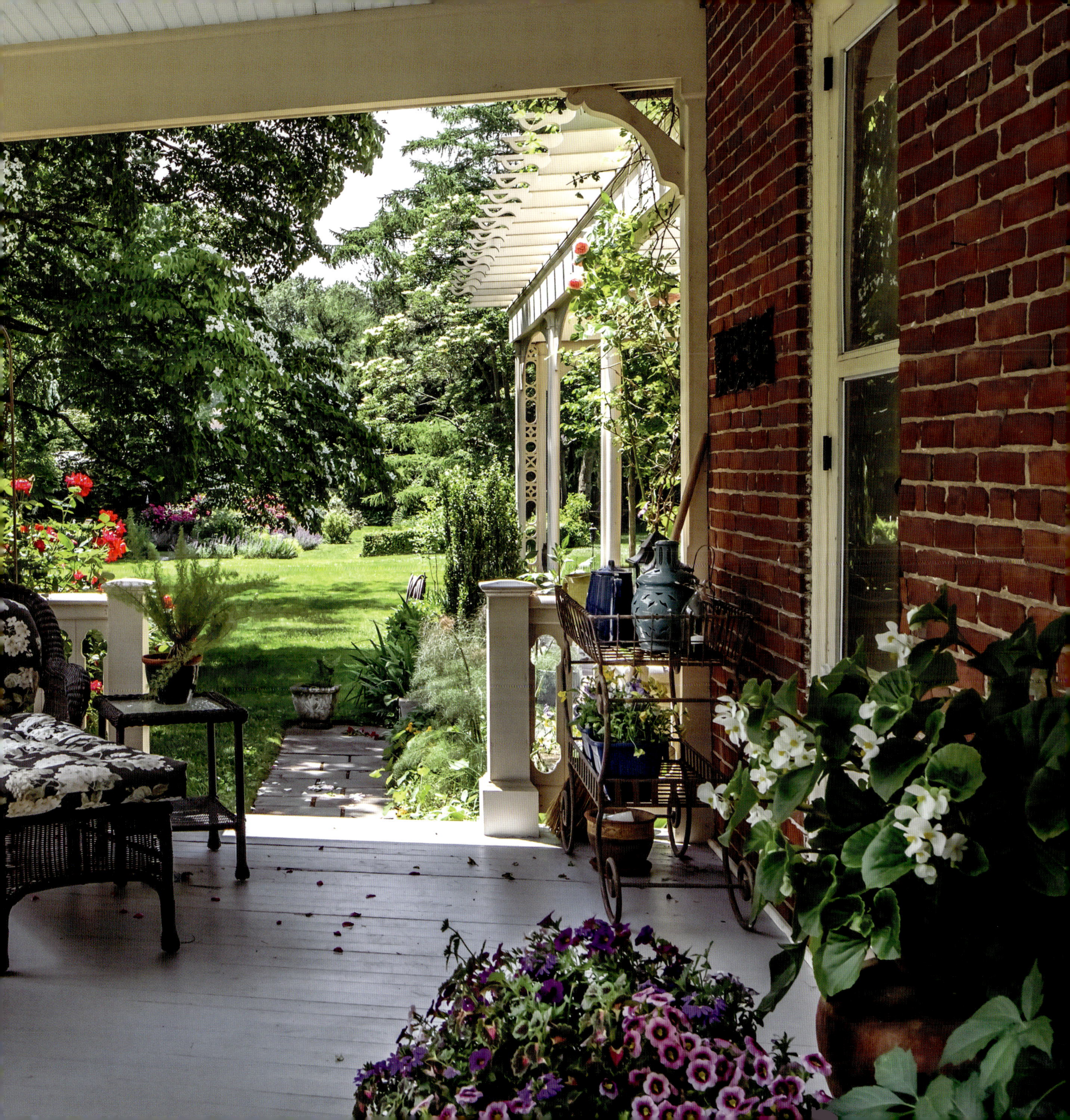

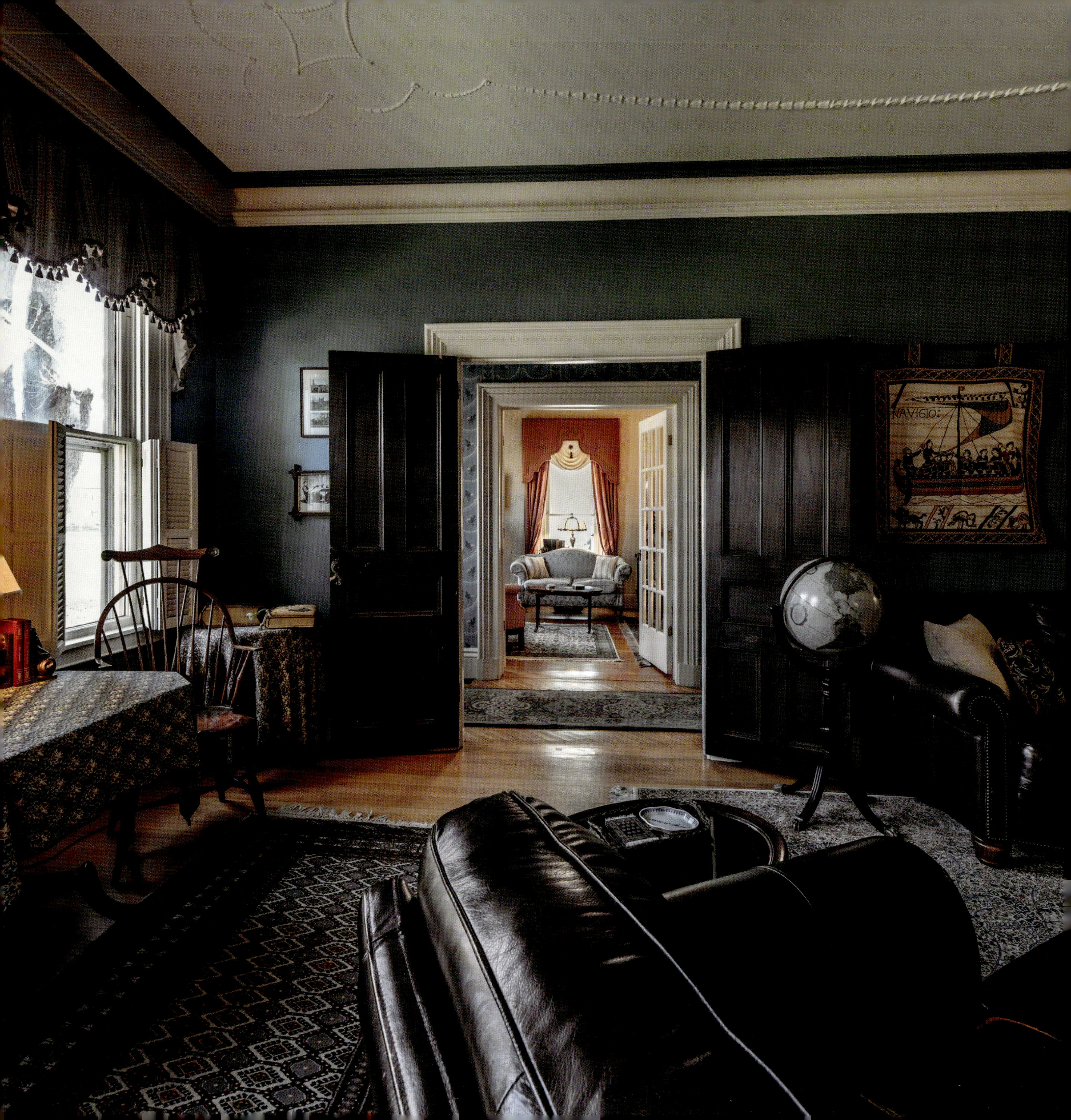
NAVIGIO:

View from the library into the parlor.

Around 1895, photographer Richard DeLamater, who lived next door at 349 Main Street, took a glass plate negative of the house. In 2007, owners Judith and Charles Melchreit used DeLamater's image to document and restore the south veranda and pergola. ♛

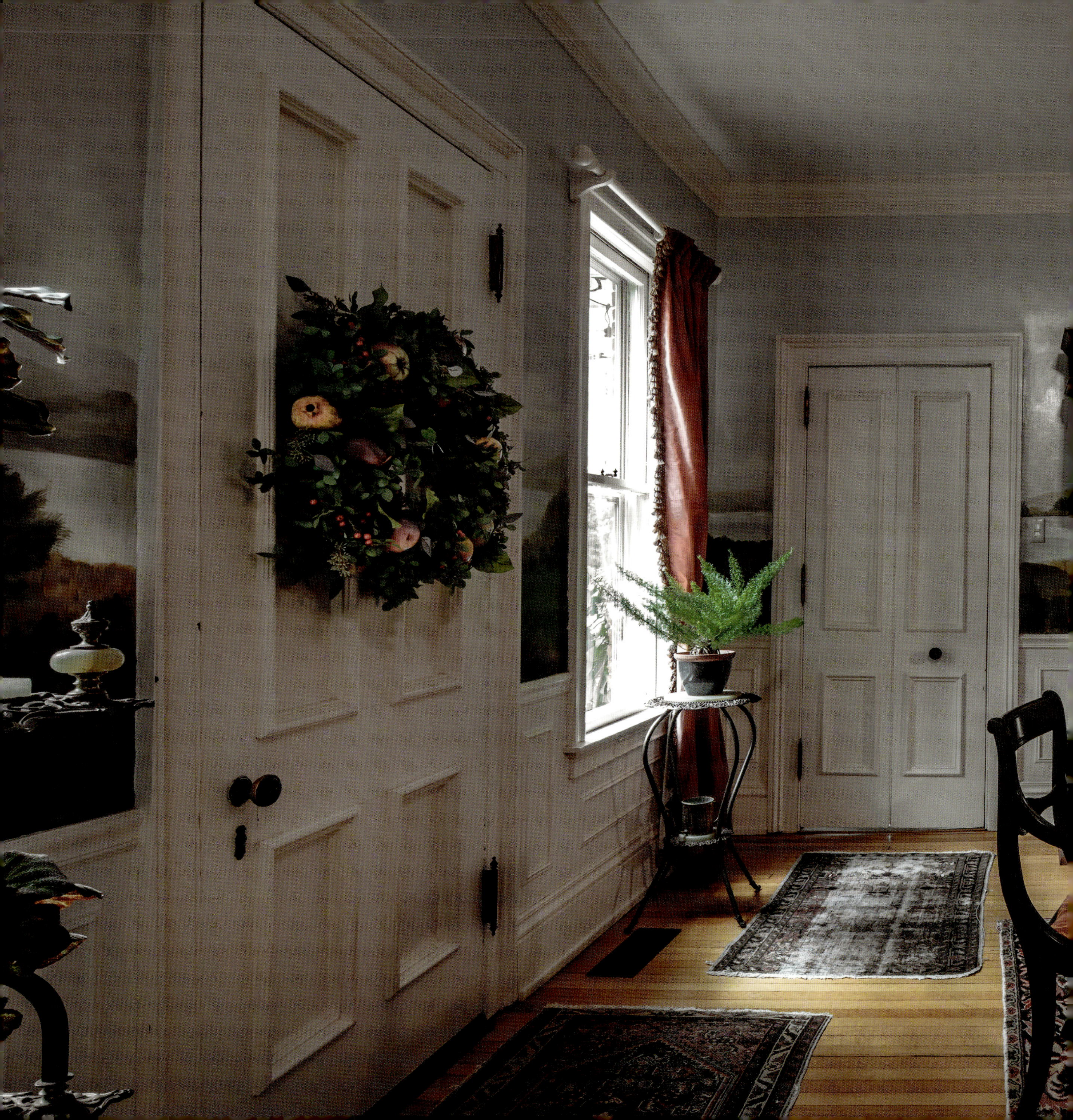

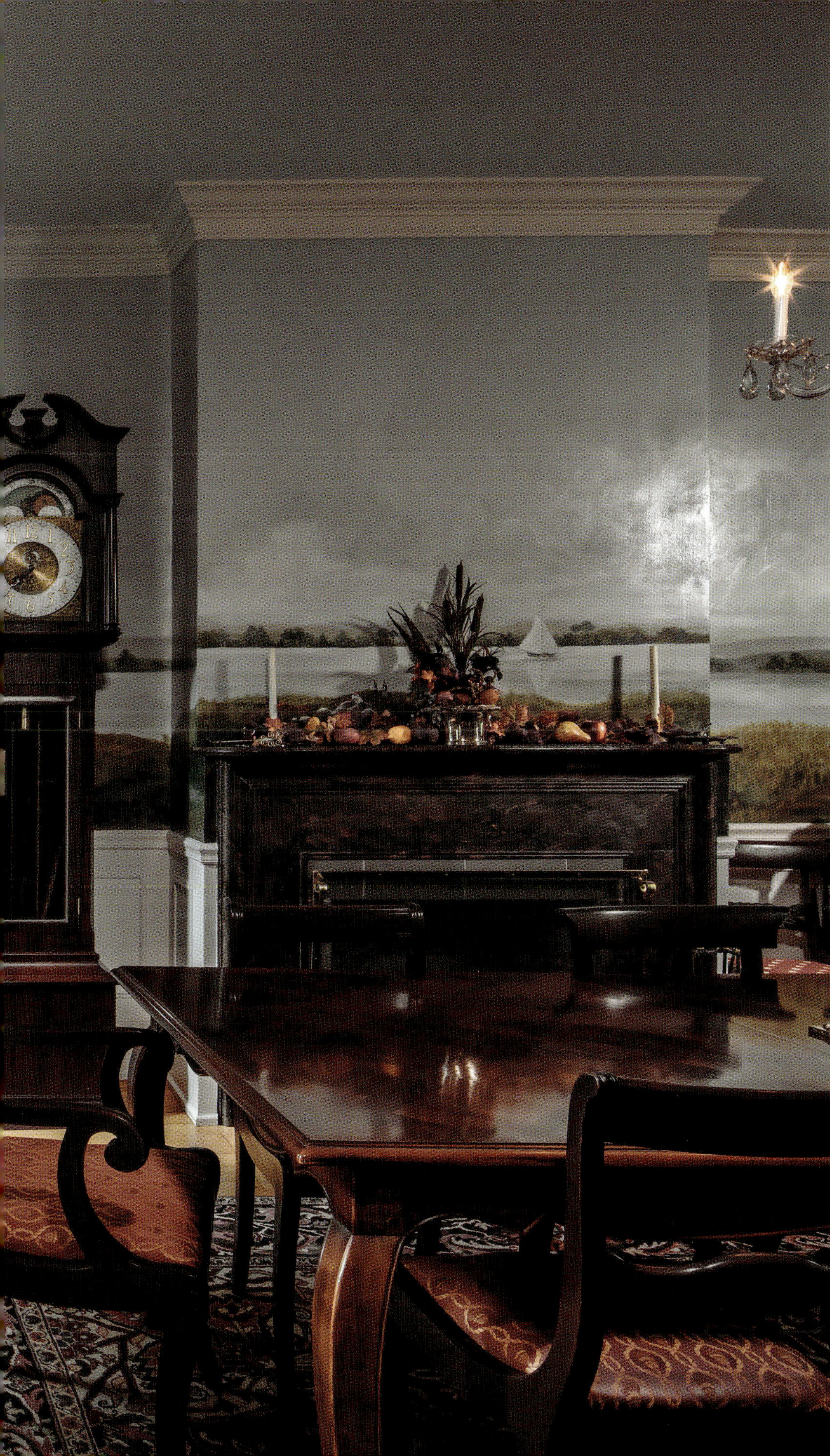

The dining room with its mural of the Connecticut River.

(following spread)
(left) Library is the northeast room of the house.
(right) The center hall and 1869 newel post.

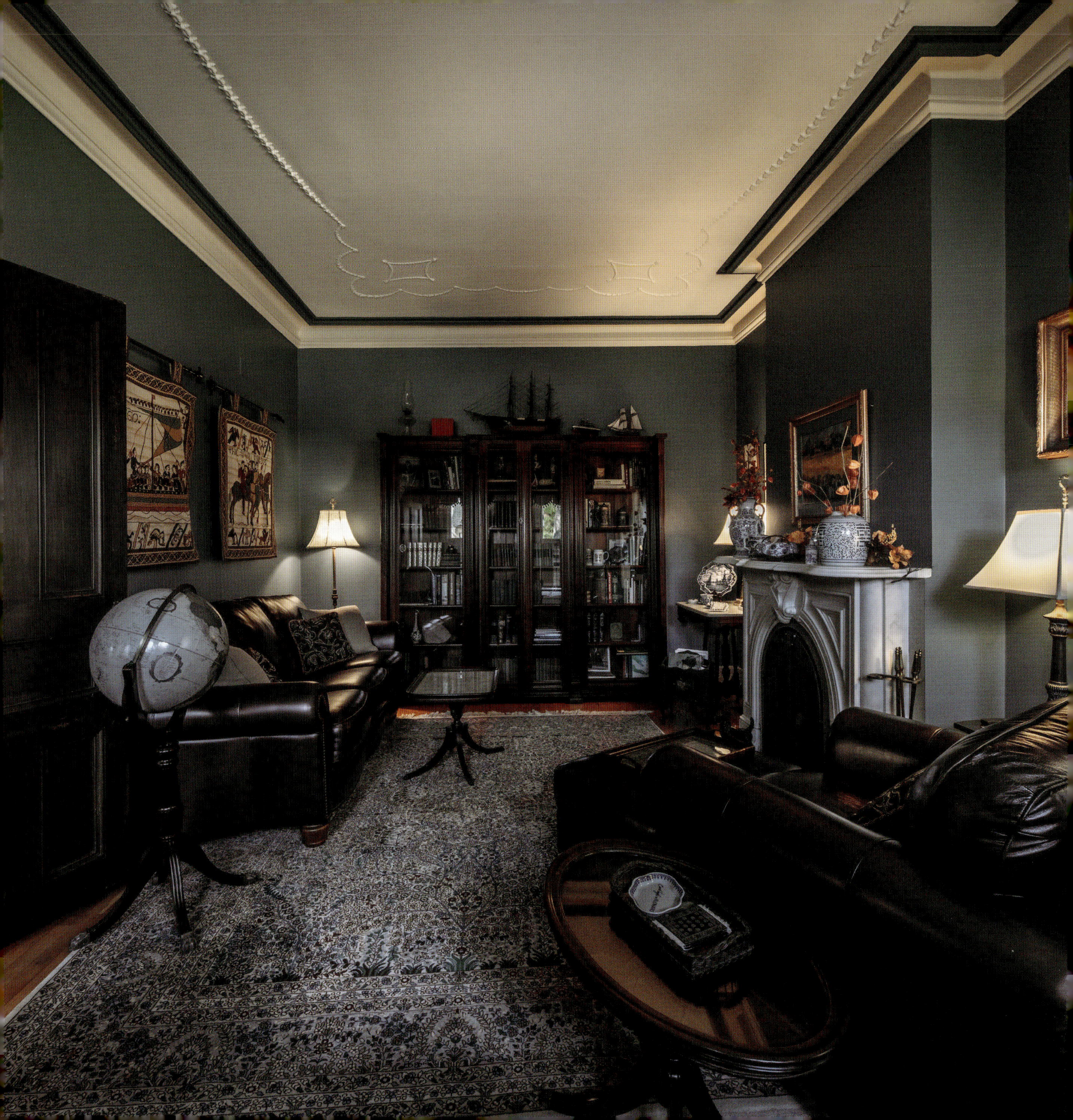

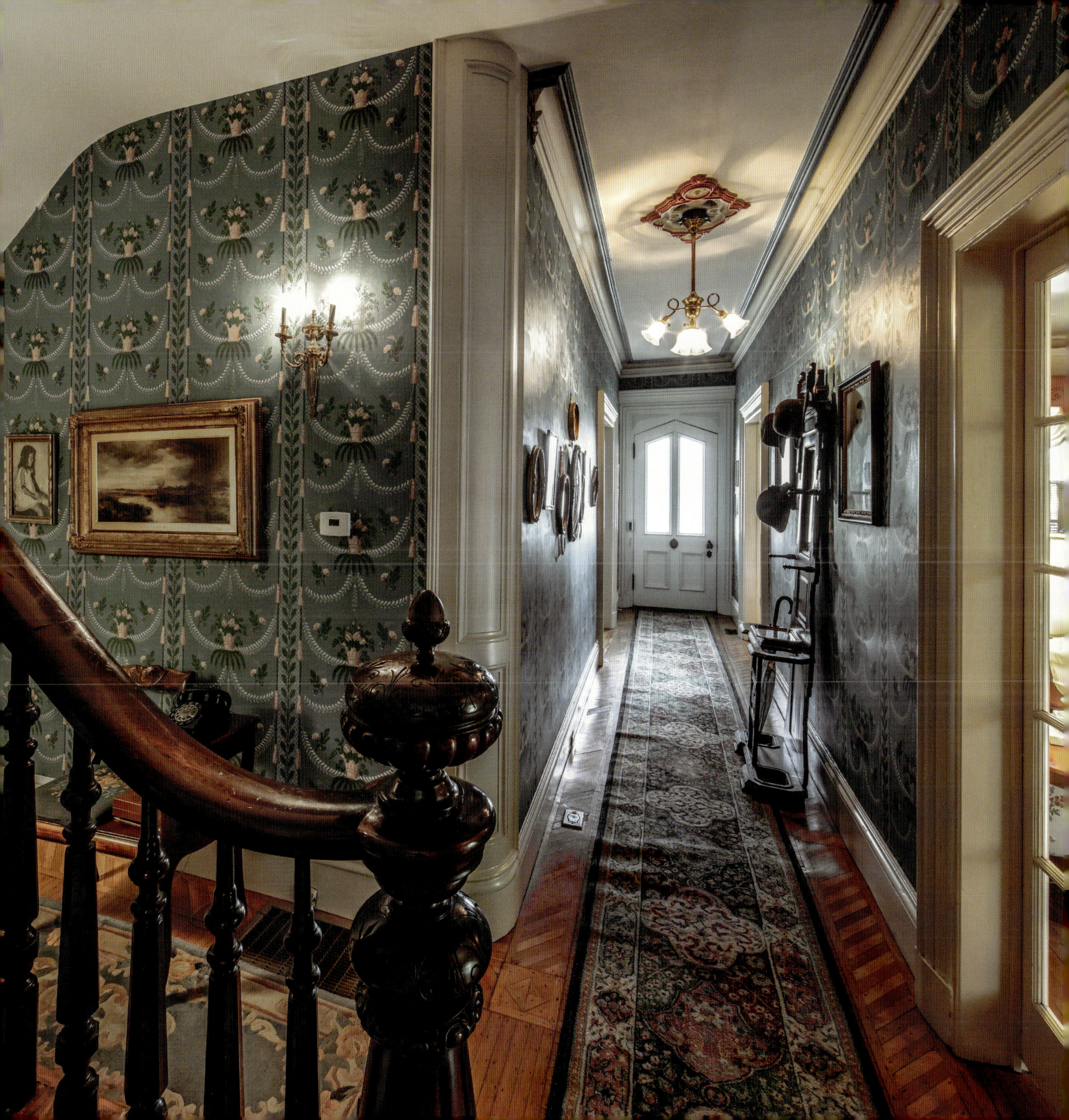

Comstock, Ferre & Co. (Heirloom Market)

— 263 Main Street —

As the U.S. population exploded in the early nineteenth century, so did the need for seed. Wethersfield entrepreneurs responded by establishing an industry to supply good seeds from Wethersfield crops quickly and conveniently to farmers and gardeners across New England and beyond.

Comstock, Ferre & Co. — the seed store was downstairs and the offices above.

Wethersfield's commercial seed industry was started in 1811 by Joseph Belden. By 1820, Belden's Wethersfield Seed Gardens at 249 Main Street—with gardens, seed houses, and barns stretching all the way to Garden Street—had become a major business. Much of Belden's operation was destroyed by fire in 1834. To replace the destroyed buildings, and a good example of Yankee recycling and adaptive reuse, the Beldens moved to the wood-framed structure that was behind the brick building fronting Main Street. Structural evidence suggests this section dates from the first half of the eighteenth century and was originally a two-story, two-room home with a gambrel roof. There is a local tradition that this structure was Silas Deane's store. It is also possible it might have been the old Wolcott House, which served as a kitchen for the Webb House before the new kitchen ell was built in 1784.

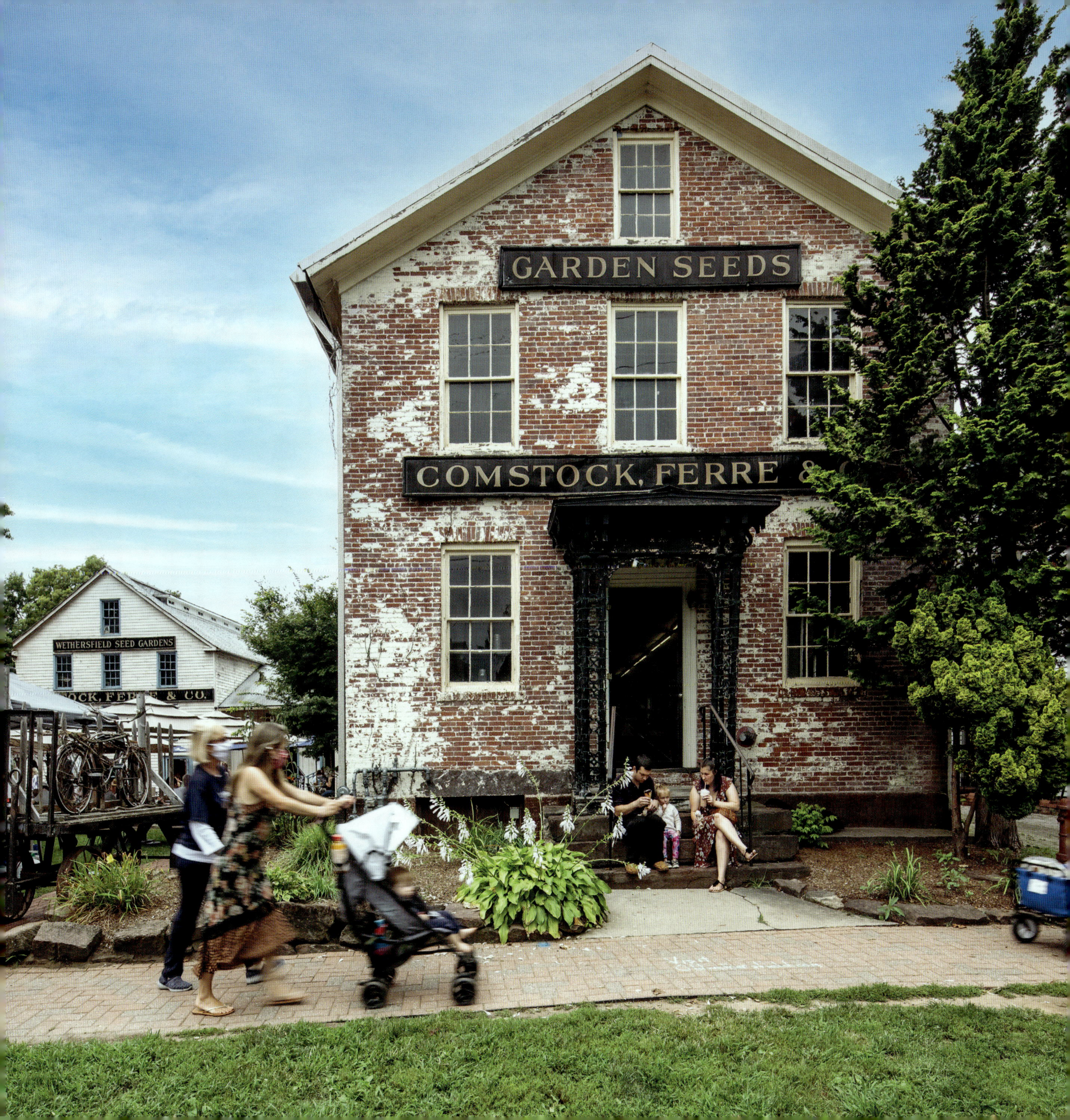
GARDEN SEEDS
COMSTOCK, FERRE &
WETHERSFIELD SEED GARDENS
OCK, FERRE & CO.

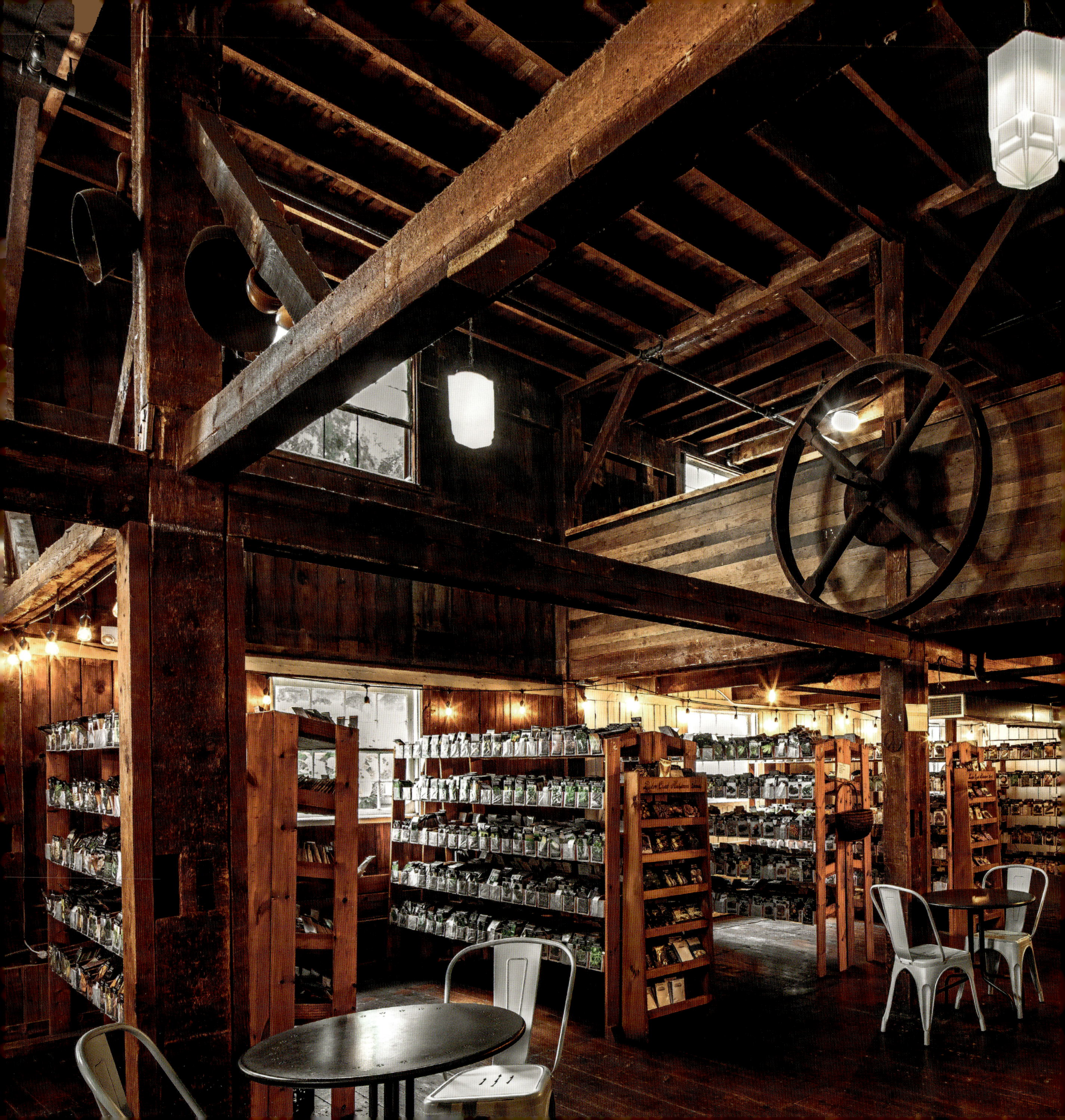

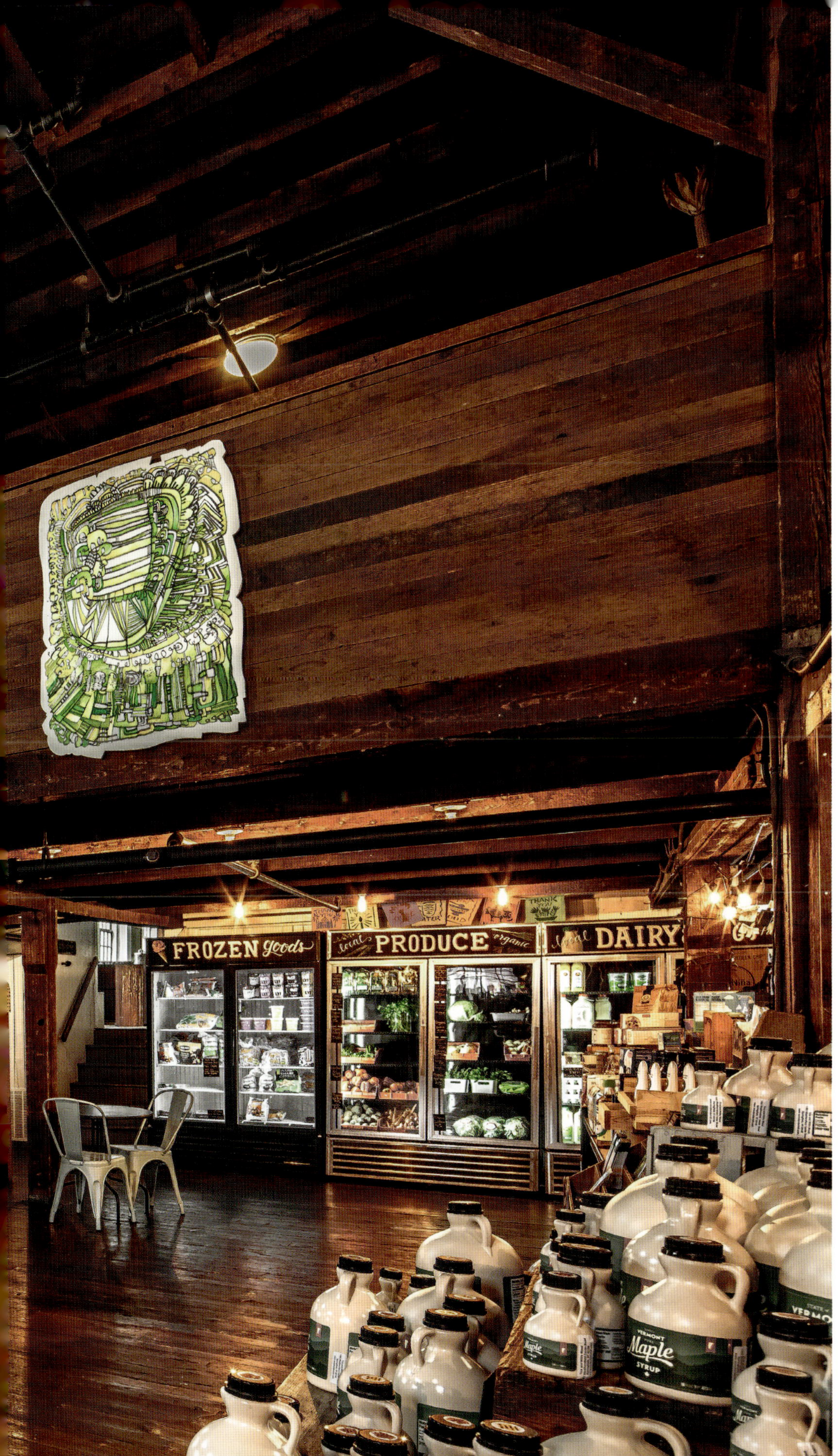

Heirloom Market is in what was the main warehouse, now opened up by the removal of the second floor.

Outside seating is a welcome addition to the community.

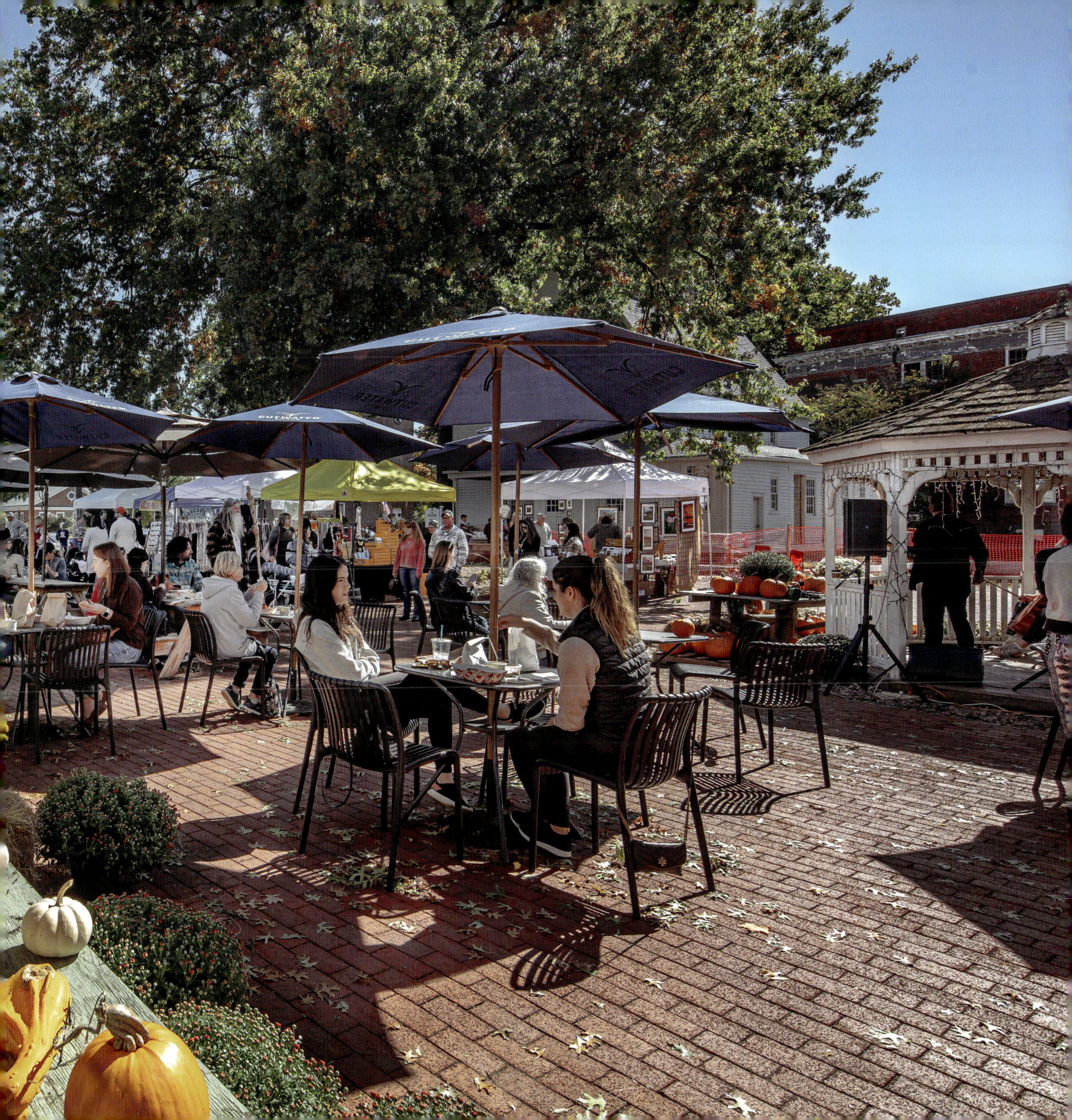

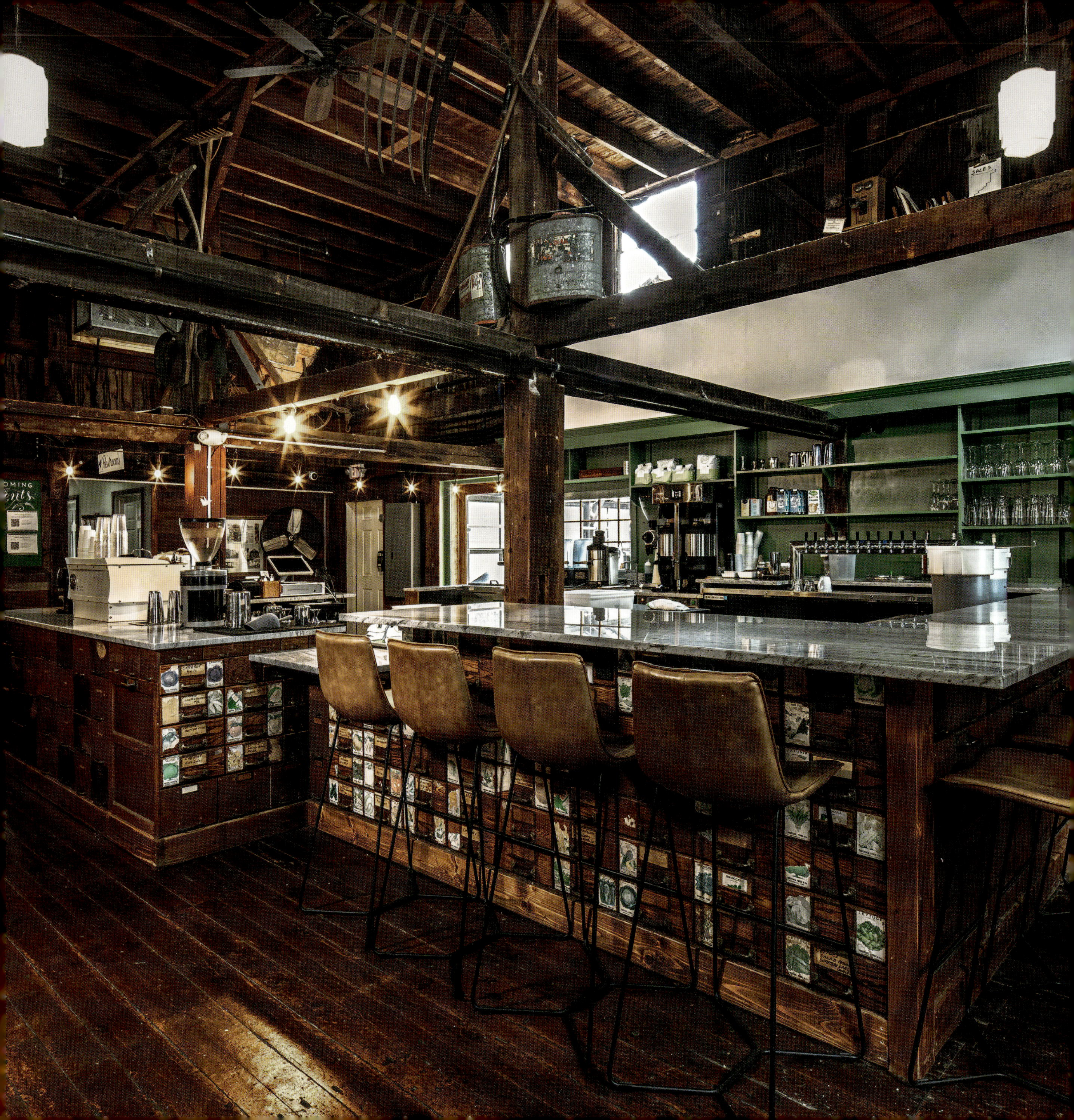

The face of the drawers that once held packages of seeds form the front of the bar counter at the café in Heirloom Market.

(following spread) Heirloom Market is still offering heritage seeds in the Comstock, Ferre tradition.

In 1838, father and son Franklin and William Comstock purchased the remaining business, establishing Comstock, Ferre & Co. The Comstocks adopted the idea of packing seeds in paper packages, following the example of the Shakers, who had a village in nearby Enfield. Comstock's traveling seed merchants then distributed commission boxes of Wethersfield seeds from the southern states to the Mississippi River and westward. At each stop, they picked up the previous year's boxes and collected payments.

Stephen F. Willard was employed by Comstock, Ferre & Co. in 1872 as a traveling salesman and soon took over management of the company. Under Willard family management, Comstock, Ferre thrived and evolved into a successful retail garden center until competition from big-box retailers forced its sale in 1991. The new owner continued the retail business but applied to the Historic District Commission in 2008 for permission to demolish the barns to the rear of the property, including the mid-nineteenth-century middle barn, and to construct two new buildings for mixed use—retail, office, and residential. The Commission heard from the Connecticut Trust for Historic Preservation (now Preservation Connecticut), a leader in promoting preservation and adaptive reviews of historic agricultural buildings and compatible new construction, who described the Comstock, Ferre connected barn complex as a particularly significant representation of the mid-nineteenth-century revolution in scientific agriculture and commercial horticulture. The Connecticut Trust encouraged the preservation and reuse of the historic barns. The Commission denied the application to demolish.

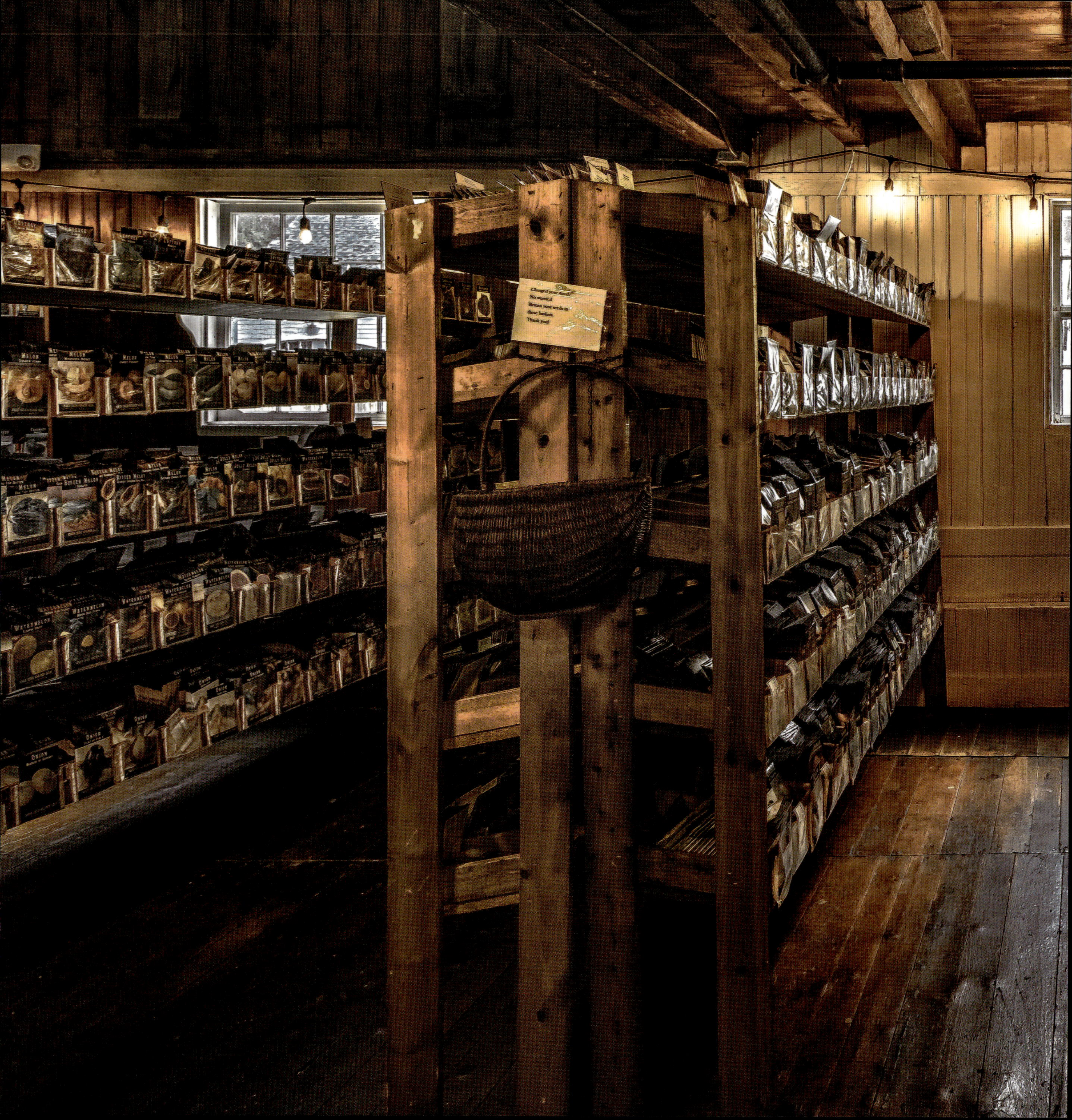
Changed your
No worries!
Return your seeds to
these baskets.
Thank you!
MELON
WATERMELON
ONION

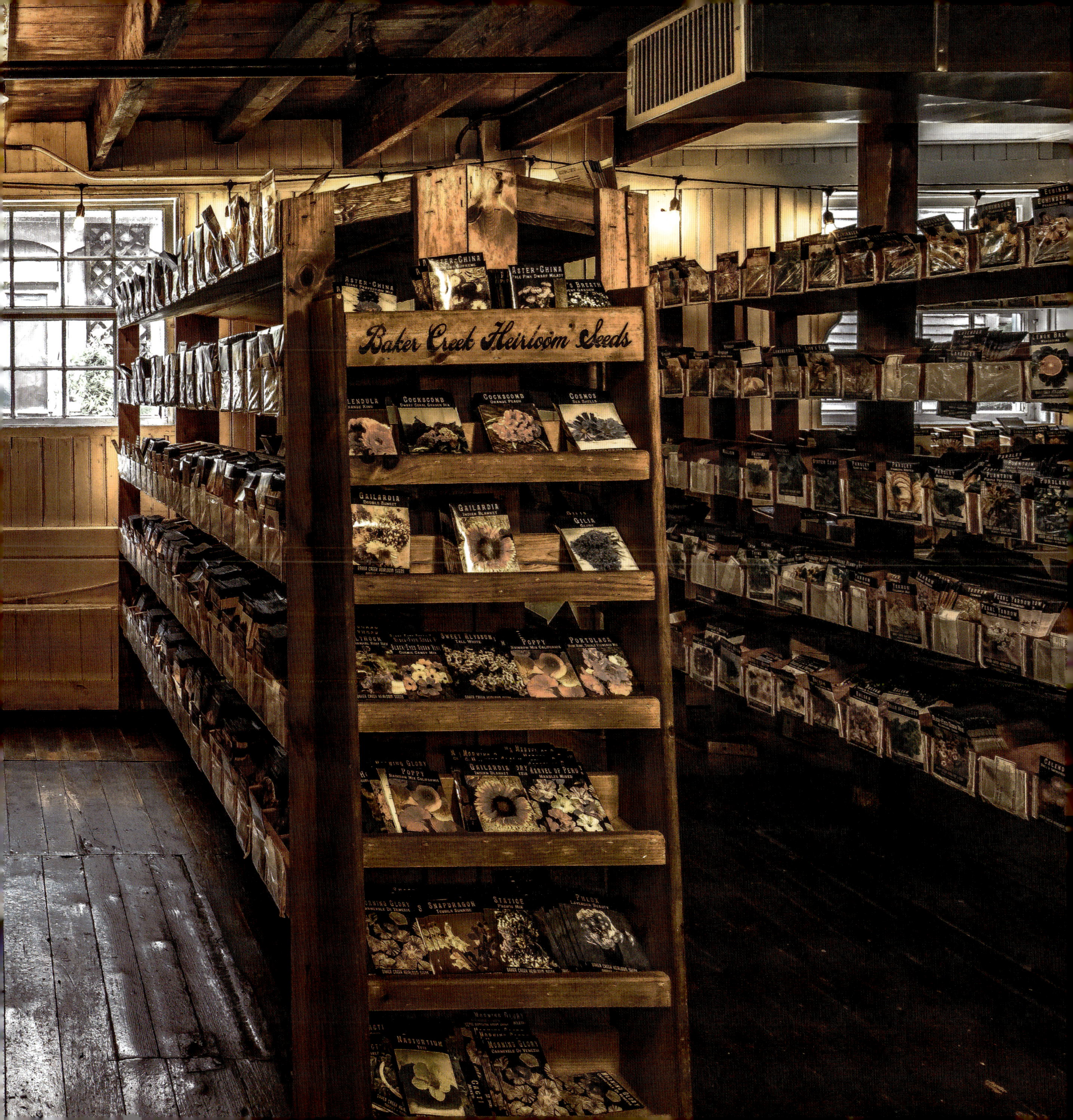

Baker Creek Heirloom Seeds
ASTER-CHINA
ASTER-CHINA
COCKSCOMB
COCKSCOMB
COSMOS
GAILARDIA
GAILARDIA
GILIA
SWEET ALYSSUM
POPPY
PORTULACA
POPPY
GAILARDIA
SNAPDRAGON
STATICE
PHLOX
NASTURTIUM
MORNING GLORY

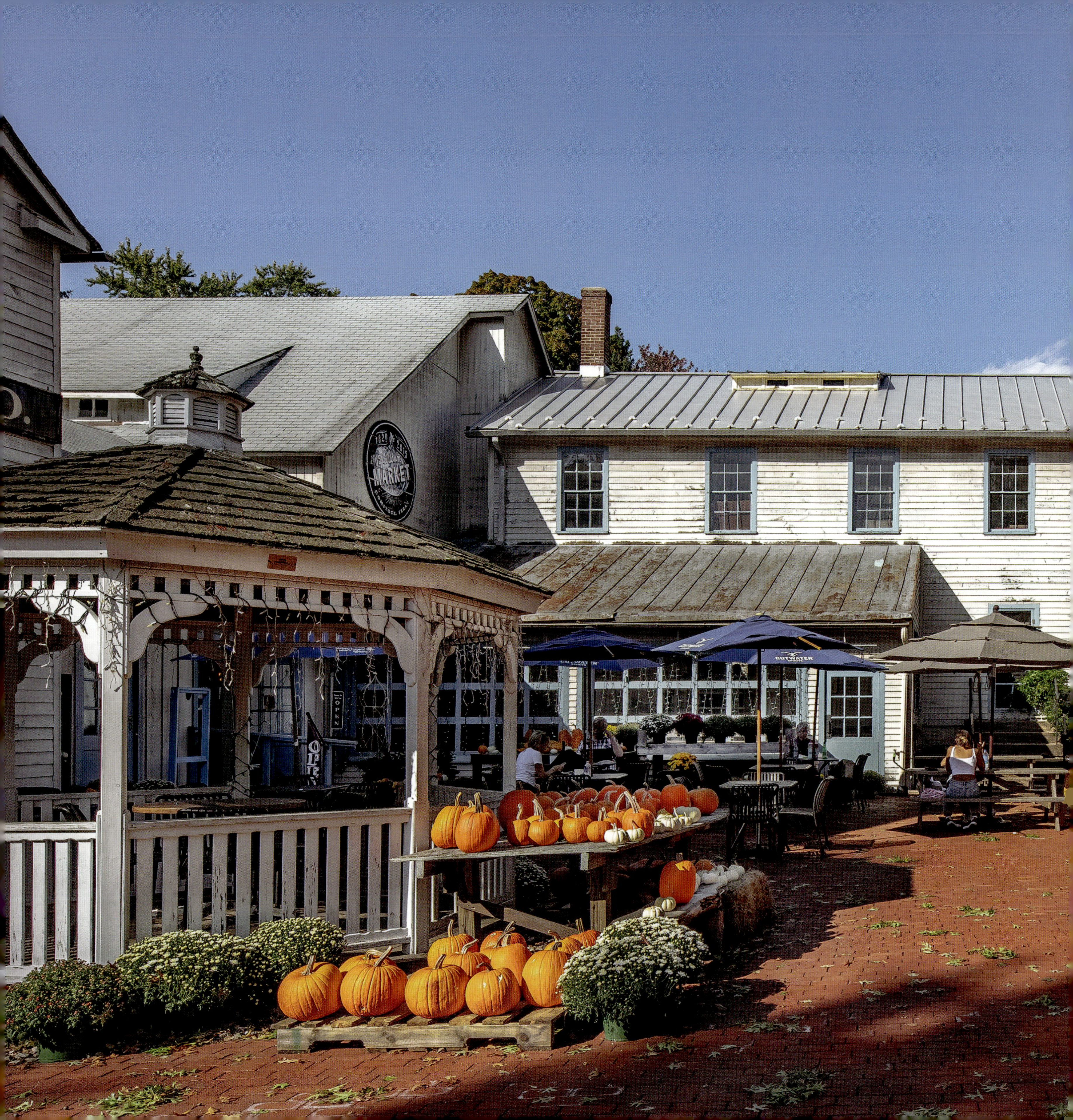
1820
2015
MARKET
CUTWATER

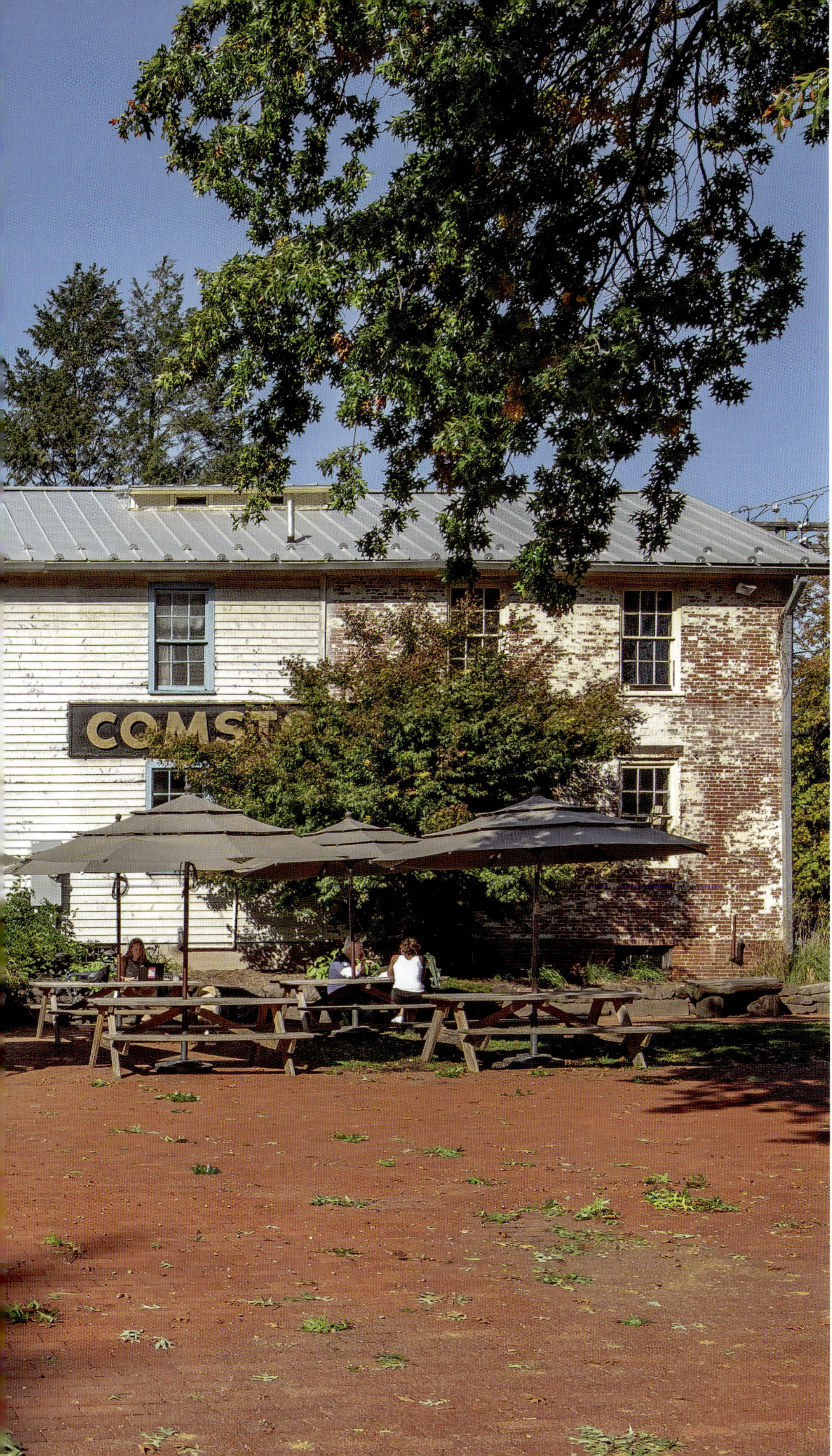

The wood-framed section behind the brick building in front, which might have been Silas Deane's store, was moved here after the fire of 1834.

The machinery of Otis Elevator Model One that operated from the basement to the second floor.

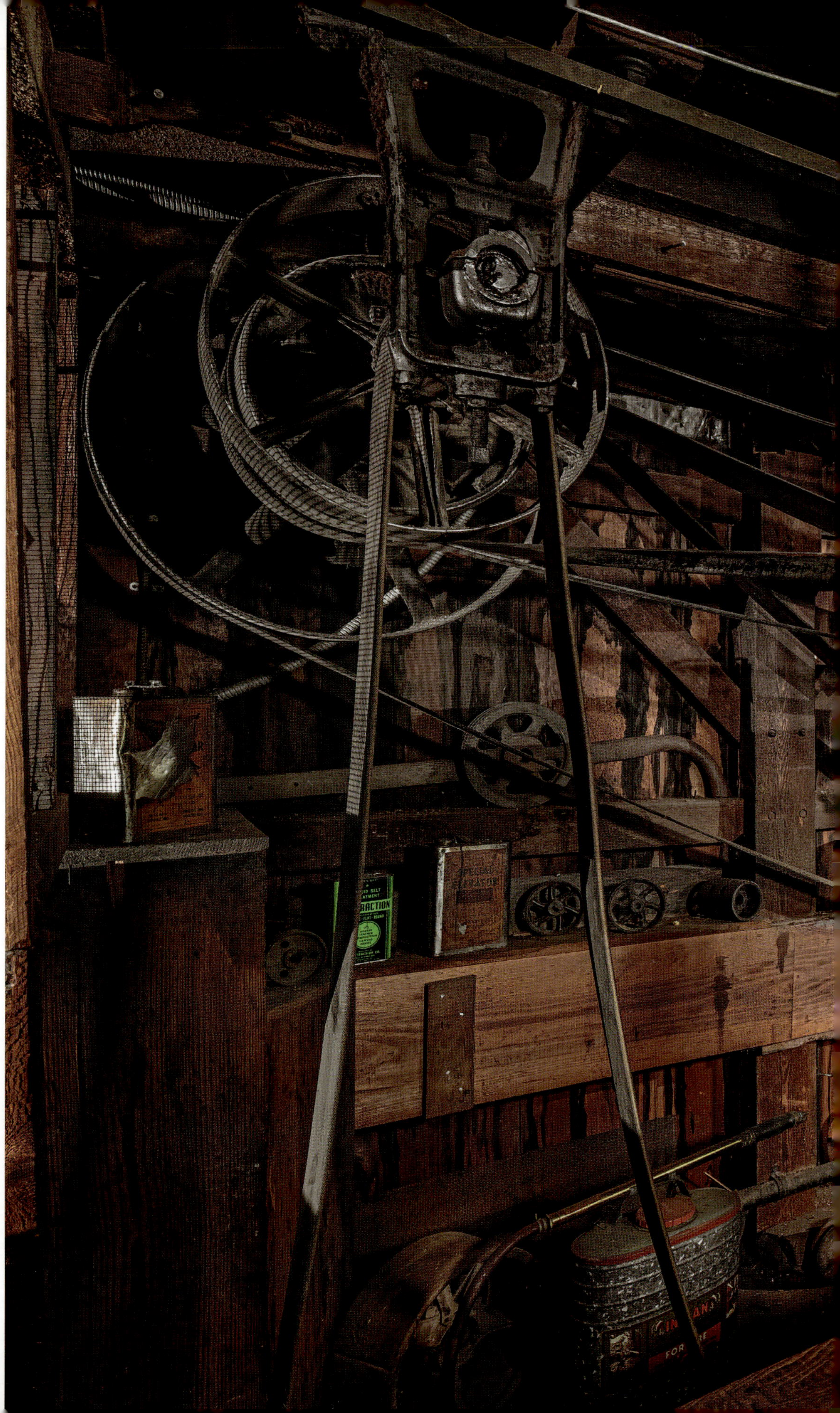

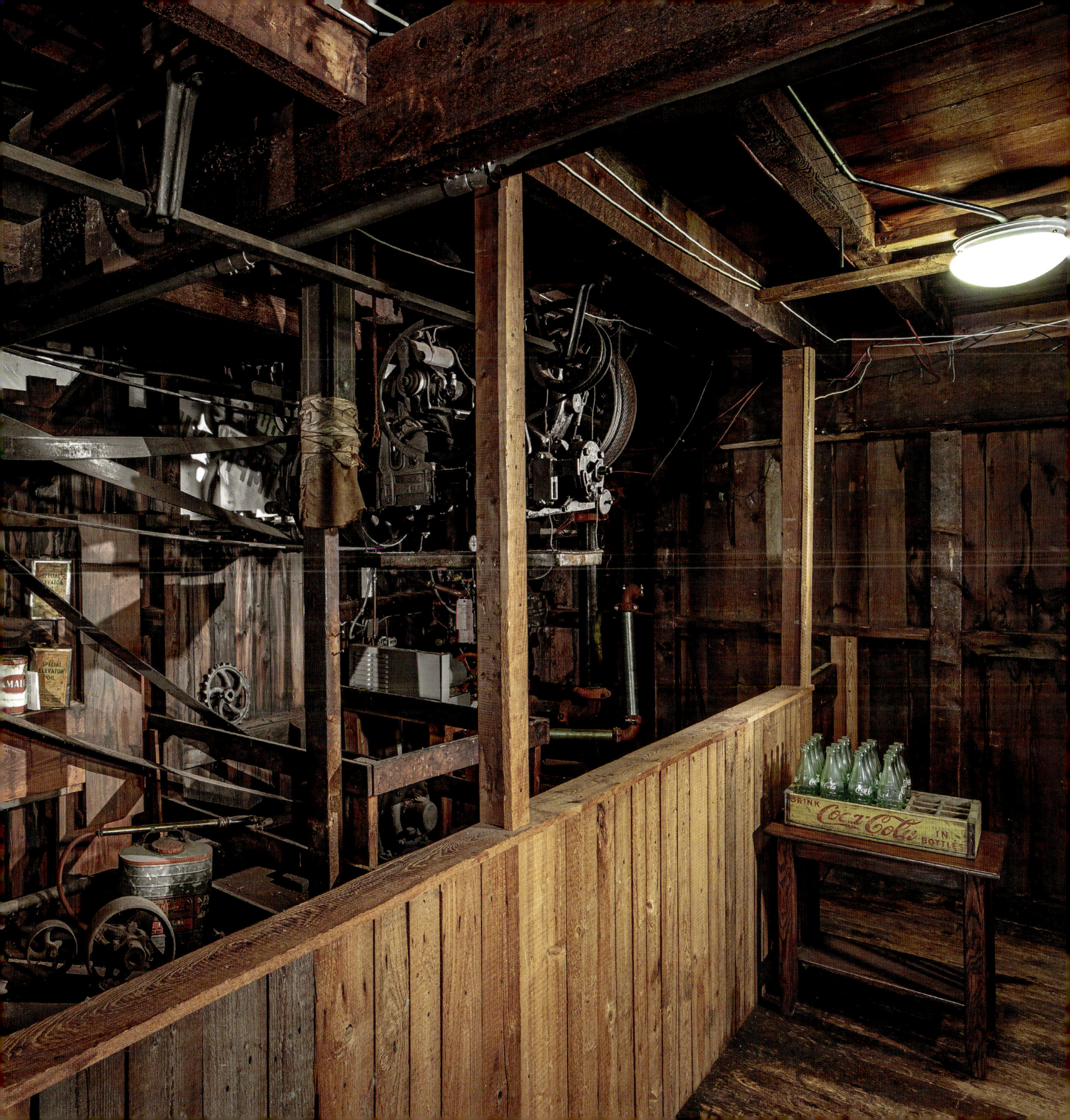
SPECIAL ELEVATOR OIL
DRINK
Coca-Cola
IN BOTTLES

In 2010, the Comstock, Ferre property was bought by Baker Creek Heirloom Seed Company, who leased it to Spiro and Julia Koulouris in 2016. They creatively reused it as Heirloom Market, a natural foods grocery store and café. After acquiring the full title, the Koulourises added an appropriately designed bar and most recently converted the greenhouse into an attractive additional seating area for the café.

Comstock, Ferre evolved into Heirloom Market, featuring organic, GMO-free groceries as well as gardening supplies and, of course, heirloom seeds. In the café, locally roasted coffee and espresso drinks are served in addition to freshly baked pastries and bread.

The greenhouse has been remodeled and repurposed for café seating.

This historic nineteenth-century agricultural complex is an excellent example of how Old Wethersfield has creatively retained, restored, and adaptively reused its architectural heritage, where each generation not only preserves the past but integrates that heritage into a robust, contemporary present. ♕

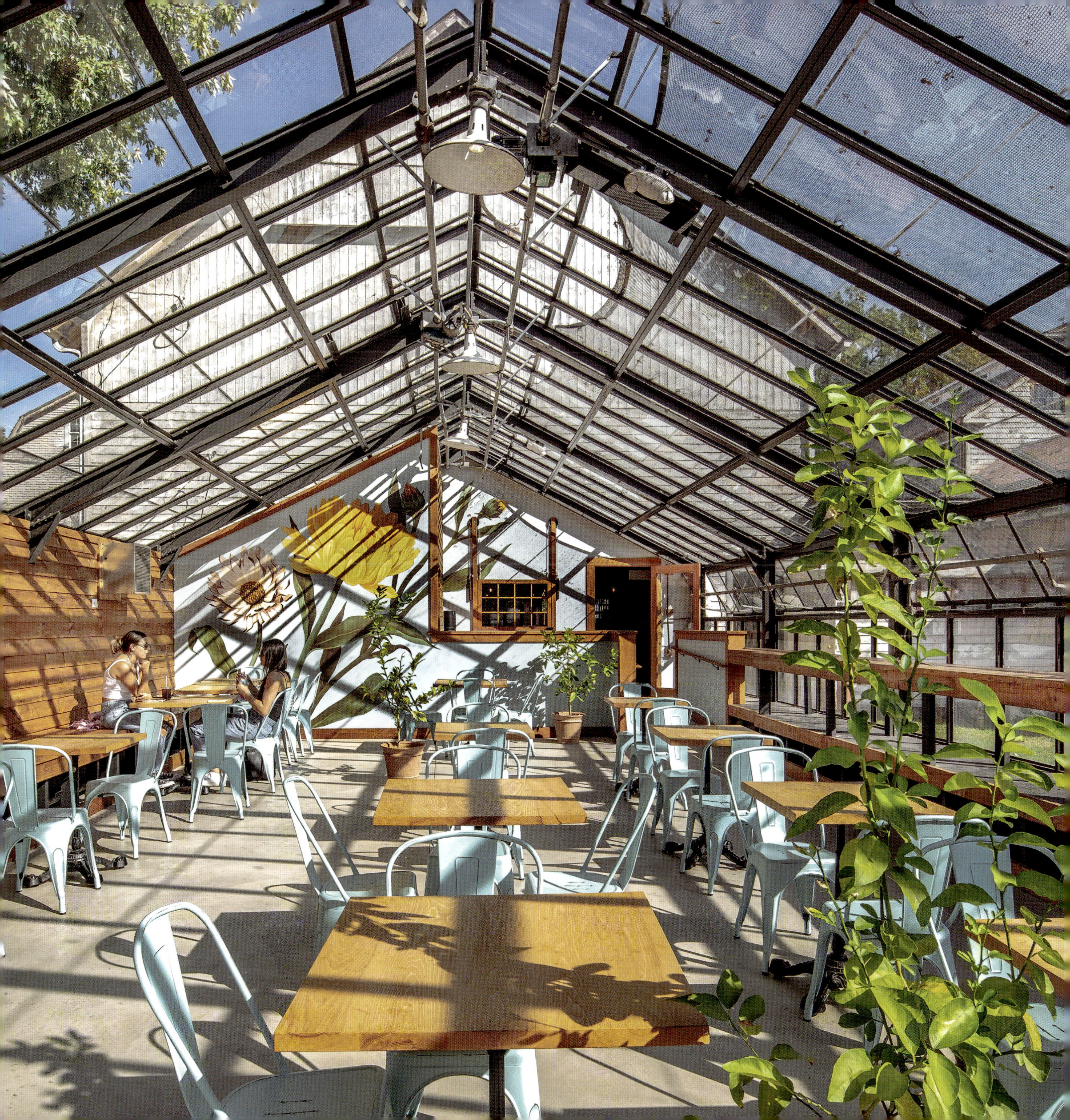

AFTERWORD *and* ACKNOWLEDGEMENTS

These stories of stewardship are largely drawn from *Old Wethersfield—History, Architecture, and Preservation* by Anne Crofoot Kuckro, (to be published by Wesleyan University Press), lightly edited for this format and to reflect changes since 2010.

To Chris Knopf, Editor of that publication and of this book, and to Jill Fletcher, Project Coordinator for both, my eternal gratitude for their heroic work in bringing this project to completion. This book would not have been possible without Peter R. Brown's wonderful and evocative photographs that bring these stories alive, and without the design vision and expertise of Don Carter.

The support of the Webb Deane Stevens Museum, and Brenton Grom, Executive Director, and that of The National Society of The Colonial Dames of America in The State of Connecticut, and Alice Hyland, its President, have been critical to the success of this project. Thanks to Amy Northrop Wittorff, Executive Director of The Wethersfield Historical Society for appointing Jill Fletcher, as Project Coordinator for the publication of Anne's work and to William Johnson, Museum Educator at the Society for his research assistance.

For their invaluable help with the captions, I am indebted to Paul Bourdon, Charles Lyle, Judith and Charles Melchreit, Cynthia Riccio, Amy Northrop Wittorff, and James Woodworth.

This book reflects and recounts the stewardship of generations of property owners, proprietors, and custodians but would not have been possible without the generous cooperation of today's owners and stewards.

Heartfelt thanks to the Town of Wethersfield for leasing the high school to the Wethersfield Historical Society, which has transformed it into the Keeney Memorial Cultural Center and Museum; to The National Society of Colonial Dames of America in The State of Connecticut, owner of the Silas Deane House; to The Wethersfield Historical Society, owner of the Thomas Chester (Hurlbut-Dunham) House; to Connecticut Landmarks, owner of the Belden House and Tavern (Buttolph-Williams House); to First Church of Christ in Wethersfield, owner of the Meeting House; to Paul Bourdon, owner of the George Hubbard House; to Olga Cherkasova and Dmitriy Gorbunov, owners and proprietors of the Silas W. Robbins Inn; to Spiro and Julia Koulouris, owners and proprietors of Heirloom Market and Cafe; to Charles and Judith Melchreit, owners of the Daniel Francis House; and to Anne Kuckro, who shared with me the restoration of the Dr. Daniel Hooker House.

Lee G. Kuckro

REFERENCES

Adams, Sherman W., and Henry Reed Stiles. *The History of Ancient Wethersfield*, Vol. 1. Somersworth: New Hampshire: New Hampshire Publishing Company, 1974.

Beaumarchais, Pierre-Augustin Caron de. Beaumarchais to Congress, March 23, 1778. New York: New York Historical Society.

Downing, Antoinette Forrester, and Vincent Scully. *The Architectural Heritage of Newport, Rhode Island, 1640–1915.* New York: American Legacy Press, 1982.

Francis, James. "Account book of Wethersfield: 1788–1815." Manuscript Collection: Connecticut Historical Society, Hartford, Connecticut.

Palmer, Frederic. "The Bulletin of the Antiquarian & Landmarks Society, Inc of Connecticut." *The Connecticut Antiquarian* Volume III, no. 1, July 1956.

Phipps, Frances. *Colonial Kitchens, Their Furnishings, and Their Gardens.* New York: Hawthorn Books, Inc.,1972

Wethersfield, Connecticut. *Land Records.* Volume 2. May 11, 1662, recorded 1672.

ABOUT THE AUTHOR

Anne Crofoot Kuckro (1945–2010) was a passionate, visionary leader whose interest in historic preservation, vernacular architecture, community planning, local history, and heritage tourism spurred transformative changes in Wethersfield. Cultural institutions, tourism, economic vitality, and civic life all benefited from her enthusiastic dedication.

As president of the Wethersfield Historical Society, Anne led the planning, public relations, and fundraising for the rehabilitation of the 1893 High School into the Keeney Memorial Cultural Center. During construction, she functioned as clerk of the works, coordinating between the architect and the contractors. Anne conceived and researched the architectural frieze *300 Years of Domestic Architecture 1637–1937*, illustrated with her renderings of elevations of a house from each decade, for the orientation room on the first floor.

Anne served as president of The National Society of The Colonial Dames of America in The State of Connecticut and presided over the initial planning and fundraising efforts for the Education and Visitors Center at the Webb Deane Stevens Museum.

To promote and share Wethersfield's history with a wider audience, Anne was a founding committee member and chair of the annual Wethersfield Weekend Festival from 1998 to 2002. She directed the annual three-day event that turned the Historic District into a living history museum with costumed artisans, enactors, musicians, and guides. She researched, wrote, and produced two forty-five-minute audio tours of Wethersfield's Colonial history and its Revolutionary history, two bus tours that provided context for specific local house museums, and two walking tours that included brochures and historic markers.

Anne also chaired the town's 350th Celebration Committee, the Cove Park Committee, the Silas Deane Task Force, and the Wethersfield Tourism Commission. She served as a delegate to the Regional Tourism District.

Students of all ages benefited when Anne shared her passion for architecture and history. She created educational programs through research and grant writing and wrote teaching materials. At the adult level, Anne developed and taught Wethersfield History, an Architectural Perspective. She employed walking tours and classroom presentations with materials about the surviving residential architecture within the Wethersfield Historic District to lead students through the town's cultural heritage and history.

Anne was the project director for Discovering Local History on Location and in the Classroom, a local curriculum for grades three, five, eight, eleven, and twelve. She developed the curriculum in close coordination with the Wethersfield

Public School's administration, art instructors, and classroom teachers along with staff from the Webb Deane Stevens Museum and the Wethersfield Historical Society. The result was thirty lessons in Discovering Local History and a sixty-six-page appendix.

Anne directed the Hartford Architecture Conservancy's survey and authored *Hartford Architecture. Volume One: Downtown*, published by Hartford Architecture Conservancy in 1978. She wrote extensively about Wethersfield including *Captain James Francis Master Builder: Brick Architecture in Wethersfield before 1840* (1974) and *Wethersfield: A Tour of Houses and History* (1984), both books published by the Wethersfield Historical Society. Several articles were printed in *The Magazine Antiques*. Anne's unfinished manuscript, *Old Wethersfield — History, Architecture, and Preservation*, surveys the history of Wethersfield, its architecture over three centuries, and its story of historic preservation with photographs and examples from the Historic District; to be published by Wesleyan University Press.

Her knowledge of and familiarity with Wethersfield land, tax, probate, and historic records; inventories; account books; and local diaries were encyclopedic. She was an unmatched resource for anyone researching local history.

ABOUT THE PHOTOGRAPHER

Peter R Brown is an award-winning architectural and fine art photographer working closely with national architects, interior designers and high-end builders. His commercial clients demand the utmost in detailed, high resolution and precision renderings. In addition, Brown also creates fine-art images that feature soft focus and atmospheric images, employing film-based Pinhole cameras and other alternative photographic methods. *peterbrownphotos.com*

ABOUT THE EDITOR

Chris Knopf's career ranged from editing and publishing to being the CEO of Mintz + Hoke Marketing Communications. An author, he has published essays, short stories, and eighteen mystery/thriller novels. His interests in building and house design led him to one of his projects: creating a home from an eighteenth-century barn. *chrisknopfmystery.com*

ABOUT THE DESIGNER

Don Carter is a nationally-recognized designer and illustrator. A 2017 Connecticut Art Directors Club Hall of Fame inductee, Don is a creative director at Adams & Knight in Avon, CT. He is also the co-creator of the *Birds & Desserts* art series with baker-turned-artist, Dora Dylanne Reyes. *slothman.cargo.site*